Harry Bertoia
Sculptor

Harry Bertoia
Sculptor

by June Kompass Nelson

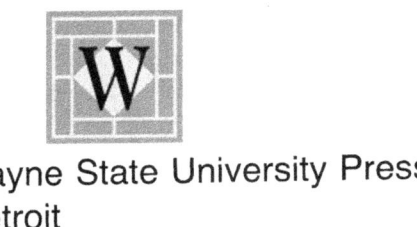

Wayne State University Press
Detroit

Published simultaneously in Canada by
The Copp Clark Publishing Company
517 Wellington Street, West Toronto 2B, Canada

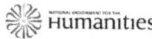

MELLON
THE ANDREW W.
FOUNDATION

The publication of this volume in a freely accessible digital format has been made possible by a major grant from the National Endowment for the Humanities and the Mellon Foundation through their Humanities Open Book Program.

Library of Congress Catalog Card Number 70-78546

ISBN 978-0-8143-4372-2 (paperback); 978-0-8143-4371-5 (ebook)

Wayne State University Press thanks Celia and Val Bertoia for their enthusiastic support of this project and generous permission to reproduce images of Harry Bertoia's works.

The Press also thanks the following individuals and institutions for their generous permission to reprint material in this book: Artists Rights Society (ARS); Bruce Ackerman; Albright-Knox Gallery; Leo Baeck Institute; Bank of America; Jeff Burgess; Dallas Public Library; Eastman Kodak Company; Esto Photographics; General Motors Heritage Archives; Knoll, Inc.; Reiko Sunami Kopelson; Massachusetts Institute of Technology; Dr. Samuel Nelson; Simon Property Group; Syracuse University Art Collection; and Dominique Tomme.

Courtesy of the Leo Baeck Institute: *Hollow Forms*, Plate 57; *Golden Screen* (1967), Plate 58; Musical sculpture (1960-64), Plate 59; Sculpture (1967), Plate 60; Musical sculptures (1968), Plate 61; *Small Bush* (1965), Plate 63; Sculpture (1960), Plate 67; *Spring* (1965), Plate 70.

Used with permission of Bank of America: Bertoia installing segment of ceiling sculpture (1968), Plate 50.

Courtesy of Esto Photographics: Manufacturers Trust 510 Fifth Avenue New York, NY (Ezra Stoller © Esto), Plate 22; and Chapel, MIT, Cambridge, MA, © Wayne Andrews/Esto, Plate 25.

Courtesy of Knoll, Inc.: Frontispiece portrait of Bertoia with pipe (George Rosenthal/Knoll); The Bertoia chair, Plate 18; Sculptures (c. 1950-2), welded metals (Herbert Matter/Knoll), Plate 20.

Courtesy of the Syracuse University Art Collection: *Syracuse Nova*, 1961, Plate 83.

From the collections of the Texas/Dallas History and Archives Division, Dallas Public Library: Sculpture screen (1955), Plate 54.

Exhaustive efforts were made to obtain permission for use of material in this text. Any missed permissions resulted from a lack of information about the material, copyright holder, or both. If you are a copyright holder of such material, please contact WSUP at wsupressrights@wayne.edu.

http://wsupress.wayne.edu/

To Samuel

Contents

Illustrations

Plate   84.   Dandelion sculptures for fountain (four of seven) (1964)
Eastman Kodak Pavilion, New York World's Fair
Courtesy, Eastman Kodak Company

85.   "Galaxy" (1964)
Golden West Savings and Loan Association, Castro Valley, Calif.
Courtesy, Mario Gaidano
Gene Anthony, photographer

Preface

The quietly poetic personality of Harry Bertoia so impressed me when first I met him on board the *Cristoforo Colombo* bound for Italy in 1957 that I became interested in learning more about his work. When I returned to America the following year, my first visual contact with the golden sculpture wall in a bank on Fifth Avenue in New York whetted my appetite and I began looking for Bertoia sculptures wherever I went, finding them in museums, churches, and business establishments all over the country. Realization came gradually of the extent and variety of his artistic output.

Surprised to discover there was no monograph available giving details concerning the sculptor and his work, I wrote Bertoia in the spring of 1966 requesting permission to undertake such a study. Permission and cooperation were freely and generously granted, even though Bertoia was (and is) somewhat reluctant to have his work summarized while he feels there is still a great deal more of it to come. His cooperation involved spending many long afternoons with me in his studio answering questions and digging through his files to provide information and photographs. It has included reading through my manuscript and correcting factual errors and misinterpretations on my part while refraining from comment on my value judgments. His patience and kindness as well as his enthusiasm for his work provided inspiration for mine.

My work began in Detroit where this study was undertaken as a master's thesis under the direction of Dr. Wayne Andrews, professor of art and art history, Wayne State University, whose courses, "The Artist in American Society," I had been following with interest and benefit. Dr. Andrews has given encouragement and help on many occasions since that time, as has Dr. Bernard Goldman of Wayne State University.

Many persons interested in Harry Bertoia and his work have patiently answered written inquiries or granted personal interviews, for which I am extremely grateful. I have received the cooperation of the art galleries representing Bertoia in New York, Chicago, Cincinnati, and Detroit. Librarians in Detroit and New York have been most helpful, and personal friends in several cities have performed indispensable services which have been greatly appreciated. My cheerful and patient husband has always provided me with good counsel when it was needed.

I wish to thank the companies (particularly Northwestern National Life Insurance Company of Minneapolis), museums, and private collectors who have either kindly given permission to publish or supplied photographs for reproduction of works in their possession. Many architects have been generous with their time in checking details, as well as with the photographs lurking in their files.

To all persons, named and unnamed, who have contributed to the production of this volume, go my sincere thanks.

J. K. N.
Kinnelon, New Jersey
December 1968

Life and Personality

Harry Bertoia was born on March 10, 1915, at San Lorenzo, a village near Udine in northeastern Italy. Except for the fact that some of his antecedents came from Pieve di Cadore, Titian's birthplace, family connections are unknown. However, there were Bertoias who had been artists of one kind or another in northern Italy for centuries. The short-lived Jacopo Zanguidi Bertoja, a celebrated mannerist painter from Parma, was active during Titian's lifetime.[1] Father and son, Guiseppe and Pietro Bertoja were noted scene designers at Venice and elsewhere in Italy during the nineteenth century. And just prior to that, Valentino Bertoja, father of Giuseppe, had been first violoncellist at Venice's Teatro La Fenice.[2]

As a boy Harry was interested in drawing, art, and artists, and was always listening to family discussions on these subjects. There was also a great deal of interest in music in his immediate family. Both his father Giuseppe Bertoia and his brother Oreste had considerable musical talent, although it was used for relaxation and not professionally.

Harry was given his English name at birth by his father, who had already been to Canada and stayed long enough to become a Canadian citizen. He hoped to emigrate to the New World with his entire family, but things did not work out quite the way he planned. Harry attended primary school in Italy, and it was not until he was fifteen that he and his father came to America, then in the first stage of the great depression. Giuseppe Bertoia worked first as a miner in Canada and later as a laborer in Detroit, where the pair went to be near Oreste, who had preceded them to this country. After a few years the elder Bertoia returned to Italy and Harry remained with his brother. He never again saw his father, who died during World War II.

At first Harry had trouble with English. (He still speaks with the trace of an accent, carefully chooses his words, and dislikes lecturing or public speaking.) But after a year of Americanization classes at the Davison School, he entered Cass Technical High School in Detroit, a public school which for the past fifty years has maintained a special program for talented students in the arts and sciences. At Cass Tech he had classes in jewelry and handcrafts, as well as in drawing and painting. Perhaps the most talented art student Cass Tech ever had, he maintained an attitude of seriousness toward his work that was uncommon to his classmates, most of whom were several years his junior. "It was not necessary to tell Harry exactly what to do to a drawing. The teacher could make suggestions and Harry would bring from within himself the solution to the problem," said one of his teachers recently.[3] Upon graduation in 1936 he won a scholarship to the Art School of the Detroit Society of Arts and Crafts, where he studied painting and drawing for a year under John Carroll and Sarkis Sarkisian.

In 1937 another scholarship, awarded on the basis of his work in metalcrafts at Cass Tech, sent him to the Cranbrook Academy of Art in Bloomfield Hills, Michigan, which profoundly affected his career. The unique character of the Cranbrook Academy in the thirties, and the effect it had on all who were privileged to enjoy its atmosphere, cannot be overemphasized. There was no rigid curriculum and consequently no degrees were awarded. There was a small number of students and a great deal of freedom. Studios and shops were accessible at all hours so students and faculty could work whenever they wished to. Cranbrook was a gathering of artists who taught and learned from each other under ideal conditions. Discussions with visiting European artists were common. One with Walter Gropius particularly stands out in Bertoia's memory. Cranbrook was a significant factor in the artistic development of Harry Bertoia, as well as in that of other well-known artists who were there at the time, such as Eero Saarinen and Charles Eames. "The basic thought was simple and good," Bertoia says. "The many artists from Cranbrook now working in their chosen fields demonstrate the worth of the idea."[4]

Harry entered Cranbrook as a student of painting and drawing. Though he called upon resident-sculptor Carl Milles many times during his stay there — just as he often visited resident-ceramist Maija Grotell — he never attended classes in sculpture. This fact may help account for the experimental freedom with which he has always approached materials and techniques.

In 1939 the architect Eliel Saarinen, father of Eero and director of the Cranbrook Academy of Art, asked Harry to stay on to start a department of metalworking. There was a metal shop in existence at Cranbrook but it had not been used for several years. Harry took on the job, reorganized the shop, and began teaching metalworking techniques to small groups of from five to ten students. Almost immediately all metals except silver became hard to obtain as a result of the war in Europe and priorities in America. Harry became an expert silver craftsman, producing a handsome tea service for Eliel, as well as quantities of unusual abstract jewelry, some of which is owned by his Cranbrook friends and acquaintances, including Pipsan Saarinen Swanson, Eero's sister.

An important part of Bertoia's work at Cranbrook was an after-hours activity begun while he was still a student and continued during the four years of his teaching career. Working in the print shop at night when other students were not around, experimenting with inks and woodblocks, he developed an ingenious method for producing inventive and varied color prints, each one different from the next.

Eager to have his work evaluated by a qualified, disinterested observer, he packed up about a hundred of these graphics and sent them to what he thought would be the proper place, the Solomon R. Guggenheim Foundation Museum of Non-Objective Painting in New York. To his astonishment Hilla Rebay, director of the museum, retained all of them, some for herself and some for the museum. Her letter asking for prices kept him up all night making decisions, as he had never before sold so many works. Given musical names by Miss Rebay, nineteen of the monoprints were exhibited in New York in 1943 by the Guggenheim Foundation. This was one of the largest representations of a single artist in the show, which included works by Moholy-Nagy, Werner Drewes, and Charles Smith, among others.

From that time on he was given frequent showings of both monoprints and jewelry at the Nierendorf Gallery in New York, always to the accompaniment of favorable critical reaction. Before the gallery closed in 1947 after the death of the owner, Bertoia was receiving a monthly stipend from Nierendorf in return for a stipulated portion of his work.

By this time he was married and living in southern California, having been lured there in 1943, by his friend and Cranbrook colleague Charles Eames, to help with the design of a chair Eames was trying to perfect. Bertoia was not yet an American citizen, his naturalization having been delayed because of the war and a technicality regarding his entry through Canada. Nevertheless, he felt a need to help his adopted country's war effort. It pleased him that in addition to his design work on the chair in California, he was able to contribute, in a small way at least, by working on the airplane parts manufactured by the Evans Products Company, of which Eames was director of research and development.

Bertoia finally received his citizenship in 1946. After the war he worked at the Point Loma Naval Electronics Laboratory, doing layouts for reports of scientific studies. Much of the work done at this laboratory was based on human engineering. Stroboscopic photos of human actions were used to help evaluate equipment and provide manuals for those concerned with its use. These photos confirmed the beauty of repetitive line which had interested Bertoia from his earliest drawings and prints. In spite of the monotony of his daily work, Bertoia's two years at Point Loma had a significant influence on his future work. His contacts there provided an exposure to the sciences for his inquiring mind—"one day talking to a marine biologist and the next day to a physicist, each one opening up whole new worlds." It was at this time that he started making sculptures, after hours.

At first Bertoia loved southern California. "We could go almost naked most of the year," he said. But after three or four years he began to realize how much he missed the variety of changing seasons. When Hans Knoll, husband of Cranbrook colleague Florence Schust Knoll, made a proposal that would permit him to return East under conditions that would insure his being able to support his growing family, he accepted with some enthusiasm. Knoll Associates Inc., an international firm promoting good furniture design, already numbered among its associates such men as Ludwig Mies van der Rohe, Pierre Jeanneret, Franco Albini, Isamu Noguchi, and Eero Saarinen. The proposal to Bertoia was a liberal one with a program for the design and development of furniture, of course, but allowing him considerable freedom to do what he liked.

Bertoia set up his studio in Bally, Pennsylvania, between Reading and Allentown, not far from a Knoll factory. He settled his family in a 200-year-old farmhouse in nearby Barto, among the rolling hills of some of the most beautiful and productive farmland of prosperous eastern Pennsylvania. He hopes never to move again.

Thus began in 1950 the years of prolific activity which have continued to the present, gaining momentum from time to time as he worked intermittently on designs for furniture and increasingly on the sculpture which is now his only interest. He works in his two-story barn-like studio most days, including Sundays, and some nights. Two assistants help with the not inconsiderable job of crating for shipment and with elements of some of the mammoth sculptures he has produced on commission in cooperation with a growing number of architects. The planning and installation of these sculptures have required trips all over the country—to Boston, Los Angeles, Minneapolis, New York, St. Louis, Seattle, and Washington, D.C., to name a few of the cities where his commissioned works have been located. Local union membership cards have often been arranged so that final joint-welding could be done by the sculptor himself on the spot. For his accomplishments in the field of architecture, Bertoia was awarded the Craftsmanship Medal of the American Institute of Architects in 1956.

Architects with whom Bertoia has worked are unanimous in describing their association with him as a delightful experience. His "extraordinary sensitivity to architectural spaces and problems" has been attested to by more than one, as has his ability to visualize from blueprints and preliminary stages of construction.[5] In the case of St. John's Unitarian Church in Cincinnati, for example, the original architectural plan specified a forty-foot sculpture to be placed outside the front wall of the sanctuary. When Bertoia was first shown the site on a drizzly day in November, the building in frame without either walls or roof, he said after careful consideration, "You don't need a sculpture on the front of the building because that large oak tree will cast a shadow on the wall and that will be decoration enough."[6]

Following an explanation by architect John Garber of the heliocentric orientation of the church plan with the altar as focal point, they clambered inside the framework. There, standing on narrow planks laid across the floor joists, Bertoia studied what would become the wall behind the altar by having a single plank held vertically in position. His pronouncement, "All right, I think I know what to do," unaccountably made everyone feel the problem had been solved. And so it had, as the completed sculpture proved (plates 1-3). Delivered four months later and designed to take advantage of sunlight and shadow on the brick wall of the interior, it became "the core of the religious services...a thing of richness and complexity in an otherwise very ascetic space."[6]

Since 1950 Bertoia has also produced an uncounted number of small sculptures which have been purchased by museums, such as the Milwaukee Art Center and the Long Beach (California) Museum of Art, as well as by other artists (Max Bill, the Swiss architect and sculptor, for one), and such well-known collectors as Robert W. Sarnoff (no less than six) and Joseph H. Hirshhorn. Art historian Aline Saarinen has said of the latter that "in sculpture his eye is almost infallible: he seems to have an intuitive flair for three-dimensional objects."[7]

Bertoia's works sold through the Fairweather Hardin Gallery in Chicago since 1950 number in the hundreds. The Staempfli Gallery in New York has accounted for a like number since 1959. His works have also been sold through galleries in other cities and direct from his studio. He has been given regular showings by these galleries and has been represented in traveling shows of the Museum of Modern Art and the American Federation of Arts, as well as in the annual sculpture exhibition of the Whitney Museum of American Art. His work has been shown in London, Paris, Amsterdam, and other cities of Europe, where it was well acclaimed.

A European trip in 1957, made possible by a grant of $10,000 from Chicago's Graham Foundation for Advanced Studies in the Fine Arts, gave Bertoia a much-needed rest from the overly-persistent commissions. It permitted him not only to visit his family at San Lorenzo, but also to see for the first time the historic art treasures of Venice, Florence, and Rome, as well as some of the famous museum collections throughout Europe. His own sculptures went on view at the Brussels World's Fair the following year.

His wife Brigitta, whom Bertoia married in 1943 just prior to leaving Cranbrook, accompanied him on the trip to Europe. The daughter of Dr. Wilhelm R. Valentiner, the well-known art historian and Rembrandt scholar who was for a long time director of the Detroit Institute of Arts, Brigitta had been schooled in Switzerland before coming to Cranbrook. The Bertoias have three children, two of whom were born in California. Mara Lesta, the eldest, graduated from the University of California,

Los Angeles, in 1967. Val Odey, their son, is studying at the Indiana Institute of Technology, and Celia Marei attends public school in Pennsylvania.

Bertoia's personality has changed very little since he wrote on his Cranbrook application nearly thirty years ago, "I am rather silent, resolute and industrious." Mrs. J. Robert F. Swanson (Pipsan Saarinen) confirms that at Cranbrook "he was a very quiet and hard working young man who showed a lot of talent particularly in metalwork."[8]

Now middle-aged, bushy-browed and balding, Bertoia has light blue eyes which communicate the sparkle of a man who enjoys living. Of medium height and stocky build, he likes to wear comfortable, loose-fitting clothing, thick soft-soled shoes, and a beret in winter, a straw hat in summer. A pipe smoker, he seems incomplete without one in his mouth. He is soft-spoken, quiet, even taciturn, except when motivated by the rapport established in conversation.

Bertoia is resolutely dedicated to working at his sculpture but always sees it within the larger framework of his complete life. His gentle sense of humor helps him maintain balance between his dedication to his art and the everyday necessities surrounding its fulfillment. When his enthusiasm is stimulated by a new project, he drives himself toward its completion. Yet he prefers an unhurried atmosphere and seeks with typical Italian patience to resolve all problems—eventually. Since 1957 he has accepted only commissions that interest him, refusing those that do not as well as those that conflict with prior commitments. Although his work is based unequivocally on aesthetic principles, his approach to it is a practical one. Architects and businessmen alike are appreciative of his willingness and ability to estimate costs and deliver finished works on time.

Modest and unpossessive about his work, Bertoia frequently has given away a piece of sculpture to one who he knows appreciates its qualities. For himself he prefers to get on with the new rather than to dwell narcissistically on the old. His analytical mind leads him to evaluate his own work critically and the confidence which has come with experience lends credence to such statements concerning his own failures and successes as "The model in the studio was beautiful, but somehow the result did not come up to expectations" (St. Louis airport project) or "This was more successful because it was done on ground already broken" (Manufacturers Hanover Trust screen).

Cranbrook-trained artist Clifford B. West recently made a film entitled, "Harry Bertoia's Sculpture." After the brief introductory script, written by his wife Eleanor T. West, the sculpture itself took over the soundtrack. Mrs. West quoted Confucius in the first paragraph of her script, then continued on her own:

"Creative endeavor without possession, action without self-assertion, development without domination, these are intrinsic virtues."

So believes the sculptor, Harry Bertoia. His works are never signed and seldom named. His sculpture seems to belong more to the people who see it than to the man who created it.

In every person, these sculptured units of form, color and sound strike an individual chord—and their range is infinite—from stars to the bottom of the sea, from mist to silver precision, from the presence of everyday things to the unexpectedness of a reality merely sensed.

The sculpture of Harry Bertoia is elemental; sometimes stark, sometimes gay. It is a rediscovery, a remembering, an experience.[9]

Experiments and Techniques

Bertoia's earliest known published work is a series of woodcuts done at Cranbrook to illustrate an avant-garde play written by a friend and privately printed in 1943.[1] These woodcuts reveal an early mastery of line drawing based on an awareness of the work of Matisse and Picasso. Having been talked into doing them in spite of his preference not to, Bertoia considers these figural illustrations a deviation from his true interest at the time, which was completely abstract. A few years earlier, however, he had been working in a much more realistic manner, as the pair of woodcuts reproduced here shows (plates 4, 5). Nostalgic recollections of farm life in Italy, they have a marvelous narrative readability and a wealth of detail. The zigzag design of the one and the horizontal strips of the other point to his later woodblock experiments in abstract composition.

Since his earliest abstract drawings (plates 6, 7, 8, 9), Bertoia has drawn what he feels and not what he sees. He has tried several times to explain what drawing meant to him.

In a statement published in 1944 Bertoia said: "Drawing is a way of learning, a way of finding a truth. A line commences somewhere, gathers momentum, spends its energy and comes to an equilibrium equivalent to a life-cycle. It could also be said that it establishes its norm of balance and dimension. I draw what I don't know in order to learn something about it."[2] A year later, in conjunction with the production of a book of eighty-four of his drawings which, he said, were "not meant to tell a story nor to represent anything but themselves," he wrote: "In a period of inaction a certain something begins to form, to ferment and to build up and around. However vague its content, its development continues relentlessly until it takes physical existence through medium, e.g., paper and ink."[3] Ten years later he revealed: "There was a time when I thought that drawing was a way of learning. I know now it is more."[4] In 1969, after more than twenty years, his drawings are still important to him. He does not like to sell any of them, for he considers them his "notebook," the basis for all his work. Each one contains the seed of ideas for a number of his sculptures.

The medium for Bertoia's drawings soon became almost exclusively printer's ink on rice paper in an unusual technique which he still uses today for working drawings of his sculpture. Ink is rolled out on a table top and the paper laid over it. He then draws on the back of the paper either with his fingers or with a pencil or stylus, causing the paper to pick up ink from below in a soft, vaporous-looking texture. Sometimes a sweep of the back of his hand produces the background, picking up a shadowy reverse of the previous drawing to form the basis for the new one. Details are filled in in a variety of ways. Lines are drawn freehand, even the precisely repeated straight lines, and occasionally they are scratched into the still-wet ink after the drawing has been pulled from the table. Many of the early monoprints were begun this way (plates 10, 11). Colors were subtly muted and as early as 1942 he began using powdered metals to harden the inks and add lustre.

Other monoprints, like one owned by the Museum of Modern Art (plate 12), were made by cutting a woodblock into small identically-shaped sections and constantly rearranging these forms, a versatile invention, somewhat like Gutenberg's movable type, for producing infinitely varied abstract patterns on paper. Light colors were laid on over darker grounds and metallic inks sometimes over all. The resulting monoprints were produced without pre-established designs. Most were done on transparent oriental paper and frequently they were framed in copper with glass on both sides so they could be hung in a window to catch the light. Some were done in series, like the movements of a symphony (plates 13, 14). Before leaving Cranbrook, Bertoia had a show, and many of the framed monoprints were purchased by his admiring colleagues.

The Museum of Modern Art print (plate 12) can be considered as either a horizontal or vertical composition. It has a background of soft greyed-blue with touches of deep navy blue, bright blue, and intense light blue. The small shapes are superimposed in muted oranges and the larger overlays are in metallic gold. The forms have a three-dimensional look and appear to be floating in space. A similar technique but different coloring and forms were used in the Guggenheim Museum's *Multicolored Trapezoids* (plate 13) and in its counterpart (plate 14).

The monoprints still in the possession of the Guggenheim Museum (at least thirty-four) represent two styles of Bertoia's work of this period —one dominated by line, the other by form. Lines are soft, or softened by the texture of the background on which they are drawn. Sometimes they are seemingly random doodles, but repetition is an important factor in holding the linear design together, as it is also in the form-dominated prints. Here are the beginnings of a life-long interest in the aesthetic effects created by identical forms repeated in varying positions in space.

Still another graphic work that combines both line and form is the Guggenheim's small *Fugue* (6½ x 6½ inches). It contains a minimum of very precisely placed elements in a beautifully balanced composition in reds, greens, gold, and soft browns. Bertoia's paintings, which were mostly oils on masonite or other board, tended to be somewhat larger than the monoprints but reveal a similar variety of abstract compositions relating line and form in space.

From the first Bertoia's monoprints received favorable critical notices. The 1943 Guggenheim show was reviewed by Carlyle Burrows for the *Christian Science Monitor.* While complaining, "There is not a great deal that one can describe intelligibly in a show of this sort even though its manifestations are varied and resourceful," with regard to Bertoia he declared it was clear his work had been invited with special confidence. "Bertoia...works with precise but graceful line and delicate color and usually avoids the somewhat general 'geometric' classification into which the exhibited work falls."[5] *Art Digest,* reviewing the same show, called Bertoia's prints "the nicest development of all the departures we found here."[6]

Early in 1945 monoprints and jewelry were displayed at the Nierendorf Gallery, "filling three rooms and several cases." One reviewer put Bertoia in Paul Klee's sphere as "the one artist, if any, he follows."[7] According to another, he was "confirmed [as] one of the most inventive and original of the non-objective painters."[8] At a later showing where his prints were presented along with Ernest Mundt's mobiles and Adolph Gottlieb's oils, Bertoia's work was lauded for its "feeling for space and texture."[9]

In a review, "Tobey and Bertoia: Fantasy and Geometry," Alfred Frankenstein wrote in the fall of 1945 about two separate shows at the San Francisco Museum of Art. Of Bertoia's work he said, "The whole thing is very subtle in tone, texture, formal arrangement, and dynamic movement, and leads one to hope that a larger Bertoia show may be forthcoming."[10]

The jewelry produced by Bertoia in the forties while he was teaching metalcraft at Cranbrook was as inventive and varied as his graphic work (plates 15, 16). Closely related in style to his monoprints and paintings, it is important in the larger body of his work as his first experimentation in designing with metal and presages the variety of form and texture of much of his later sculpture.

His fascination with the effects of light led Bertoia, while still at Cranbrook, to construct models, first in cardboard, then in metal, based on a uniform modulus (not unlike some of his cutout woodcut forms) wired together but spaced apart on different vertical planes. Though all parts are painted a stark white, when the model is placed in a window (plate 17), the gradation of values that the light imposes on the forms creates a varied pattern. This model formed the basis of one of his major concepts out of which later grew a group of important sculptures.

The path from monoprints and jewelry to furniture design, and finally sculpture, had a more logical progression than at first appears. The saga of the chair (or more appropriately, chairs) is an interesting one. It all began back in 1940-41 when Charles Eames and Eero Saarinen won a first prize in an industrial design contest sponsored by the Museum of Modern Art in New York, with the design for a molded plywood chair they had entered as a joint venture. After winning the award, they went their separate ways, developing chairs in different directions. Saarinen's famous "womb chair" was the final result of his part in that project.

Eames, on the other hand, moved to California to solve the problem of the high cost of the molding process which was preventing manufacturers from producing his chair. In addition to Bertoia, he persuaded Don Albinson, who now works for Knoll, Herbert Matter, a photographer, and Gregory Ayn, an architect, to work on the project. All contributed something. Drastic changes in the shape of the plywood and the metal frame resulted from Bertoia's efforts to avoid torturing the wood.

Thus it was not "out of the blue" that the proposal came from Knoll Associates in 1950. Hans and Florence Knoll were very much aware of Bertoia's activities in the field of design and the Knoll policy that "everybody here gets credit for his work" was guaranteed to appeal.[11] Also, according to Knoll policy, the artist receives a royalty on each piece of furniture designed by him that is manufactured and sold.

The Bertoia chair (plate 18), which came on the market in 1952 and is still being sold through Knoll International, is completely different from the Eames chair, both aesthetically and functionally. Made of a web of wires welded into a basically diamond shape, then bent to form a graceful receptacle for the body, it is suspended cradle-like in a wire frame. It can be completely upholstered or merely seat-padded, leaving the backrest portion free to reveal the repetition of the basic diamond shape in its criss-crossed wires. It is an excellent design, functional yet full of grace.

Hans Theodor Flemming, author of several books and since 1946 art critic for *Die Welt,* wrote an article in 1960 surveying the American "pioneer spirit" in art which, he said, "caused more dismay than admiration in Europe, and especially in Paris." Among other observations, in the course of which he complimented Bertoia's architectural sculpture as "a happy synthesis of 'free' and 'applied' art," he commented, "The metal chairs designed by Bertoia for Knoll International may also be works of art on a level with the allegedly 'free' creations of his colleagues."[12]

Bertoia also designed for Knoll a high-backed chair and ottoman, a side chair of criss-crossed wires with a square rather than diamond shape, and a bench made of metal and slats. By 1953 Bertoia had ceased thinking about furniture, although he remains to this day available to Knoll for consultation, and was devoting his full time and energies to sculpture.

Since Bertoia had worked with metals at Cass Tech, and at Cranbrook during his jewelry designing days, and with metal rods and wires for furniture both in California and Pennsylvania, it was natural that his creative talent should assert itself with these materials. Some of his earliest sculptures, done in California in 1947-48, have a spindly look and show his concern for vertical balance (plate 19). Many of those first exhibited in New York at the Knoll showrooms in the early fifties were based on line and repeated modulus in a variety of space planes (plate 20). Some were an almost direct translation into three-dimensional actuality of his illusionary graphics of the preceding decade. "The structures have a cellular regularity, organic like honeycombs, chemical like crystals. With neither a beginning nor an end, they lace through space without enclosing it, are jagged, unfinished, with a magical suggestion of continued movement," wrote one observer.[13]

"One prevailing characteristic of sculpture is the interplay of void and matter, the void being of equal value to the component material units," Bertoia has said.[14] From the beginning his sculptures were constructions in metal using rods and wire to define space and to support abstract shapes usually cut out of flat sheets of enameling steel. He uses an acetylene torch for the cutting as well as for melting other metals—brass, nickel, copper—which he flows onto the forms and rods to obtain textured surfaces. He employs industrial metal shot to enhance the textures. His works are sometimes gilded and frequently lacquered to preserve their surfaces. He is constantly experimenting with different metals and his experiments have often led him into entirely new areas of sculpture.

When Bertoia became interested in bronze casting, for instance, characteristically he began by experimenting and developed a direct casting process all his own. Following is a description of this technique published recently in Craft Horizons:

Harry Bertoia experiments with pouring the molten metal with a minimum of limiting mold, or with no mold at all. This takes us back to an aspect of casting so ancient that its origins are unknown, except that it must have preceded lost-wax and sand casting. It is also putting to serious use the foundryman's game of pouring out the metal at the end of the day and remarking on the free and evocative shapes it assumes in hardening.

Bertoia pours his molten bronze in a shallow, concave pit, and then works on the surface of this metallic pond as it cools by scraping, cutting, punching, and adding water to cause parts of the metal to cool more rapidly than others. The end result is a large, flattish, torn relief puckered, blistered, and otherwise textured and with a curiously fascinating color.[15]

This is a fairly accurate description of his "action sculpture" technique, except that for reasons of safety, water is not poured until after most of the action is over. In addition, Bertoia likes to relate stones to metal and collects a pile of smooth and rough ones of varying sizes in his studio, to be plunged into the molten mass at the proper time.

30

Large Scale Commissions

Unlike many American sculptors today who shun the utilitarian, Bertoia likes to work with architects. Their projects give him the opportunity to do large-scale works he couldn't otherwise afford. He considers it a challenge, an intellectual exercise, to cope with the requirements of architectural commissions. He has not sought them, but rather they have come to him, at first through his acquaintances and later, in greater abundance than he has been able to handle, through architects unknown to him, as a result of his early successes.

Eero Saarinen was the first to call upon his talent. One of the buildings in his enormous Mondrian-like layout for the General Motors Technical Center in Warren, Michigan, needed a device to enhance both its lobby and the functional part of its main floor. Bertoia set to work on the problem and the result was the golden, textured metal screen sculpture which divides the entryway from the dining area in the main restaurant building (plate 21). Visible from the outside through the glass façade, from far away it is seen as a large horizontal rectangle of brilliant gold. On closer inspection it becomes a myriad of small gold rectangles placed vertically on three different planes, connected by rods, with an occasional "trill" of smaller, more open forms placed where they add the most interest to the design. From the other side, the screen provides the dining employees with privacy (sheltering them from the street outside) as well as the interest of its variety in texture and contrast between space and form.

This, his first of several architectural screens, obviously related to his 1943 experiments (see plate 17), was an exercise in large scale design incorporating space and light. It was finished in 1953. There are two unfortunate aspects. First, its proximity to the dining tables permits people to use its projections for coat racks (Bertoia says this is all right but does not help the design), and second, from the inside looking out it loses some of its color and texture as the forms are silhouetted against the outside light. From the lobby, however, the piece is effective both in its architectural serviceability and as sculpture. The individual panels are related to each other through the shadows cast from plane to plane by the light which acts, along with the repeated modulus and varied textures, as an element of design. Here we have

the first large-scale three-dimensional result of the
Guggenheim monoprints.

There followed almost immediately a commission from the
Manufacturers Trust (now Manufacturers Hanover Trust) Company for
a screen with a similar purpose for their building at 43rd Street and
Fifth Avenue in New York City, then being built by the architectural
firm of Skidmore, Owings and Merrill. This enormous sculpture wall
(sixteen feet high, seventy long, and two deep), which serves to
separate the public from the private portion of the main banking floor,
was completed and installed in 1954 (plate 22). It contains more than
eight hundred separate forms placed in five different vertical planes,
with a network of connecting and supporting rods and braces, the
whole anchored to both floor and ceiling. It weighs more than five tons
and was constructed and shipped in seven 1,500-pound sections. It is
golden in color and textured with copper, bronze, and nickel fused
together on the metal plates.

Generally similar in purpose and design, the screen for the General
Motors Technical Center and the Manufacturers Hanover Trust
sculpture wall beg to be compared. Almost twice as big and with its
component parts scaled accordingly, the latter has a greater proportion
of open to closed forms, a more complicated five-plane structure, and
more favorable overhead lighting, which reveals clearly the interlacing
of its structural members. (Plate 23 shows the intricacy of its welded
construction as well as the textural variety of some of
the individual units.)

Both screens act as backgrounds for their own presentations of
sculptures-within-a-sculpture—the invented abstract structures which
appear here and there in intervals between the panels. Each one is a
sculptural gem which could stand alone. They show to best advantage
in the General Motors screen, perhaps because there are fewer of them,
perhaps because each one is more delicately detailed than in the
larger screen, perhaps because the smaller size of the repeated
modulus gives greater uniformity to the background, thereby
emphasizing the contrast. This uniformity carries with it a certain
monotony, however, which is altogether lacking in the bigger and
bolder Manufacturers Hanover Trust screen. Profiting from the lessons
learned in working on its prototype, Bertoia here combined innovation
with repetition in a buoyant manner which leads the eye along a
bouncing course from one end of the wall to the other, up and down,
back and forth, and yet does not destroy the unity of the whole.

The Manufacturers Trust screen received instantaneous critical
acclaim. Instantaneous possibly because of its location (within easy
access of New York-based art critics), but it was unanimously
acclaimed for its intrinsic beauty, technical excellence, and the
inventive variety of its design—one of the first successful collaborations
in modern times between sculptor and architect. Ada Louise
Huxtable wrote:

The screen wall is a note of Byzantine splendor in an otherwise austerely elegant interior. Brilliant gold in color, primitive in texture and pattern, it is the perfect accent for the polished surroundings....The result, here, has been the successful integration of two of the major arts.[1]

More recently, it has been described as "undoubtedly the outstanding example of welded metal sculpture in architectural use."[2]

A year later, after some preliminary experiments with cloudlike sculptures (plate 24), Bertoia completed another large screen, quite different from its predecessors, for Eero Saarinen's unusual interfaith chapel at the Massachusetts Institute of Technology. Here the screen, more appropriately called a reredos (plate 25), serves to separate the back of the altar from a stairway to a lower floor where vestments and religious objects are stored. It utilizes and magnifies the dramatic effect of the only direct light in the chapel, a shaft that descends from a skylight or lantern onto a starkly simple three-foot high block of solid marble, which serves as an altar.

The sculpture is made up of twenty-four metal cords spaced equidistantly in an arc, stretched from the skylight to the second step of the three-step circular platform of travertine marble on which the altar slab is placed. Small, textured, flat, rectangular brass plates, as well as a number of open rectangles and triangles made of wire, are welded to the rigid vertical cords at different heights and angles to catch or deflect the descending light. (The lantern also provides artificial light for night use.) The effect is of a twinkling cascade of light caught in tiny pockets quite like moonbeams reflected on the ripples of night-darkened water. The dimly lit chapel gains spirituality from this evanescent reredos which changes constantly, sometimes dramatically, as the sun traverses the sky or emerges from behind a cloud.

Other commissions followed in profusion for screens, fountains, and free-standing pieces in cities as far apart as Miami, Florida, and Tulsa, Oklahoma, but it was not until 1962 that Bertoia started working on the large bronze panel for the Dulles International Airport at Chantilly, Virginia. Dedicated by President Kennedy in the spring of the following year, the building had been designed some years earlier by Eero Saarinen. When Saarinen died prematurely, Kevin Roche took over and it was he who contacted Bertoia concerning a sculptural work. They ultimately agreed on a large mural-like poured bronze panel in the new casting technique Bertoia was experimenting with at the time. It was to be placed in front of the entrances to the restaurant, on the main floor of the south wing of the air terminal. The geophysical nature of the completed sculpture was also decided at that first meeting with Roche.

Bertoia looked upon the Dulles Airport commission as a great opportunity, culminating his experiments in working with molten bronze. After a year of preparation, an original rejection by the committee, and later acceptance of the proposed sculpture, the actual casting of the nine eight-foot by four-foot sections of the mural was accomplished within twenty-four hours, using the method described in *Craft Horizons*.[3] Four tons of bronze were consumed in the process, which involved the firing of two furnaces simultaneously to a temperature of close to 2000° F. The contents of both furnaces were then poured on a flatbed of sand and manipulated according to plan during the brief liquid state of the metal—a matter of minutes. Many of the carefully laid plans evaporated with the pouring when immediate, frenzied, direct action took over. It was a physically exhausting undertaking. Originally, all the casting was to be done the same day in order to avoid noticeable differences among the panels which Bertoia felt would occur if some of the work were carried overnight. However, having started early in the morning of what turned out to be a very hot day, they had to call a halt at four o'clock in the afternoon, with two panels yet to be poured. Bertoia and his two assistants, as well as the foundrymen, were completely enervated. The differences he feared show up as minor flaws in transitions between the last two panels, but generally it all worked out very satisfactorily.

The result is a multi-colored metal mural which, in a purely abstract manner, creates a suggestion of the continuing formative processes of our universe throughout time (plate 26). The surface of the sculpture is rough and dry. The panels have a dark brown background providing a foil for the light colored swirls and encrustations in shades varying from light brown through yellow-green to blue-green. Many jagged holes and an occasional polished bronze highlight enliven the work, which has a painterly quality seldom seen in sculpture. For each viewer it creates a different vision—perhaps an agitated, boiling upheaval of the earth's surface in the process of evolution, or a greenish milky way swirling through the darkness of outer space. The tactile sensations it engenders are so powerful and the sense of movement created by its swirling energies is so overwhelming that the spectator feels himself to be a part of the action. It is truly a monumental work, from conception to completion.

Bertoia, who had occasion to view the mural again in 1966, three years after its installation, said he had the unusual feeling of seeing it for the first time, almost as though it had been done by someone else. He was pleased by what he saw and said in a considered, deliberate tone of voice, "I have no doubt that it is a unique work in our age."

About the time of the Dulles Airport bronze, several non-functional sculptures were done on commission through architects who availed themselves of Bertoia's talent to enhance their buildings. In 1962 the Banker's Trust Company commissioned, through Henry Dreyfuss & Associates, a delicate wall-hung piece of welded brass rods for their headquarters building in New York (plate 27). At the instigation of President Clarence P. Bryan, the Cuyahoga Savings Association of Cleveland, Ohio, ordered a ceiling-suspended stainless steel wire hemisphere, completed in 1965 (plate 28). For Minoru Yamasaki's

Woodrow Wilson School of Public and International Affairs at Princeton University, Bertoia created on a pedestal a rugged fifty-inch globe of bronze rods emanating from a central core, the outer ends forming a rippling, penetrable surface (plate 29). Though the globe is massive, Bertoia wanted to do it without a solid surface in order to hint at the realities of atmosphere. Its complex character, as well as the implication of its setting in the center of a glass-enclosed sky-lighted lounge-lobby, make of it a globe of the modern world (plate 30). It seems to represent a planet in turmoil, almost about to burst asunder by force of its internal struggles, yet somehow serenely contained in all its lumpish contours.

That same year (1964) saw the completion and installation of another large sculpture (fourteen feet high, forty-six long, and four deep) in the lobby of Yamasaki's elegant building for the Northwestern National Life Insurance Company in Minneapolis. This was an enormous undertaking requiring a full year for construction. Photographs were made to document the work as it progressed.

The commission resulted from a recommendation by the architect, who accompanied Northwestern National's President John Pillsbury Jr. to Bally, Pennsylvania, to examine Bertoia's work. Bertoia then made preliminary drawings and a scale model (plate 31). He worked from architectural plans furnished by Yamasaki, and once the commission was approved, experimented with methods of construction.

The Northwestern National sculpture is composed of thousands of textured metal rods welded together in groups like loose bundles of straw which jut out in different directions.

Six months were spent in coating individual steel rods with a brass alloy to produce a textured surface something like that of a dripping candle (plate 32). Designed to be seen overhead like a Greek frieze, the piece was suspended from the ceiling of the studio in order to get the proper perspective during construction (plate 34). This also facilitated the welding process, which required two men for each operation, as the rods had to be made rigid at the proper angle (plate 33). Some time later Bertoia met with Yamasaki and Northwestern National officials to look over the architectural space in the nearly finished building (plate 35). When completed, the sculpture's 600-pound sections were shipped to Minneapolis by flatbed truck (plate 36). After being hoisted onto the ledge in the building's lobby (plate 37), the sections were mechanically joined together (plate 38).

The completed sculpture seems to float in space, although it actually rests on tiny feet, which are invisible from the ground level (plate 39). Its position, two feet away from the wall against which it is placed, allows light to penetrate around the rods and reveal the complicated woven structure (plate 40). The focal point of a white marble lobby, this sculpture is delicate and lacy in appearance in spite of its enormous size. It faces the viewer in close proximity overhead as he enters the building through a glass wall, and his attention is caught by the warm gold of its rough, dry texture contrasted against the smooth coldness of the marble walls. The color, dryness and texture of the rods combine with the contrasting bits of turquoise, like the flash of a butterfly's wings, and the airiness of the whole effect, to suggest the totality of the Midwest farmland—its spaciousness and its bountiful harvests.

The only major Bertoia sculpture to be given a name, this one came to be called *Sunlit Straw* by a rather complicated process. When the people at Northwestern National pressed him, Bertoia asked each member of his family to make a list of suggestions. They came up with a total of thirty-three names, from which he chose three to submit to the company. From the three, John Pillsbury chose *Sunlit Straw*. The story circulated by Northwestern National's public relations department —that the name was given after a group of Amish people visiting the studio while work was in progress commented on its appropriateness for the Midwest because of its resemblance to a field of golden grain— is at least partially true. Amish people living in the vicinity of his studio did see the sculpture and make such a comment. The members of Bertoia's family were aware of this.

"Reaction to the work has been almost universally favorable, in fact, more often enthusiastic," wrote Kenneth K. Wunsch of Northwestern National.[4] Professor Laurence Schmeckebier, dean of Syracuse University's School of Art, called it "one of the most significant examples of twentieth century sculpture in America," and wrote Bertoia a letter to that effect.[5] Certainly it represents another successful architect-sculptor collaboration, and one that is completely different in both tone and technique from his previous large commissions.

Another major work was completed and installed in September 1966. It is the fountain sculpture for the River Oaks Shopping Center at Calumet City, Illinois, done at the request of the center's architects, Loebl Schlossman Bennett and Dart. "I am a great admirer of Bertoia's work and have one of his pieces in my home," wrote Jerrold Loebl. "In doing the shopping center, we naturally envisioned the possibility of having Bertoia do a piece of sculpture for the fountain.... Through Fairweather Hardin, Bertoia came and spent some time with us. All we could show him at the time were our mall and landscaping drawings and the general concept we envisioned. He came back a month later with several different schemes. We decided on one which was then created for the space."[6]

The River Oaks fountain was based on Bertoia's studies of sound in sculpture (plates 41, 42). Made of one-half inch thick Tobin bronze rods welded into a vertical position side by side on a thin metal base, the piece weighs about 4,500 pounds, and is nine feet high, ten wide, and eight deep. The rods are of differing lengths and are free at the top so that when the wind moves them against each other there should be a deep reverberating sound, like that of many bells. Tobin bronze was especially chosen as the material for the rods because of the sound it produces. Since the winds of the region are reputedly very strong, Bertoia used fairly heavy rods and was prepared to muffle them if necessary. Apparently he overcorrected for Chicago's windy conditions as, unfortunately, the sound is heard only occasionally. He calculates now that he could change that situation by extending the rods.

Such an extension would, of course, change the basic proportions of the sculpture and would improve its relationship to its surroundings. The River Oaks center is one of the most beautifully landscaped shopping centers in the country. However, the buildings surrounding the Bertoia fountain are all low and architecturally undistinguished, except the Marshall Field building, which has an arcaded façade of very high archways. A more vertically oriented sculpture would balance nicely between the archways and the repeated horizontals, and would be a more prominent feature of the general landscape.

The pool in which the piece is installed is circular and the fountain is limited to six two-foot high jets around its outer edge, so that the play of water has little or no bearing on the effectiveness of the sculpture. The color of the oxidation (a bright turquoise) and the repeated verticals of the rods give their own suggestion of water, which a directed spray would merely detract from.

Two very different pieces—one for the center of another fountain and the other a functional architectural screen in color—were completed in 1967. The latter, in the Federal Court Building in Brooklyn's Civic Center (plate 43), was commissioned by the General Services Administration on the recommendation of the architects, Carson, Lundin & Shaw and Lorimer Rich, who had the problem of coping with an unattractive view at one end of a long marble hall (one hundred and twenty-five feet). Bertoia's solution was a screen composed of uniform twenty-four inch squares of laminated asbestos, each textured and finished in a flat paint on both sides in one or another of three shades of yellow, or white. The squares are mounted in vertical positions on four different planes in front of a glass window-wall (plate 44). The choice of colors and the positioning of the squares were carefully calculated to allow for the reflection of light from the back of one form to the front surface of another, thus multiplying the range of color values.

The finished screen is twenty-four feet high and thirty-six feet wide. A sun-colored design that changes by the hour as well as by the day according to the changing light, it provides the only bright color in the enormous marble hall. Viewed from inside or outside the building, the shadows formed by the squares in one plane reflected on those in another plane create an intricate and constantly shifting display of large and small rectilinear patterns in a variety of tints, reminding one once again of the 1943 experiments at Cranbrook. "Of the many possible shapes, the square offers the greatest variety of combinations,"

Bertoia has said.[7] The Brooklyn Federal Court screen demonstrates intriguingly the validity of that statement, in spite of the incongruity of the materials of which it is made with the materials of its interior setting.

A fountain piece, the other major 1967 commission was arranged for according to the standard procedure of the city of Philadelphia, which has an official policy for the "aesthetic ornamentation of city structures" and an art commission which must approve expenditures. Edward Durell Stone, in consultation with the architect for the new Philadelphia Civic Center, Davis, Pool & Sloan, wrote a letter to the Philadelphia Art Commission recommending Bertoia. Upon approval by the commission of a preliminary sketch, Bertoia's contract was drawn up with the architect.

The fountain structure is made of copper tubes, bronze-welded together to form a wildly undulating membrane-like surface and a central stem (plates 45, 46). Water does not flow through the tubes but is played onto the sculpture from six large jets close to the piece and about eighty smaller jets encircling it and playing onto its fantastic form from the outer perimeter of a waist-high pool, forty-five feet in diameter. The sculpture is the focal point not only of the pool but also of the entire plaza, an elevated square open to the street on one side and otherwise enclosed by the contiguous buildings of the Civic Center. These white-walled buildings are of different heights, the lowest between the other two, but they have the same severely rectilinear ornamentation. In its saucer-like pool the dark (almost black) fountain structure is well-porportioned and provides a maximum contrast to its setting as its form swoops and swirls like the most fantastic mushroom of a forest before the stark white geometry of the center's façade. A walk around it reveals new descriptions of positive and negative space with each step.

The height of the water jets is controlled by a wind sensor placed in a nearby flagpole. At its highest setting the water splashes over and into the sculpture, almost obscuring its form, running down and out of its mysterious convolutions, and adding animation to the scene (plate 47). People often break into smiles as they approach and circle round the fountain. The first winter of its existence it choked up with tons of ice one night when someone failed to turn off the water. The structure withstood the added weight without damage and Philadelphians were treated to an unusual sight until the thaw.

In 1968 another fountain based on the same technique was completed and installed in front of Yamasaki's skyscraper for the Manufacturers and Traders Trust Company in Buffalo (plates 48, 49). This one is in an oval pool surrounded by a large open plaza. Since Buffalo has long winters with too much wind and ice for splashing water jets to be practical, the fountain is constructed with an open center and water pipes emerging therefrom unobtrusively follow the contours of the sculpture, some underneath and some on top of its surface membrane.

Water drips lazily from its amply curved or cut edges as from a full-blown flower in a light rain. The variegated patina of pastel shades of blue-green and brown is as appropriate to the flower-like unfurling of this sculptural form as black is to the more tumultuous form of the Philadelphia fountain.

Also in 1968 an enormous project was undertaken for Seattle-First National Bank through the architectural firm of Naramore, Bain, Brady & Johanson—a ceiling sculpture thirty-two feet in diameter, consisting of thirty-six stainless steel wire sprays of varying diameters and lengths, suspended singly and in groups of two and three, one within the other, from twenty separate points of support. A photograph taken in November of that year shows Bertoia installing one of the sprays (plate 50). The sculpture hangs from a twenty-six foot high ceiling in a fifty by seventy foot glass pavilion which forms part of the main banking room. It is visible from an approach at a higher level and also as one descends an escalator to the banking floor.

In addition to the works already mentioned, Bertoia has completed many other commissions of varying size and importance since 1953. A 350-pound, fourteen-foot hanging piece, made for W. Hawkins Ferry's lakeside home in Grosse Pointe Shores, Michigan, was conceived during the processing of the Northwestern National commission and comes to grips with the same concepts (plate 51). Its construction helped clarify the physical procedure for the larger Minneapolis piece.

William H. Kessler of Meathe, Kessler & Associates, architects of the Ferry residence, which houses a remarkable collection of modern art, suggested a sculpture for the area near the entry to the dining room. When Mr. Ferry asked Bertoia to do one, he at first hesitated, being occupied at the time with the paper work for the huge piece for Minneapolis. However, on seeing the Ferry house under construction, while in Detroit for the opening of the J. L. Hudson Gallery's showing of his late father-in-law's art collection, he decided to accept the commission. He did six drawings, from which Mr. Ferry made his choice.[8]

Having more color (red and brown as well as turquoise in irregular flower-like shapes at the ends of the rods), it is also more intricately interlaced than the Minnesota sculpture. Though it is hung by a supporting rod from the second story ceiling, Bertoia also provided it with feet so it could rest on the floor if desired. At night the light from an overhead spot appears to emanate from the golden rods themselves, and the sculpture is reflected, along with a nine-foot tall, columnar Giacometti figure of a woman, in the glass window wall across the living room, creating a marvelous effect.[9]

Among Bertoia's other commissioned works, the following were done in cooperation with the architects indicated (a checklist of commissioned works is provided in the Appendix):

Edward Durell Stone, a ten-foot sphere of twenty-four karat gold-coated wire which swayed on a slender twenty-foot steel stem above a lagoon in front of the Perpetual Savings and Loan Association Building in Beverly Hills, California (plate 52). This sculpture, composed of 84,000 parts, was a project in engineering as well as design balance.[10] Light and fluffy in appearance in spite of its enormous size, it seemed to be reaching for the sun through a cloud of mist created by fine jets of water at the base of the fountain, according to one description.[11]

Victor Gruen Associates, two vertical metal screens made in the manner of the Manufacturers Trust screen, but composed more freely, for the Dayton Store, Southdale Center, Edina, Minnesota (plate 53).

George Leighton Dahl, a sculptured metal screen, for the Dallas Public Library, Dallas, Texas (plate 54).

I. M. Pei, a balanced sphere and a free-standing metal "tree" screen, for the lobby of the Denver Hilton Hotel (plates 55, 56).

Kevin Roche John Dinkeloo & Associates, three four-foot cubes made of poured bronze panels, used as tree planters in a glass enclosed space at the Rochester (New York) Institute of Technology's new campus.

Investigations

Quite naturally some of Bertoia's commissions were more successful than others, and this applies also to the hundreds of smaller sculptures he created during the same period. One characteristic, however, that stands out among them all is their variety which, paradoxically enough, is particularly evident in whole groups of sculptures having great similarity, like the screens or the series of small bush-like forms. Like musical variations on a theme, they display the sculptor's virtuosity. For Bertoia does work principally in only four major areas or themes, into which almost every one of his sculptures can be categorized. "The validity of an idea is tested each time it takes physical shape. As long as new shapes keep forming, the idea has not yet reached fulfillment," he says, and his work attests to his continuing investigations into those concepts which, from the beginning, have interested him the most.

First are his studies in light and space which began with the monoprints and their "movable type" method of using repeated small forms. This technique led to the three-dimensional experiments described and illustrated above (plate 17). The introduction of metal for the screens kept the work monochromatic for a while, but light and its changing effects were always important (plates 21, 22, 25). The Staempfli Gallery's *Hollow Forms* is another result of these studies (plate 57), as is the small screen owned by the Theodore Lyman Wright Art Center at Beloit College, Beloit, Wisconsin. The latter was shown in a remarkably representative though succinct exhibition, "Sculpture 1950-1958" (twenty-three pieces), at the Allen Memorial Art Museum, Oberlin College, Oberlin, Ohio. In his catalog commentary Forbes Whiteside alluded to Bertoia's work:

Open constructions, which so strongly suggest steel and glass-enclosed buildings, have this in common with modern architecture: both are more concerned with modulating space than mass. If some sculptured works seem to lack a proper amount of bulk, contemplate the negative as well as the positive masses. Rods and bars define the edges and corners of the masses while each thin plate establishes the position and angle of one plane of a transparent volume.[1]

Later experiments in light and space became airier and airier as the modulus itself became a textured rod. While maintaining a basic monotone, Bertoia brought some color into play in the Northwestern National piece (plate 39) and in the one for W. Hawkins Ferry (plate 51), as well as in the *Golden Screen* owned by Robert W. Sarnoff (plate 58) and another small one owned by the Graham Foundation of Chicago, which Bertoia considers the most successful of all. From the St. Louis Airport screen of 1955 (plate 76) to the Brooklyn Federal Court screen of 1967 (plate 43), color has added further interest as his studies in light and space continue. In a rare speech given in 1955 at the International Design Conference in Aspen, Colorado, Bertoia revealed some of his thoughts with regard to color:

What happens when structure and color get together? Exploration of the possibilities of color leads to a new and very significant function. Structure enables color to attain higher intensities. It gives color a chance to receive light from more than one direction. The reflective possibilities attain an unbelievable degree of intensity and opalescence.

Architecture can benefit greatly by the use of color in ways that can give poetic expression to the thinking mind.[2]

A second investigation has been conducted over the years into the possibilities of both sound and motion in sculpture. Stemming from his lifelong interest and that of his family in music, Bertoia's experiments along these lines have elicited sculptures which produce sound as they shiver and shake when rubbed or touched by the wind or any slight disturbance. The River Oaks fountain was a not completely successful large-scale attempt in this direction (plate 41), but many smaller sculptures, like the untitled bronze in the collection of Mr. and Mrs. Irving Castle (plate 59), reverberate for a long time, setting up a strange cacophony as of ocean waves crashing and receding in a metal cave. In his show at the Staempfli Gallery in the spring of 1968, several musical sculptures were grouped together (plate 61). Each one produced a different sound when set into motion by a touch and the gallery was kept ringing with a variety of mellow tones. His experiments with various materials—bronze and beryllium copper rods and nickel alloys, to mention a few—have revealed that sculpture can produce musical sound, a fact which was effectively demonstrated in the soundtrack for Clifford B. West's film on Bertoia.

These experiments have also produced pieces like the one in the Joseph H. Hirshhorn collection—a forty-eight inch high sheaf of stainless steel wires embedded in the center of a fourteen-inch diameter steel-encircled concrete base. A half-inch wide steel collar with an adjustable key can be slid down to create a spreading motion at the top, like that of a slowly opening flower. The sheared ends of the released wires catch pinpoints of light as they wave to and fro to the accompaniment of a light metallic rattle. Other sculptures made of sheaves of wires are also designed to move slowly and gracefully when touched, like the one in the collection of Mr. and Mrs. Martin Roaman (plate 60), or are twisted and bound top and bottom so that they produce an undulating motion like that of a human muscle (plate 62).

A third theme which has interested Bertoia for a long time has to do with the concept of "the interpenetration of space." It involves the arrangement of points in space which, by their juxtaposition, appear to form a contour line, although no actual physical surface exists. Explorations of this idea have led Bertoia to create an enormous series of generally somewhat spherical sculptures, like the one at Princeton's Woodrow Wilson School (plate 29), *Small Bush* owned by Mr. and Mrs. Edwin Jaffe (plate 63), and others (plate 64). In these pieces the rods radiating from a central core have globules on their outer ends, which form the illusion if not the actuality of a surface plane. Bertoia says these sculptures attempt to deal in a mathematical sense with what he calls "the two infinities"—one of his initial thoughts in this concept. "No one knows where the center (the one infinity) is," he says, "and the rods proceeding from this source could be extended to fill the cosmos (the other infinity)." The "bushes" and the Princeton globe are also attempts to get closer to the basic relationship between light, space, and structure.

In one series based on this theme, some of which were called *Dogwood*, the sculptures look more like trees than bushes, being somewhat taller and bearing larger forms at the ends of their radiating rods. Such a one is the forty-inch high steel, bronze, and chrome piece entitled *Flower*, included in the Museum of Modern Art's traveling exhibition, "Recent Sculpture USA," of 1958. The Virginia Museum of Fine Arts' *Gold Tree* (plates 65, 66), first exhibited in the American Pavilion at the Brussels World's Fair, is another. The entire group of so-called dandelion sculptures—ranging from the twenty-foot tall former Beverly Hills installation to the forty-four inch one owned by the Des Moines Art Center, and including the eight-foot one in the artist's possession (plate 67)—comes from these investigations, though it bears the mark also of his work in sound and motion, and his interest in vertical balance.

A drawing of a proposed fountain for the McCormick Building in Chicago (never executed) shows a mammoth "dandelion" about forty feet tall, to judge from the man at its base (plate 68). The proposal was for water to be pumped up the stem into the central orb and from there, under pressure, out each of the radiating tubes to nozzles at their outer ends. Each nozzle was to function like an ordinary lawn sprinkler spraying the water in radiating directions in a fine mist. A seven-foot sculpture done previously, owned by Mrs. Florence Knoll Bassett, creates the spray effect with wire (plate 69).

The Philadelphia and Buffalo fountains (plates 45, 48), on the other hand, begin to define space in terms of an actual surface formed by a membrane. The convolutions of this surface produce positive and negative spaces which are really the *same* space looked at from one or the other side of the membrane. The aesthetics of these fountains lies somewhere between the concept of the interpenetration of space and a fourth long-standing area of interest which Bertoia has called the concept of "interior space."

This involves the idea of a dark and restful interior place, having no relationship with what is outside and therefore providing a kind of sanctuary. He describes what he envisions as "like being inside an egg." While no actual large-scale work has yet been done along these lines, the idea is embodied in a drawing on his study wall showing a globular form with an underground entrance. One would go downstairs and come up again into a windowless interior. Such a method of entrance would help insure a subdued atmosphere and provide the feeling of detachment and humility necessary to a sanctuary. A glimpse of what it might be like inside such a globe can be obtained by peering into a small bluish-green model whose surrounding membrane is constructed of fused metal shot, creating a bumpy surface inside and out, with a few tiny irregular holes allowing the penetration of small spots of light here and there. From this model it can be readily seen that an atmosphere of hushed reverence results from the subdued light, not unlike that experienced on entering Capri's Blue Grotto or the crypt of the Church of St. Francis at Assisi. More work needs to be done along these lines, Bertoia feels, but the idea, which has been with him for a long time, is slowly taking shape.

A fifth area in which Bertoia is interested involves a medium rather than a concept—the medium of working bronze while in its liquid state, as described previously. Though he has spent less time on this activity than on any other, he considers his large panel for the Dulles International Airport his best work to date (plate 26). His ability with molten bronze is confirmed by many smaller works done both before and since, such as Furrow, 1962, at the Cranbrook Academy of Art, and Spring, 1965 (plate 70), in the collection of the Chase Manhattan Bank, N.A., and shown in the 1966 annual Whitney Museum sculpture exhibition.

The medium is an exacting as well as an expensive one, requiring large quantities of molten metal. The nature of the process produces a mural-like result. The artist's role is much like that of a watercolor painter in that all direct work must be done in the few minutes which elapse between the pouring and the hardening of the bronze. The accidental effect must be quickly turned to advantage or the process must begin all over again. Bertoia's method of using water and rocks helps to give these pieces their look of association with man's basic primeval environment. Their encrusted surfaces look like cave interiors with dark cul-de-sacs and unexpected openings. There is an aura of mystery about them. It is an intriguing medium for Bertoia and he expects to do more in this field. But meanwhile other ideas crowd his fertile imagination.

One old idea that keeps returning, and may yet some day have its consummation, is a group of earth-bound bells with long antennae protruding like flagpoles from their tops many feet into the air (plate 71). This model was made as a proposal for a church whose overseers did not go through with it. The sound of the bells would come from a reverberation of the rods, which would be set into motion from the ground. The installation is envisioned for a park-like area in front of a church where people could walk around and touch the bells. The model for the bells is related to his studies of vertical balance which began nearly twenty years ago.

Bertoia's studies of sound in sculpture, he feels, have only just begun. Currently he and his brother Oreste are continuing experiments with rods and wires of different metals in an effort to produce a full range of tones bearing no relationship to our present musical scale. They have cleared out the barn at his home in Barto and it has been refinished inside to serve as a sounding box (surrounding, rather than within these instruments of music). Bertoia has constructed sculptures of varying metals, thicknesses, and heights, which have been placed inside the barn for further experiments with a tape recorder "to develop the range, autonomy, rhythm, and continuity of the sounds" (plate 72). A concert is the goal.

Among specific works projected for the future are a sculpture for a public school in Baltimore and a huge indoor piece for Yamasaki's World Trade Center in New York. Then Bertoia plans to turn his attention to some ideas he has for the embellishment of his own environment—the woods and fields surrounding his home.

When asked if he ever expects to design any more furniture, Bertoia at first said "No," feeling that for some time now he has known where he is going as a sculptor. On reflection, however, he said that if he ever did design again, it would be some type of disposable furniture. This is an outgrowth of his recent concern over the unsightliness of automobile graveyards and other junk heaps containing the refuse of modern civilization. He feels that when we are through with the things we use, like automobiles and furniture, we should be able to burn them or otherwise dispose of them in a manner that will not create an ugly sight for the eyes of future generations.

Ideas such as these abound in Bertoia's creative imagination. Where each will lead he does not now know, but the longer they stay with him, the more likely it is that they will come to fruition.

Concepts and Critiques

Over the years Bertoia's vast output of creative endeavor has taken such varied forms as drawings, paintings, graphics, jewelry, furniture design, and sculpture, the latter both architecturally functional and purely for aesthetic enjoyment. Since 1953 all other media of expression have given way to sculpture, but the earlier work has been very influential in determining its character. The rhythmically repeated lines and forms of his monoprints are seen again and again in his chairs and screens. The inherent nature of jewelry, his early work in metal, is reflected in the essential frontality of much of his sculpture. Even the textured surfaces of his molten bronzes were previewed in some of his silver work. (See plate 15, second from bottom, right hand column.) Bertoia's early preoccupation with light and space and their illusionary and three-dimensional effects has stamped its mark on all that comes out of his studio.

Since his student days Bertoia has always worked in the abstract. Aesthetic ideas and intellectual concepts have led him to create abstract forms which were later identified with such things in nature as bushes, trees, flowers, dandelions, dogwood, sunbursts, galaxies, reeds, and straw. But it should be noted that the names were applied after creation, not before, and usually by someone other than Bertoia who translated the abstract into his own familiar terms or applied the label as a convenient reference. Like other nonobjective painters and sculptors, Bertoia had his difficulties with the slow public acceptance of this form of artistic expression. One notable hassle was created by the Dallas Public Library screen, which was installed, removed, and reinstalled, as mayor, city councilmen, architect, taxpayers, and devotees of modern art argued over its merit.[1]

The reactions of professional art critics have not always been favorable either. One reviewer climaxed an unflattering description of Bertoia's sculptures with this statement: "In any context they are execrably banal, but if they are sculpture they lack any formal embellishment, content to emulate the structure of natural form in a totally imitative way."[2] The addition of color to his work made it "almost cheap" for another critic.[3] Still another wrote the following subtly uncomplimentary report:

Harry Bertoia's metal sculpture projects a sense of installed decoration; as such it represents a kind of contemporary Victorianism for an over-industrialized bourgeoisie, steel and bronze counterparts of the aspidistra and the potted palm. A dry-cleaned marsh of singing bronze reeds; a stainless steel puff-ball eight feet high; metallic shrubs and sycamores all seem to spring from the humus of marble lobbies and the photosynthesis of fluorescent lighting. They suggest the glinting frontage of sun-shot office buildings, the coolly sagacious precincts of executive anterooms, the echoing vault between the revolving door and the information desk. It is always some kind of delight to see a perfect manifestation, perfectly related; in this case we have the aesthetic of a realm whose perfect expression is Fortune magazine, the universe of burnished Lucidity. Bertoia's work reflects the brilliant clean summary of the neutral engineering that structures and decries the Xanadus of affluent society.[4]

This erudite rhetoric, which endeavors to condemn by association, demonstrates a kind of condescension that has often been lavished on artists who, like Bertoia, have sometimes worked on functional objects such as architectural screens or furniture. It reflects a romantic attitude prevalent in twentieth century America that "the artist must be isolated from society and its needs." As pointed out in a recent article by B. H. Friedman, "for many established artists...the idea of a commission is anathema. The adjective 'decorative' has become increasingly pejorative....The American artist has tended to pride himself in his own uselessness." All this, "despite Picasso's pottery; Giacometti's lamps; Calder's kitchen utensils; surrealists' chess sets; etc."[5]

For some critics Bertoia's work with architects has tainted all his output with the horrid stain of "commercialism." For others, the results of many of his collaborations have been eminently successful without compromising his artistic integrity or that of the architect. This has influenced debates current in the art world concerning the possibility of a new Golden Age incorporating the perfect synthesis of all the arts, as in ancient Athens or the Middle Ages. Whereas some historians believe that modern architecture precludes sculpture, others say that the post-Renaissance concept of individualism has made each artist too eager to demonstrate his own uniqueness to allow for the required cooperation.[6] Still others take a more optimistic view.

Bertoia took part in one of these debates, a colloquium conducted by mail among such figures of the modern art world as Pietro Belluschi, Reg Butler, Eduardo Chillida, Jimmy Ernst, Walter Gropius, Le Corbusier, and Richard Lippold, for the *Journal of the American Academy of Arts and Sciences*. In it he revealed a belief in the possibilities of the present as being equal to those of the past, the past having been helped toward its apparent unity by the selectiveness of time. Also apparent in his writings during this 1960 debate-by-mail is a strong belief in the capabilities of modern man to use creatively the materials of his own era. "Man's deepest thoughts," he wrote, "perhaps remain unexpressed, but he surely can exercise his intelligence for choosing, among the various media, the one best suited in coming closest to what he wants to say."[7] For the most part undisturbed by the controversy and disinclined to assert his own will over others, Bertoia prefers to continue his investigations into the ideas and materials which interest him and leave the judgments to time. The high professional regard in which he is held by the architects with whom he has worked gives answer enough to his critics.

"An intellectual exercise" is perhaps the one phrase best suited to generalize about the whole of Bertoia's work to date. For each of his sculptures originated in the mind—from a well formulated but constantly evolving idea or concept based on his perception, not on observation of nature—and was brought to fulfillment through the exercise of his intelligence in making decisions during the process of creation. This is why his work has such a strong appeal to the intellect. It represents an intellectual process leading toward the universal in art. Much of it is obviously willed, brought about by engineering, carefully calculated. It is the product of a modern man's use of his sensitivity and intelligence on materials which are specifically related to his twentieth century world—industrial materials, mass produced where possible, metals that have been refined and extruded into flat sheets, rods, wires, shot. In some cases, machined parts have been designed and utilized—but always designed. Bertoia rarely uses junk, found objects, or parts originally made for other purposes.

"Precision" is a word that has been applied to Bertoia's sculpture and it is aptly descriptive. His work reveals the precision that went into it, not merely in the mental calculations of engineering details, such as stresses and strains and perfect balance, but in the finishing details of craftsmanship. Patinas, sprays, lacquers are used to advantage, and he has been known to spend weeks cleaning a finished stainless steel sculpture of the black marks left by the industrial process of extrusion of the wire. His pieces gleam where they are meant to do so and have a dry, matte surface where it is willed so. Bertoia's hand craftsmanship, an unusual blend of "tender, loving care" applied to precisely chosen modern industrial materials, adds the warmth of personal attention to what otherwise might seem cold and inhuman. His sensitivity to aesthetic considerations such as color and texture, proportion and balance, makes itself felt in every piece.

There is a baroque quality, too, in most of Bertoia's work, which keeps it from being categorized as coldly calculating. The voluptuous curves of the Philadelphia and Buffalo fountains are obvious examples; so also are the painterly details of his poured bronzes—all seemingly so disparate as to be incomparable to the straight lines and rectilinear forms of the architectural screens, particularly the most recent example in Brooklyn. But here, color is the most important factor, adding a touch of flamboyance to the squares, which are otherwise so ascetic as to seem allied to the minimal trend in sculpture. A look at other pieces reveals details of rhythm, color, and texture, which link them to the baroque dynamic tradition, as well as to that of Constructivism (plates 25, 28, 39, 41, for example).

An experimenter by nature, Bertoia was encouraged along these lines by the Cranbrook atmosphere. Reflecting this freedom in its variety, his work has always been characterized by its refusal to be kept within rigid bounds. "Breaking arbitrary fences is one of my delights," he says, "I enjoy doing that." For instance, he sees no reason why color cannot be an element of sculpture – or sculpture an element of painting.

The hues Bertoia most frequently uses are yellows and blues, with yellow generally predominating and ranging from light brassy tones through brilliant golds to deep bronzes, with occasional digressions toward oranges and reds. His blues tend toward turquoise or blue-green, the natural colors of weather-oxidized bronze. Whether in paintings, monoprints or sculpture, the colors associated with metals have always been preferred. This may be a result of his happy boyhood experience of watching gypsies repair copper and brass utensils over an open fire near his home in Italy.

Sound and motion, too, are incorporated in many of Bertoia's works. Most of these are related to the early studies in vertical balance which began to intrigue him nearly twenty years ago. The actual, physical motion of the rods of the sculpture creates the sound, which is related to the avant-garde music of the twentieth century, while evoking thoughts of the primeval in its echoing sonorousness. Bertoia's appeal to the aural as well as the visual sense is unusual in sculpture and stems from a desire to involve all of man's senses in aesthetic enjoyment. In some sculptures motion alone is the object, and in still others only the illusionary effect of motion is created by designs based on changing light conditions.

Another essential of music, rhythm, is an important characteristic of all Bertoia sculptures. The repeated modulus or line, straight or curved, is always very carefully controlled by the composer-conductor, even where it seems most random. Repetition is the key to the unity demonstrated in his more successful pieces.

All Bertoia's sculptures have an overwhelming appeal to the tactile sense. They are obviously meant to be touched or rubbed. Their alternately uneven or smooth surfaces convey a feeling of the primitive (plates 22, 29, 65) or a sense of delicate, refined elegance (plates 25, 27, 69). In either case, the palms itch and the fingertips respond pleasurably to the invited investigation.

Bertoia is also very much concerned with space and the interplay of void and matter. Many of his works tend to be airy, some even lacy in appearance. His studies in density, in which he incorporates the voids into a sculpture made of criss-crossed wires or rods, culminated in the mammoth Northwestern National piece, a closeup of which reveals it to be the counterpart in sculpture of a Jackson Pollock painting (see plate 40). One of the first such studies in density was a rather remarkable head done about 1958 or 1959, now owned by Mr. and Mrs. Matthew Leibowitz of Rydal, Pennsylvania (plate 73). Like Picasso's Cubist head of 1909 and Naum Gabo's Constructivist head of 1916, it was an experiment in a new sculptural concept. The planes of the hair, forehead, nose, cheeks, mouth, and chin are recognizably outlined in space, and the actual volumes are created "out of thin air." Its four tiny gold feet are a whimsical finishing touch. This head is notable as the only Bertoia sculpture intended to be representational.

The constructed screens, too, incorporate space as an element of design. "Component parts held together as if by a magnetic force," Bertoia once called them. Light, with the changing shadows it induces, is always a prime consideration in his sculptures. Even the works in molten bronze are affected by his feeling for light and space, with their jagged holes and the cast shadows of the inserted rocks and crusty projections.

Much of Bertoia's work is designed for places where it can be viewed only frontally (see plates 25-27, 39). Even many that can be walked around are forced by architectural conditions to have essentially a back view and a front view rather than a continuing motion in the round (see plates 21, 22). This preponderance of frontality in his sculpture to date, while it is determined by the placement of the pieces, is attributable to his early work in paintings, monoprints, and jewelry, and to his first three-dimensional studies in light effects. For it was this work which prompted his first architectural commission and many of those which followed were along similar lines. Exceptions are the Princeton globe, the so-called bushes and dandelions, and the River Oaks, Philadelphia, and Buffalo fountains—indications that in his later work he is getting away from this restriction.

These, then, are the components of Bertoia's sculptures—metals, texture, color, light, sound, motion, rhythm, line, and modulus—all related to the surrounding and incorporated space, making it seem almost tangible. The essential spirit with which they are imbued is an exuberance of life, of dynamic energy. Some are blatantly gay, made for sheer delight in the beholding. Many have a shimmering quality developed with color, light, and motion. His bronzes are more elemental. Composed of fire, water, air, and earth, they seem mysterious and are meant to evoke thoughts of man's beginnings and of the dark recesses of his soul or inner spirit. These two types—the joyful, the bright, and the stark, the elemental—demonstrate Bertoia's abiding interest in dualities, such as the two infinities. To him, the bright and open ones have to do with the sky, whereas the dark and crusty ones pertain to the earth. Individual sculptures combine other dualities, or paradoxes, such as power and gentleness, strength and delicacy, massiveness and airiness.

Bertoia feels strongly that an artist should not allow himself to be a man set apart from the society in which he lives. He is very much concerned with the modern world, its new sensations, and its new materials and techniques. He seeks always to use to best advantage the materials and methods of our industrial society to produce "life-enhancing" objects—objects of beauty and interest to modern man. Essentially abstract and nonfigural, his sculptures are nevertheless very much concerned with relating man to his immediate environment as well as to his universe.

Illustrations

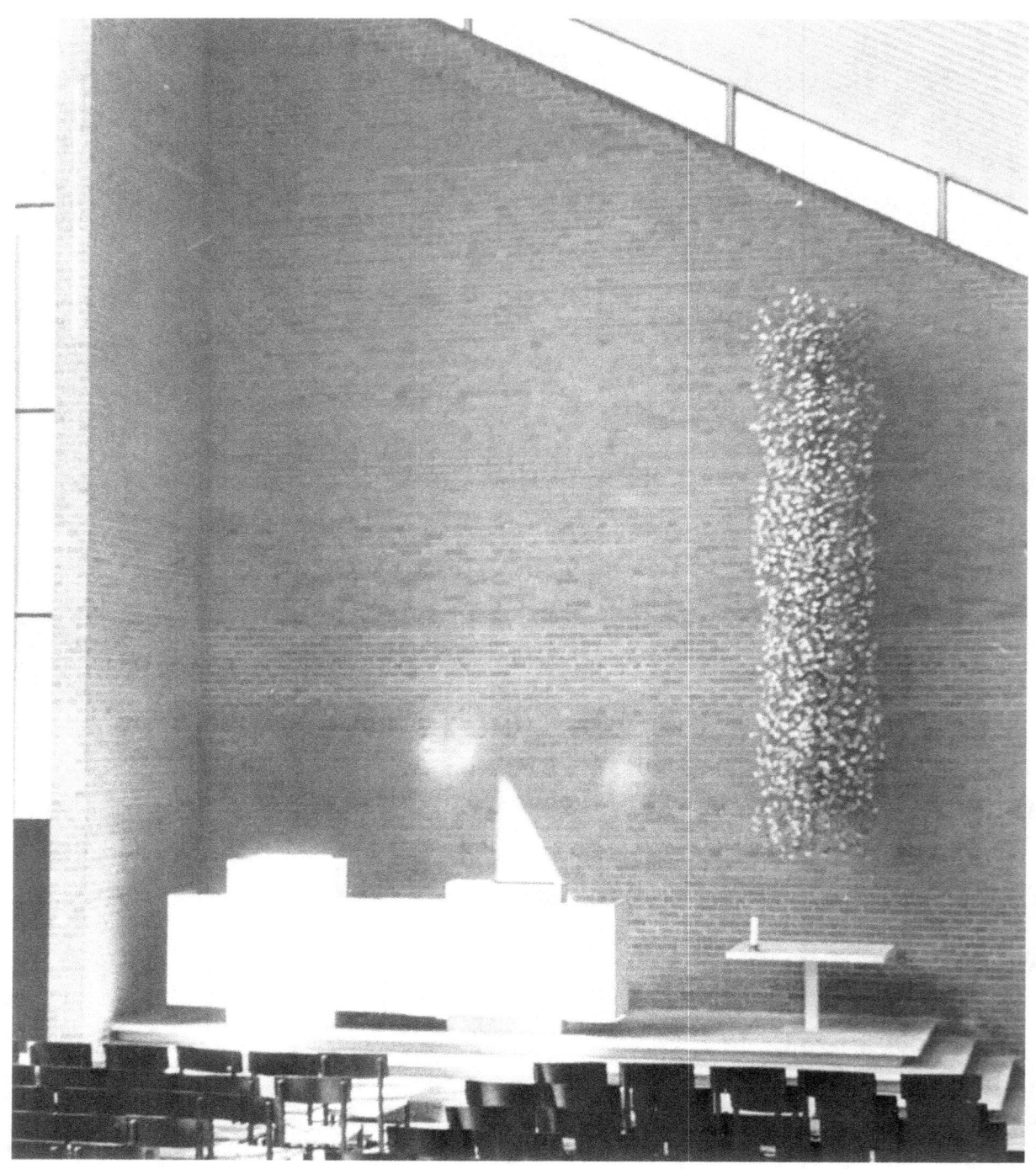

1. Wall hanging (1961), brass rods and sheet metal, about 12 x 2 ft. St. John's Unitarian Church.

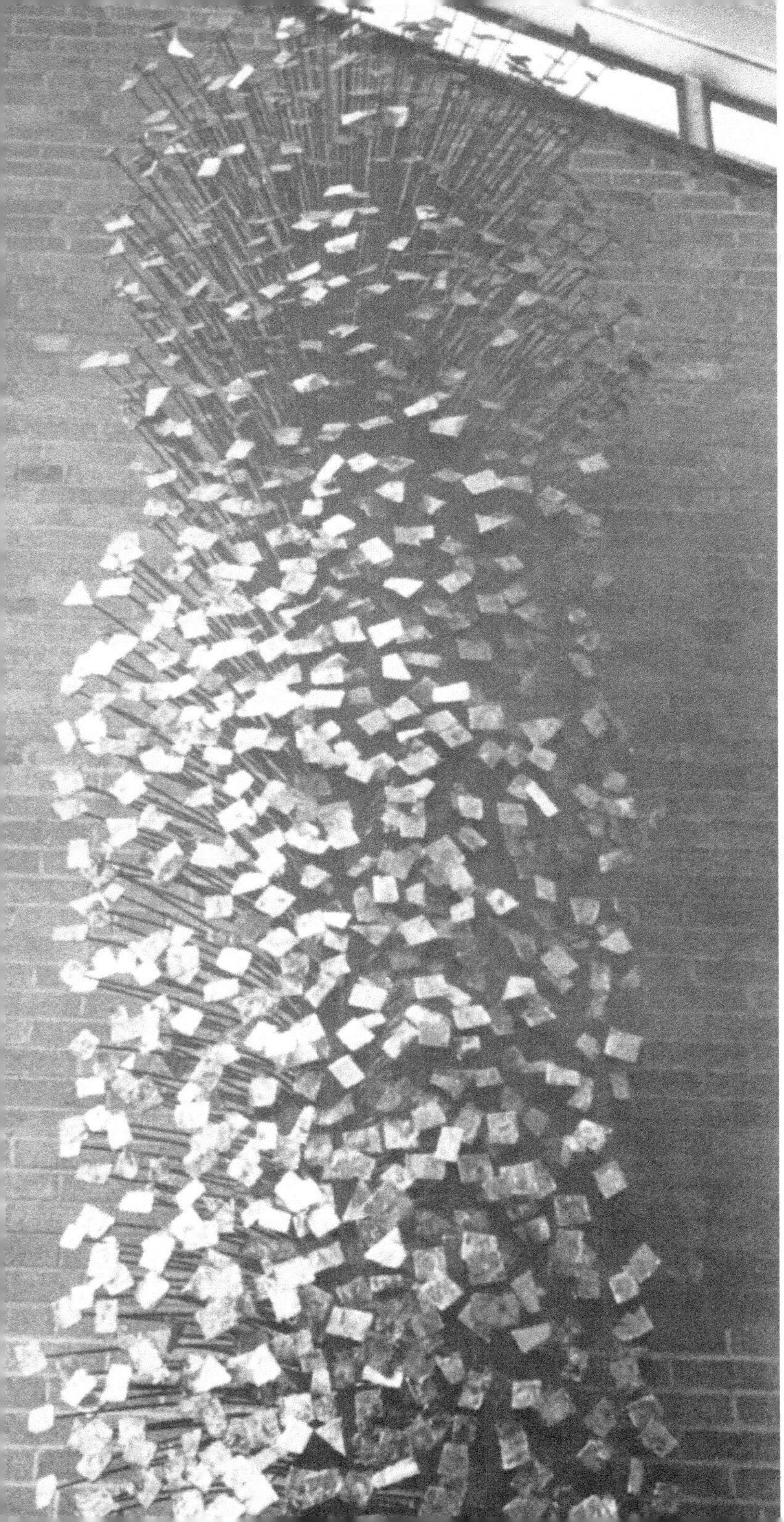

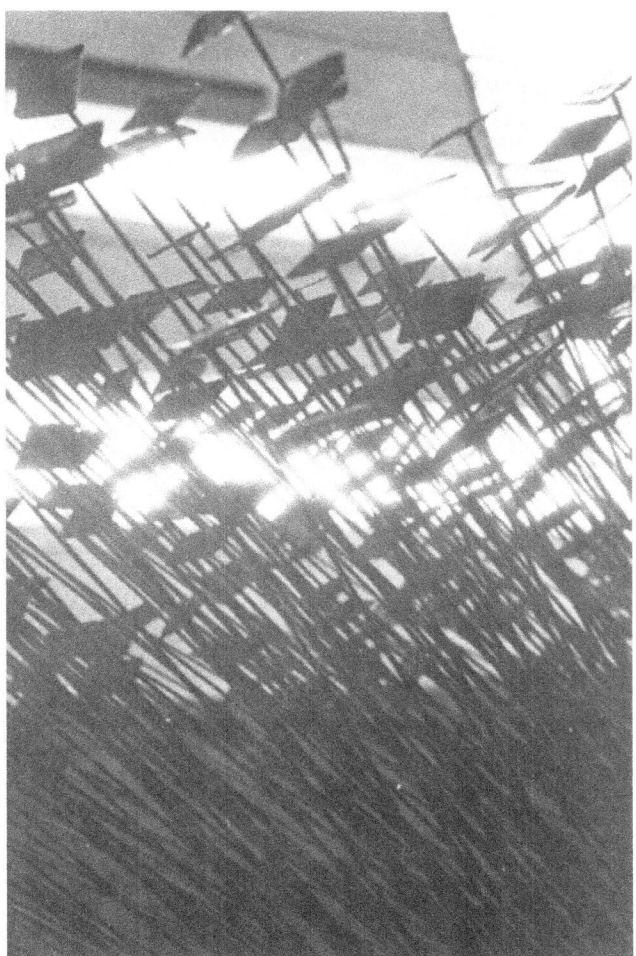

3. Detail of St. John's Unitarian Church sculpture.

2. Detail of St. John's Unitarian Church sculpture.

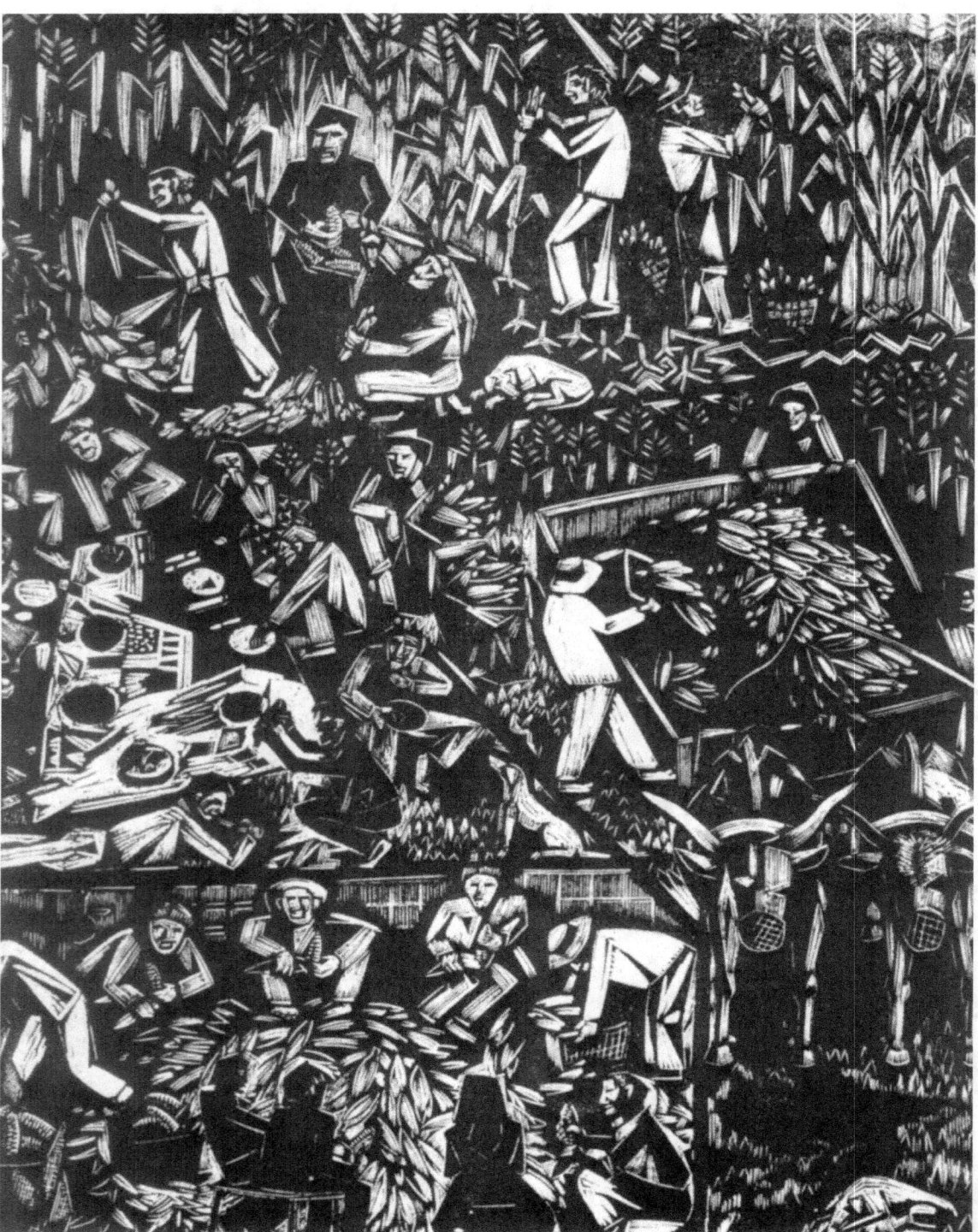

4. "Corn Harvest" (1941), woodcut, 10¼ x 8¼ in. Mrs. Elfriede Fischinger.

5. "Grape Harvest" (1941), woodcut, 10¼ x 8¼ in. Dr. and Mrs.
Samuel J. Nelson Jr.

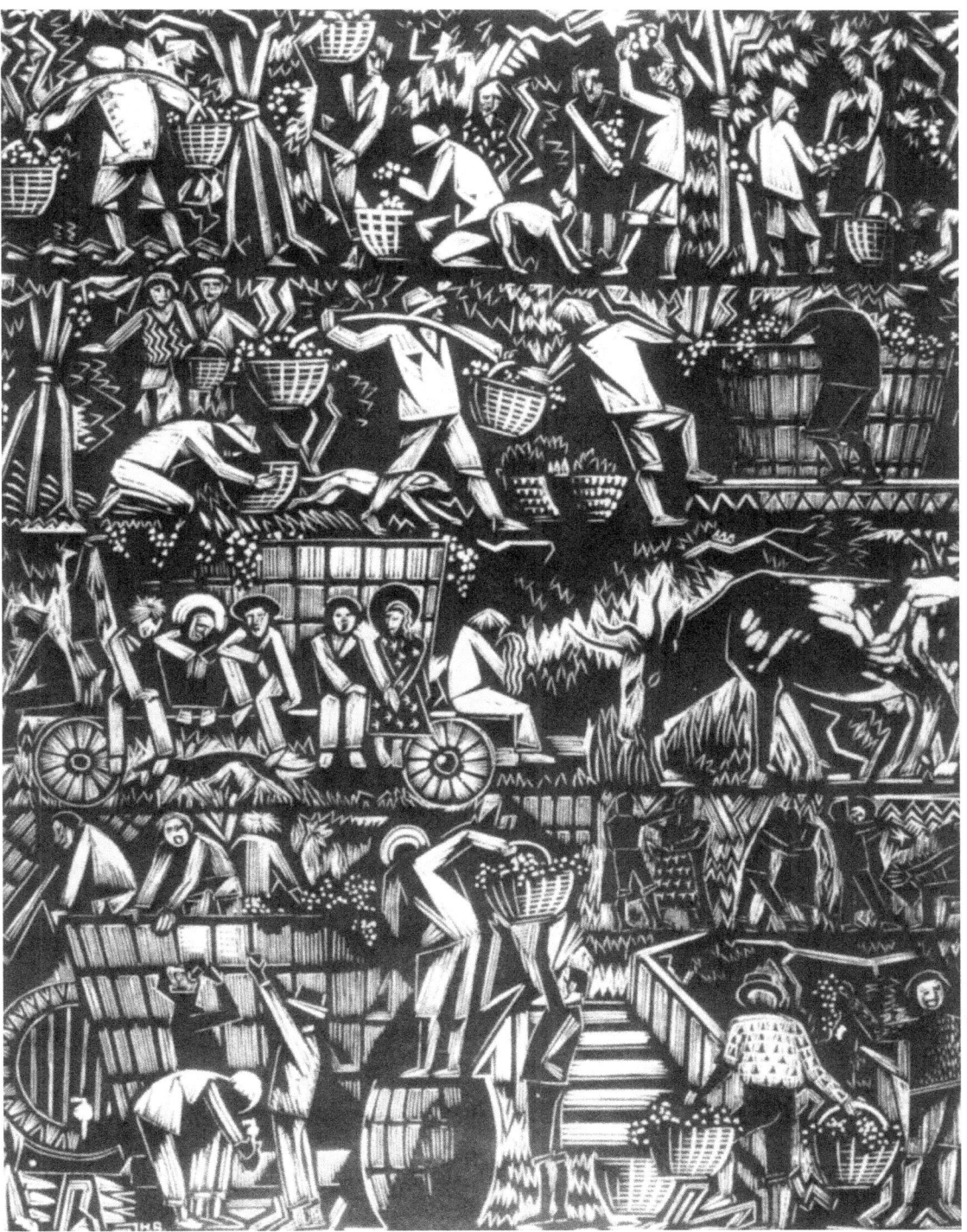

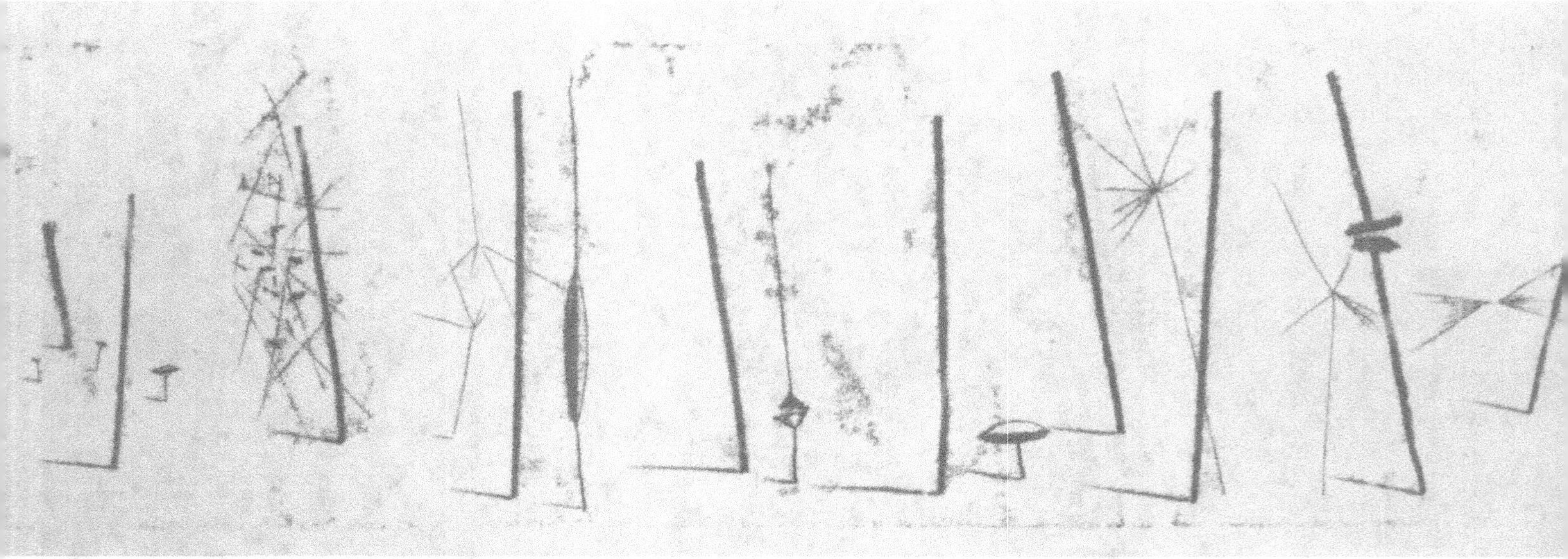

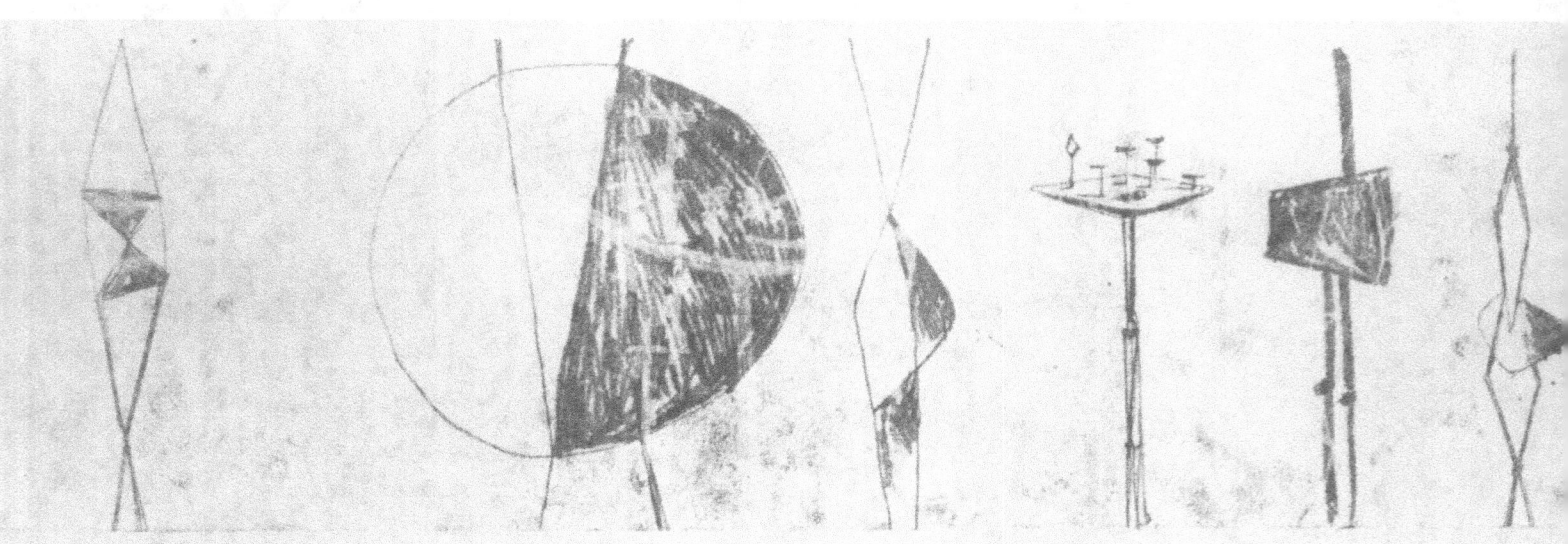

6. Drawing (c. 1943), printer's ink on rice paper.

7. Drawing (c. 1943), printer's ink on rice paper.

8. Drawing (c. 1943), printer's ink on rice paper.

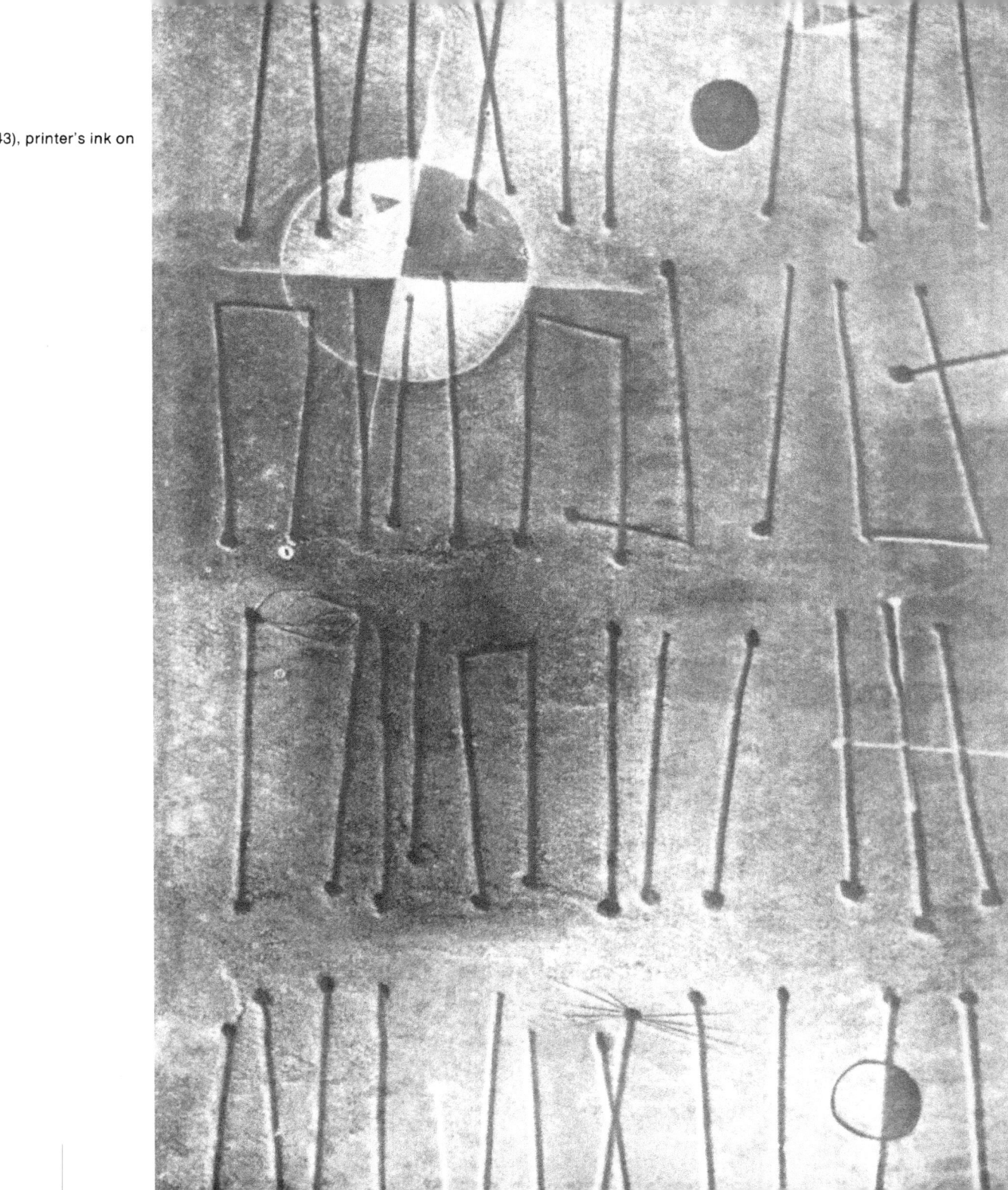

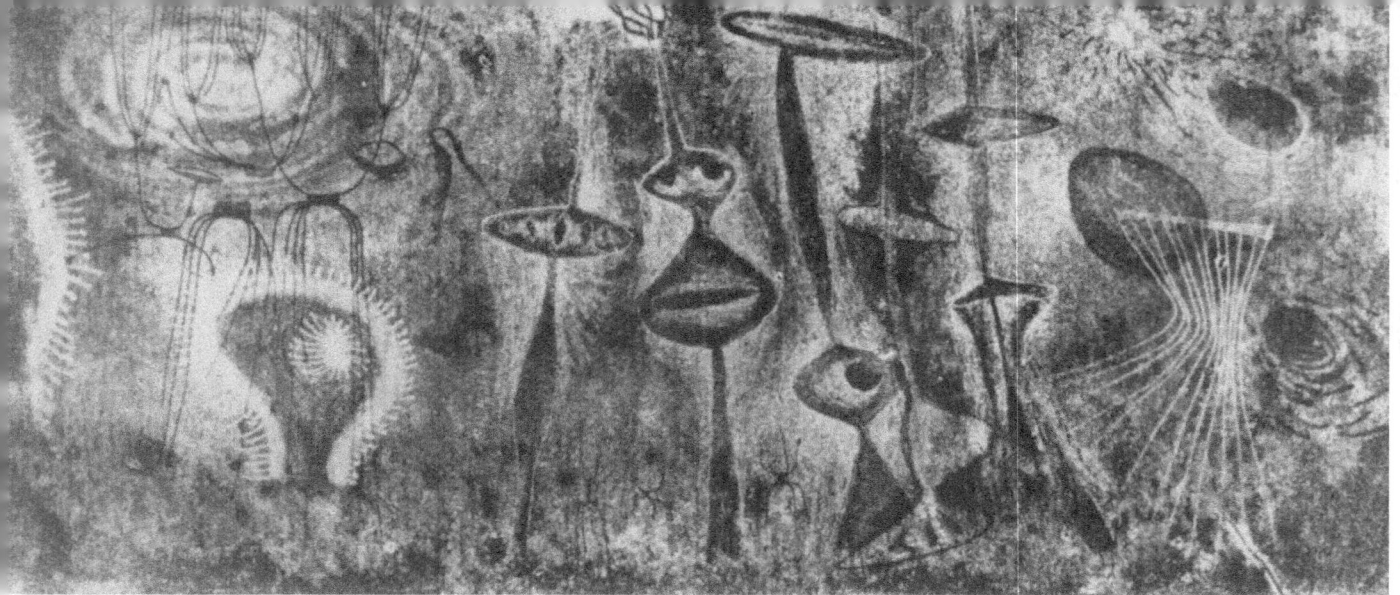

9. Drawing (c. 1943), printer's ink on rice paper.

10. Monoprint (before 1948).

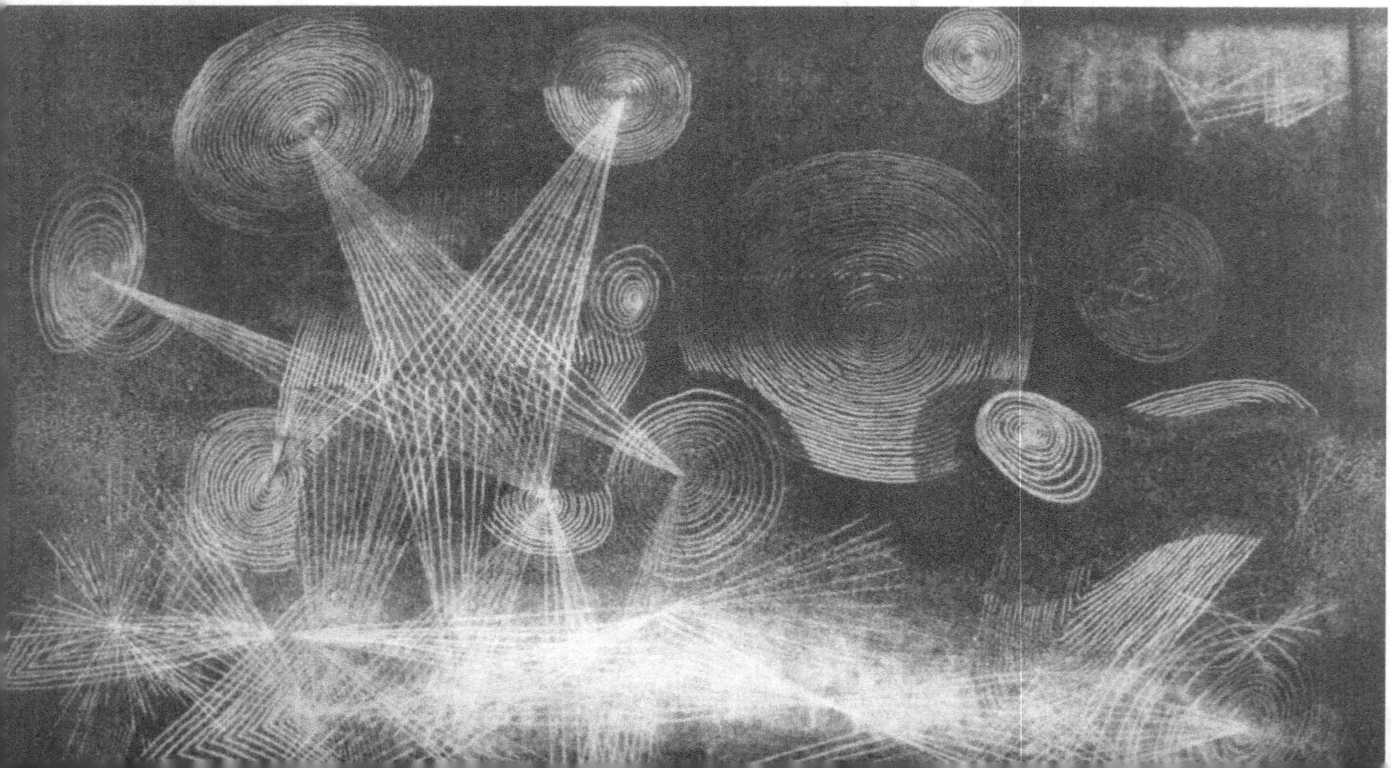

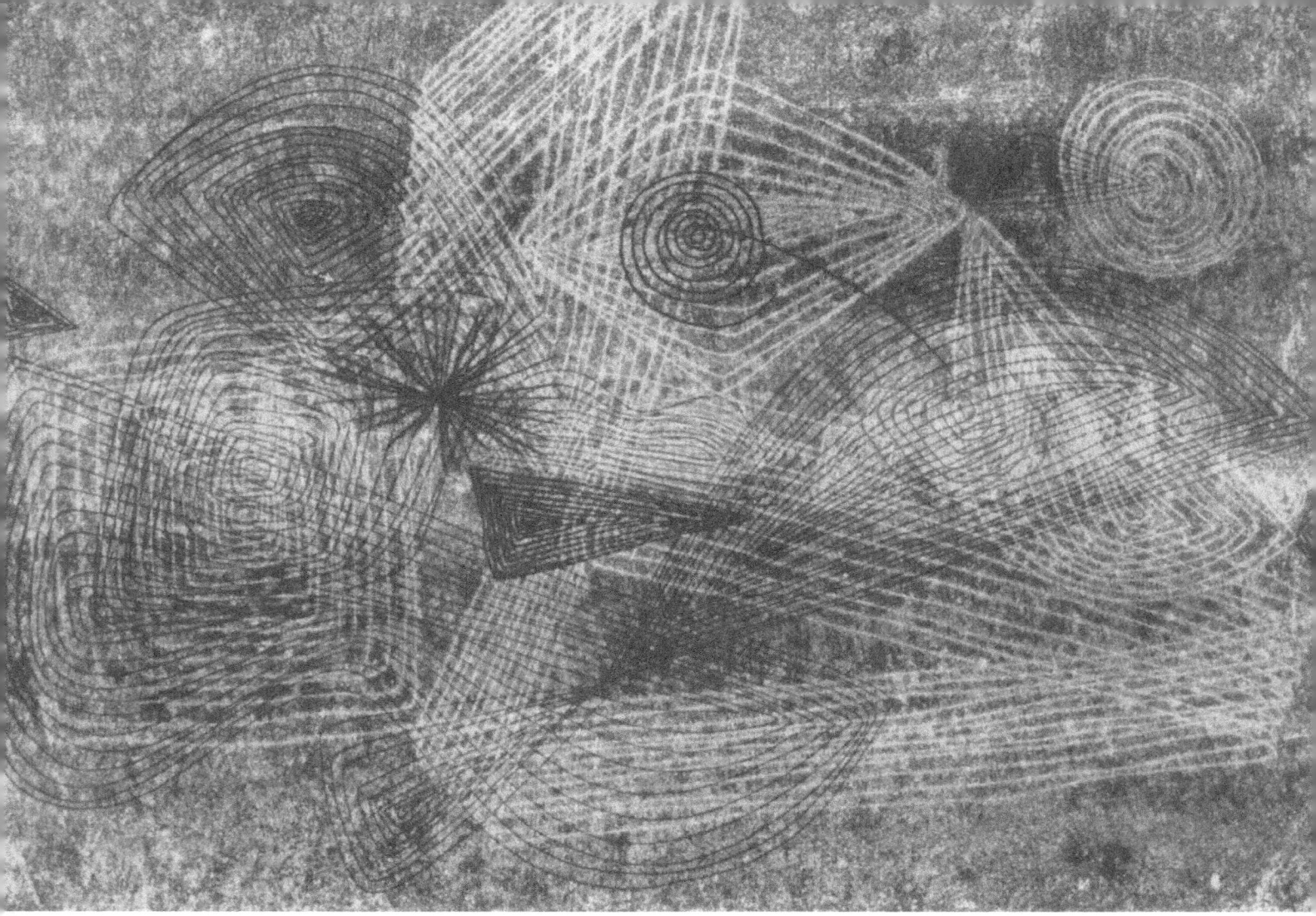

11. Monoprint (before 1948), 14⅛ x 20 in. Solomon R. Guggenheim Museum.

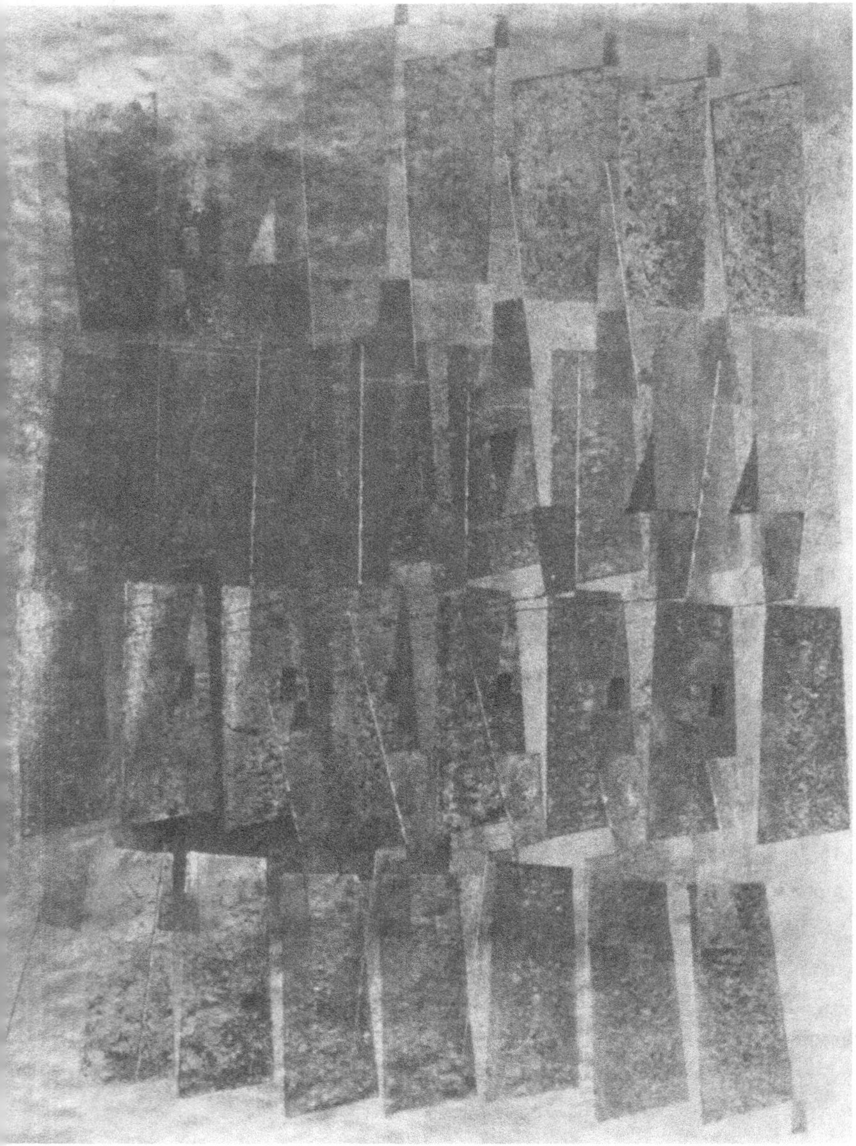

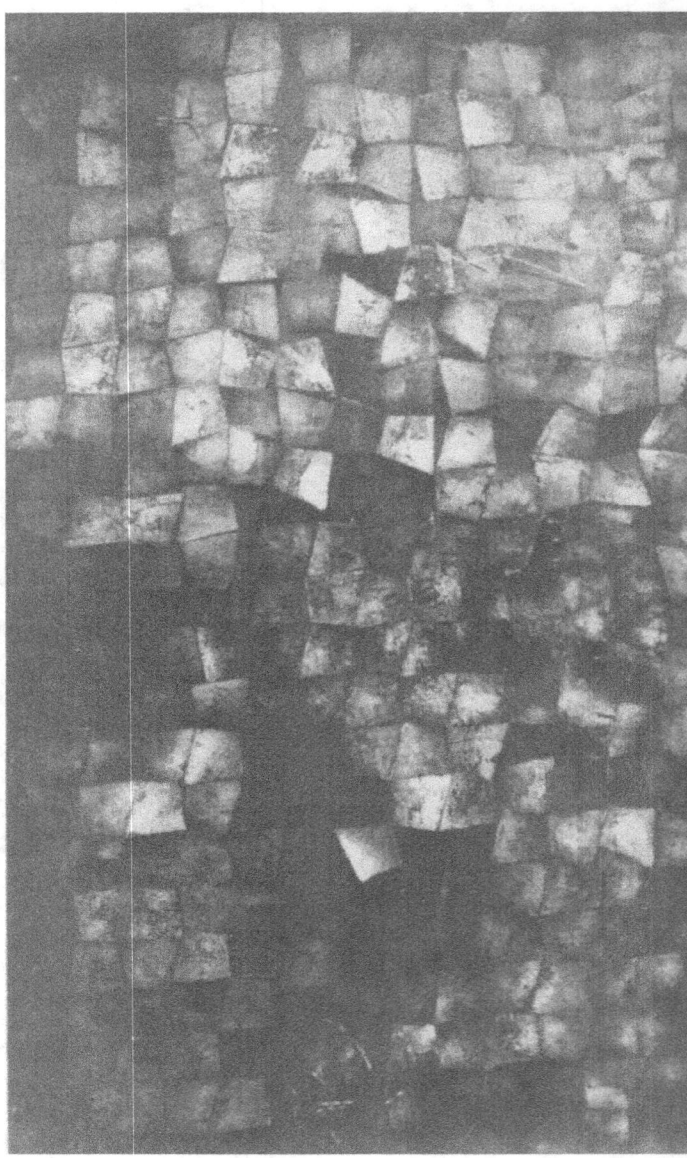

12. "Composition" (1943), monoprint, 24⅞ x 18⅞ in. Museum of Modern Art (James Thrall Soby Fund).

13. "Multicolored Trapezoids" (before 1948), monoprint, 37 x 24 in. Solomon R. Guggenheim Museum.

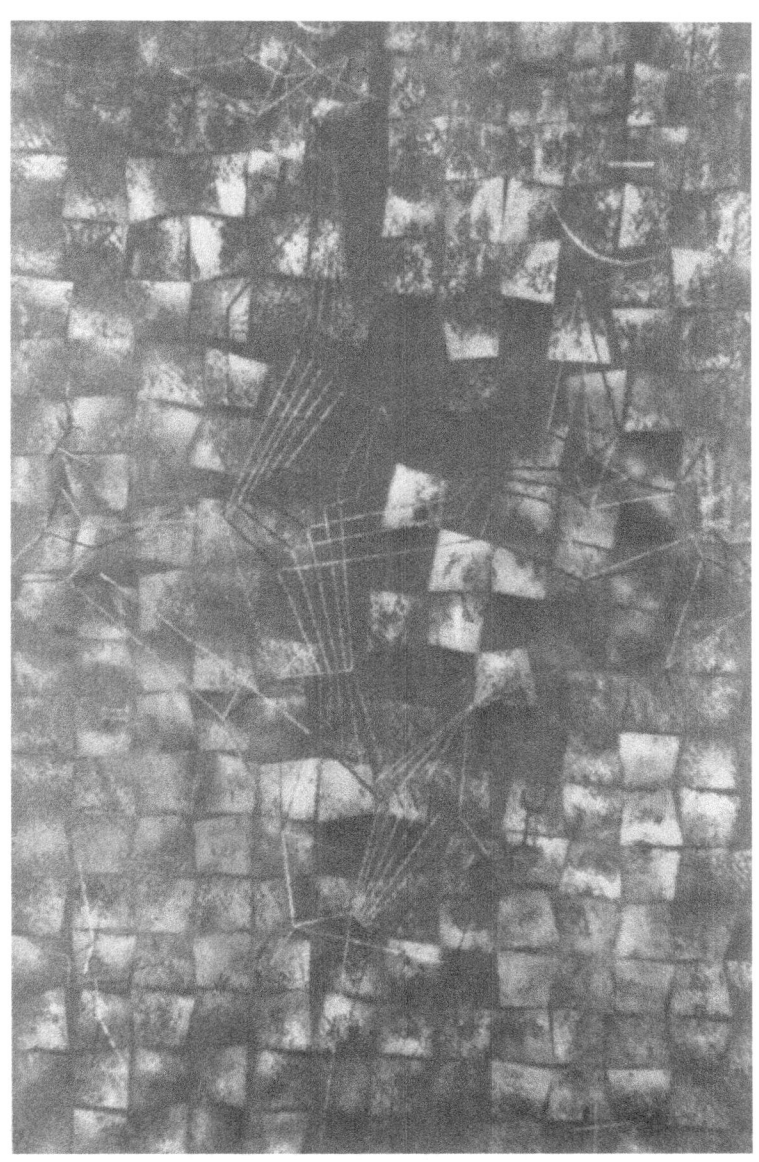

14. Monoprint (before 1948), about 37 x 24 in.

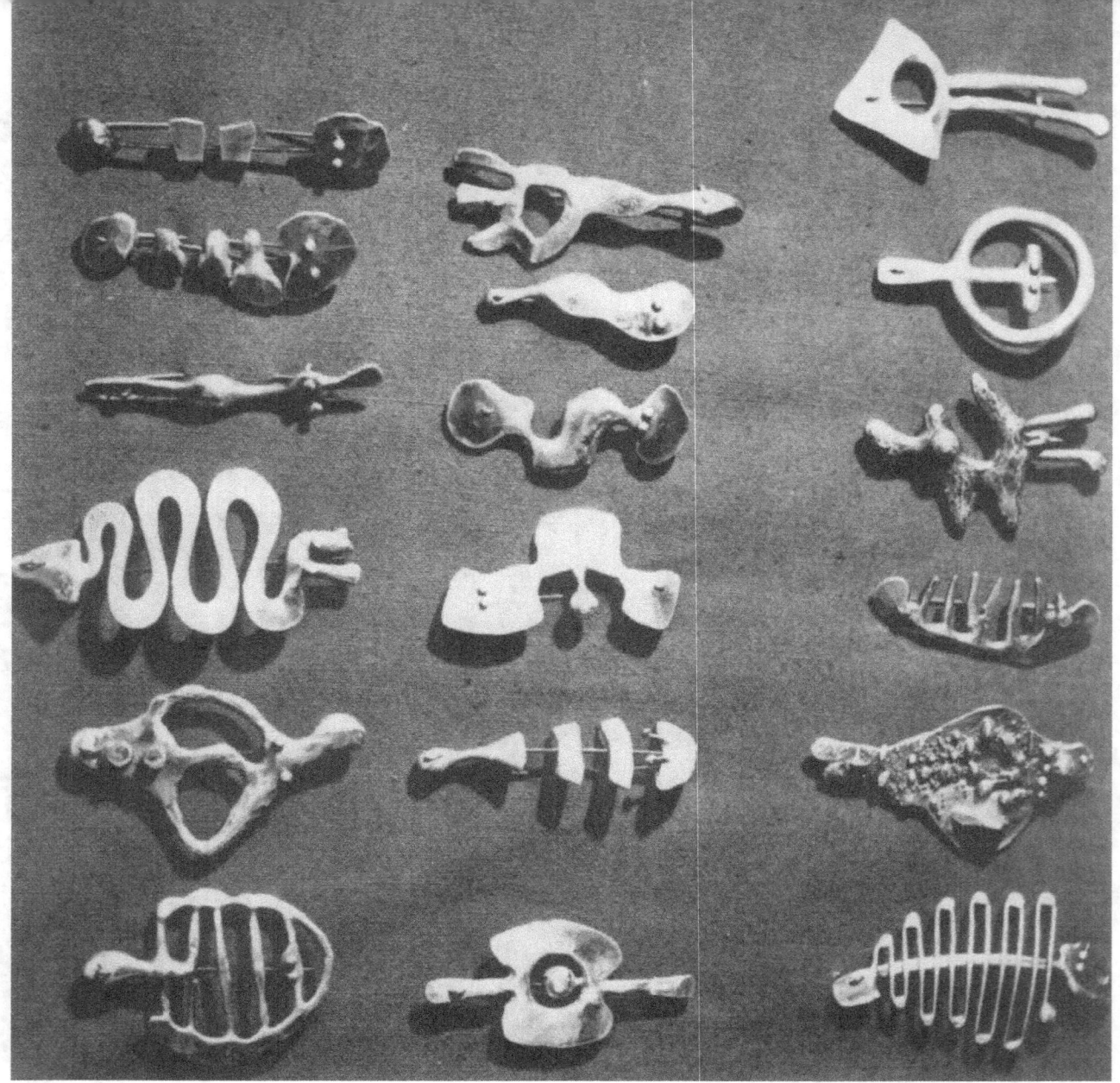

15. Silver Jewelry (c. 1943).

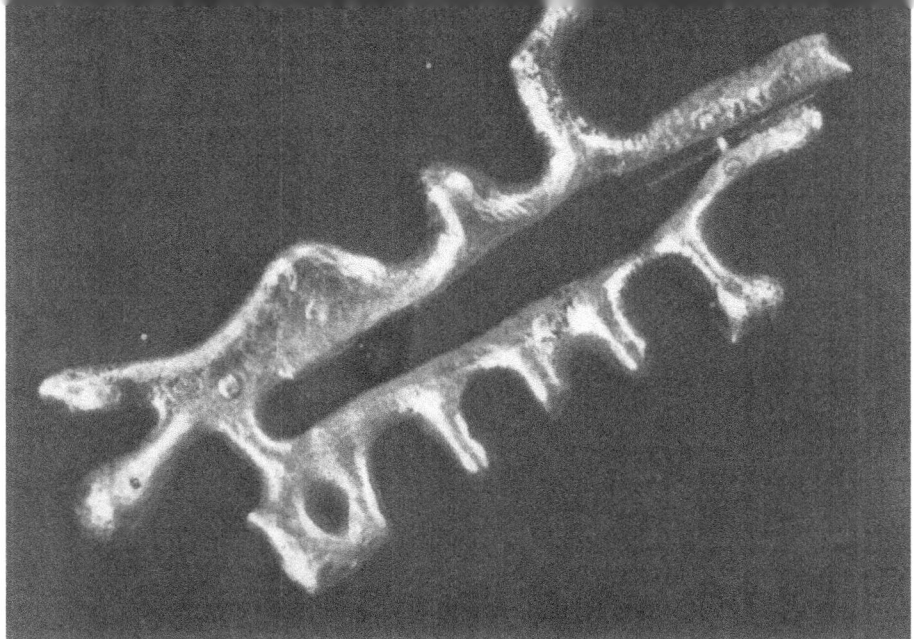

16. Silver brooch (c. 1943).

17. Study of light and space effects (c. 1943), metal painted white, about 15 x 30 x 3 in.
Collection, the artist (photographed in window of studio).

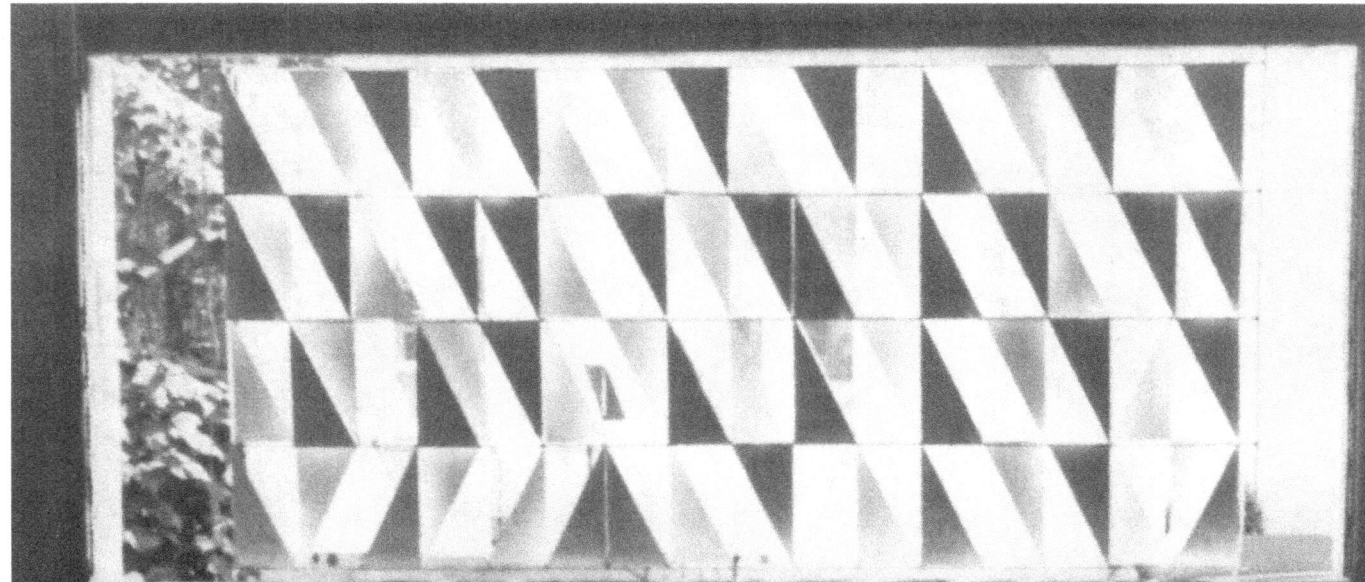

19. Sculptures (c. 1947-48), metal rods and wires.

18. The Bertoia chair (1952).

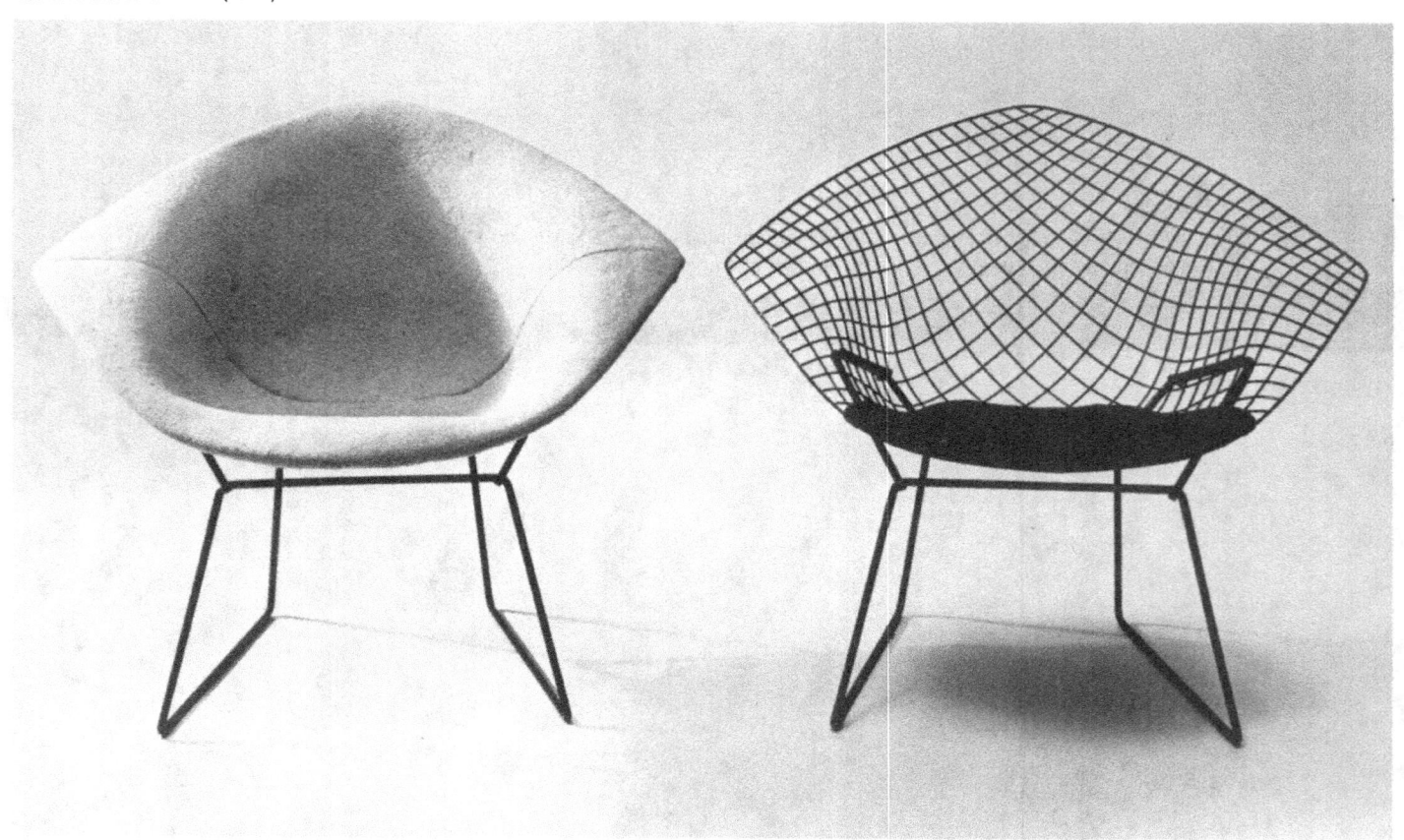

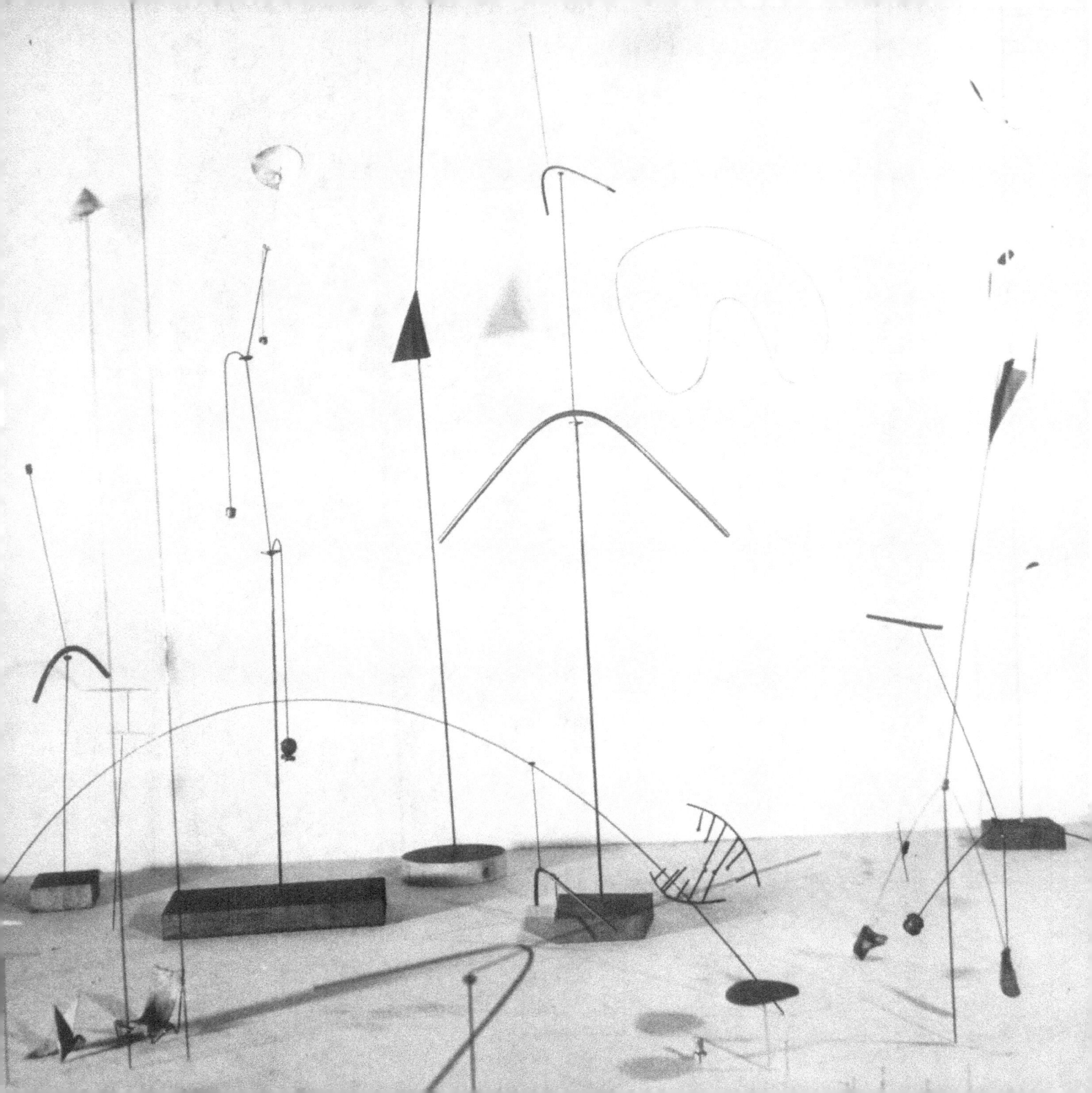

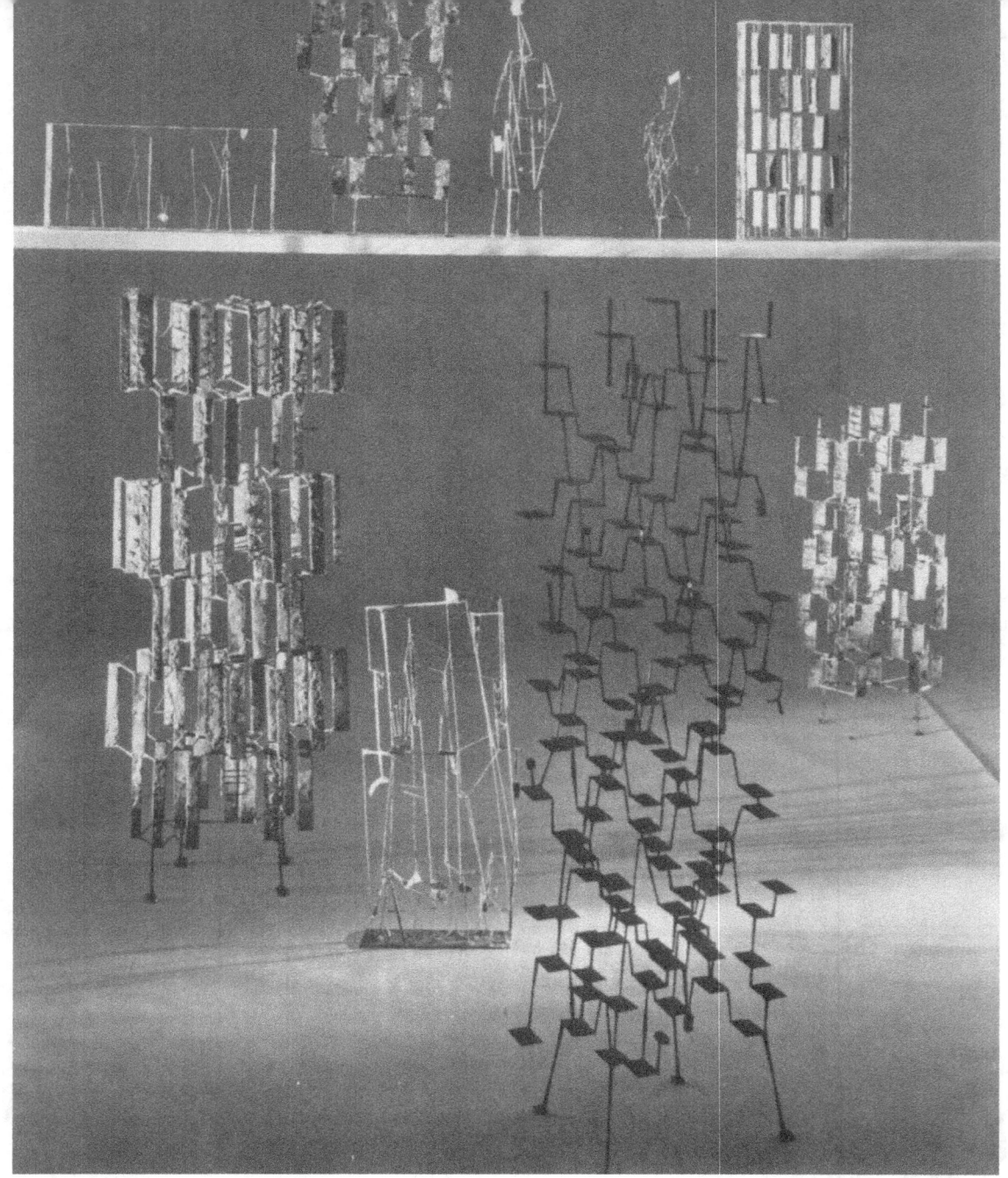

20. Sculptures (c. 1950-52), welded metals.

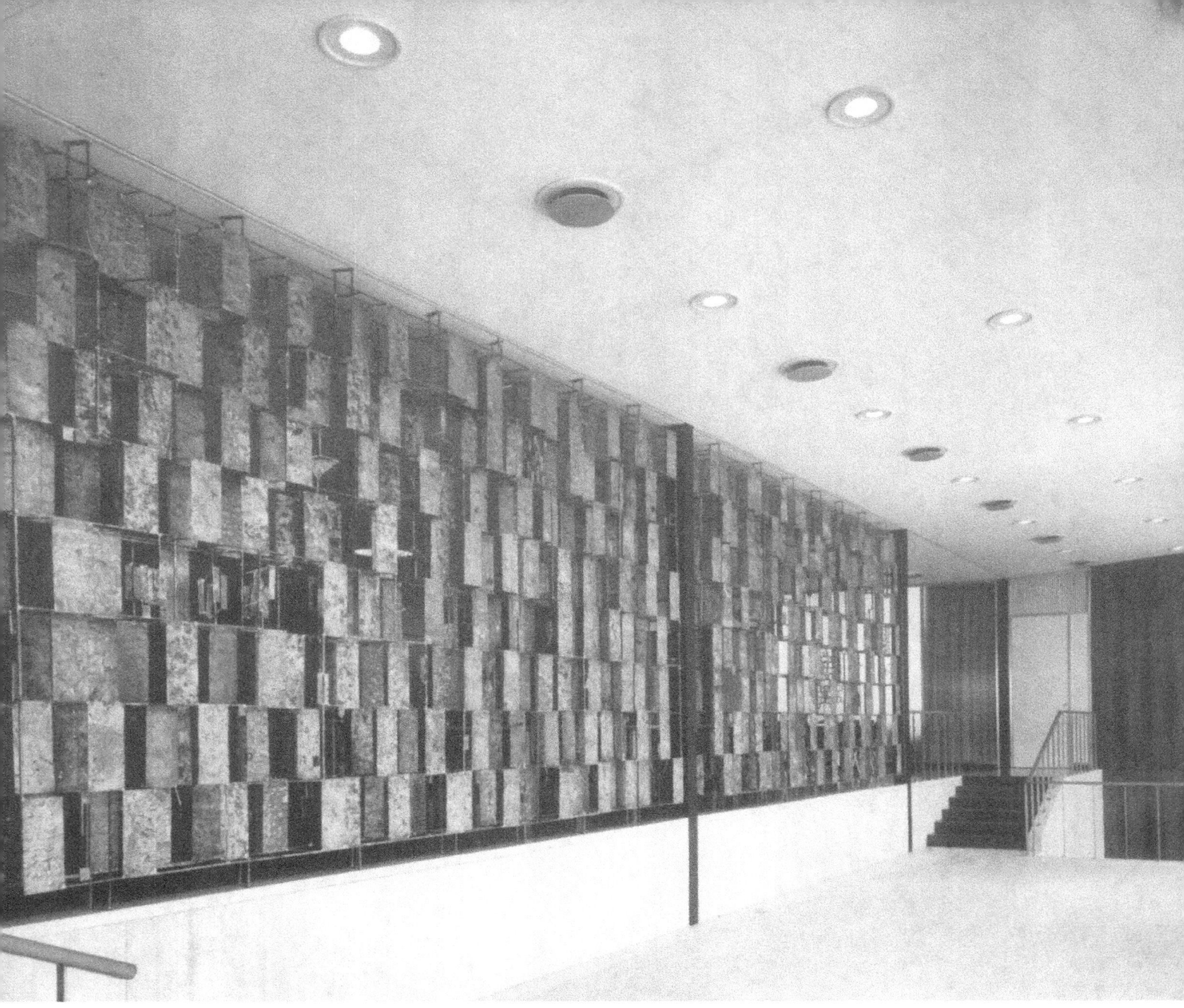

21. Sculpture screen (1953), welded metal, about 10 x 36 ft. x 8 in. General Motors Technical Center.

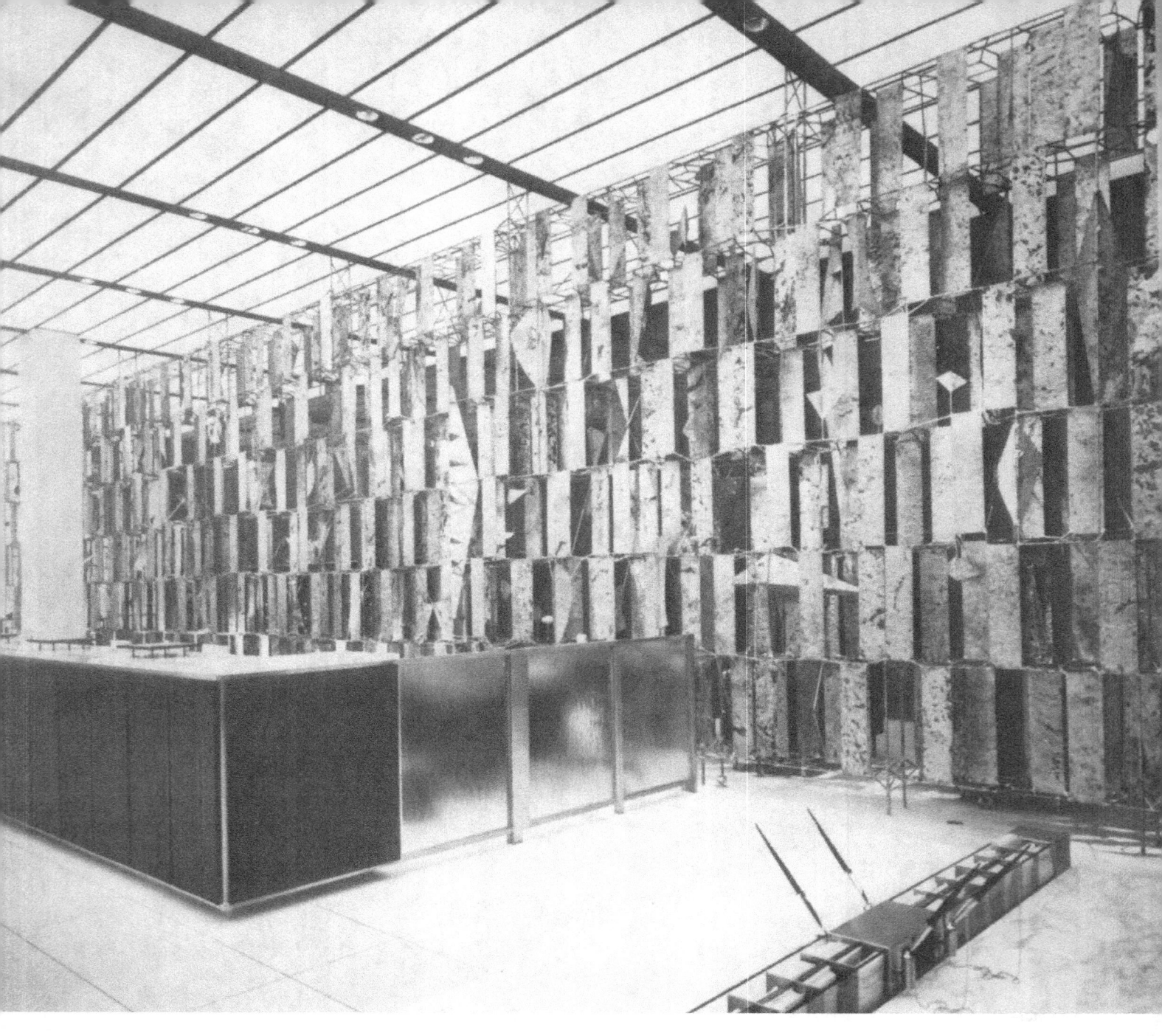

22. Sculpture screen (1954), welded metal, about 16 x 70 x 2 ft. Manufacturers Hanover Trust Co.

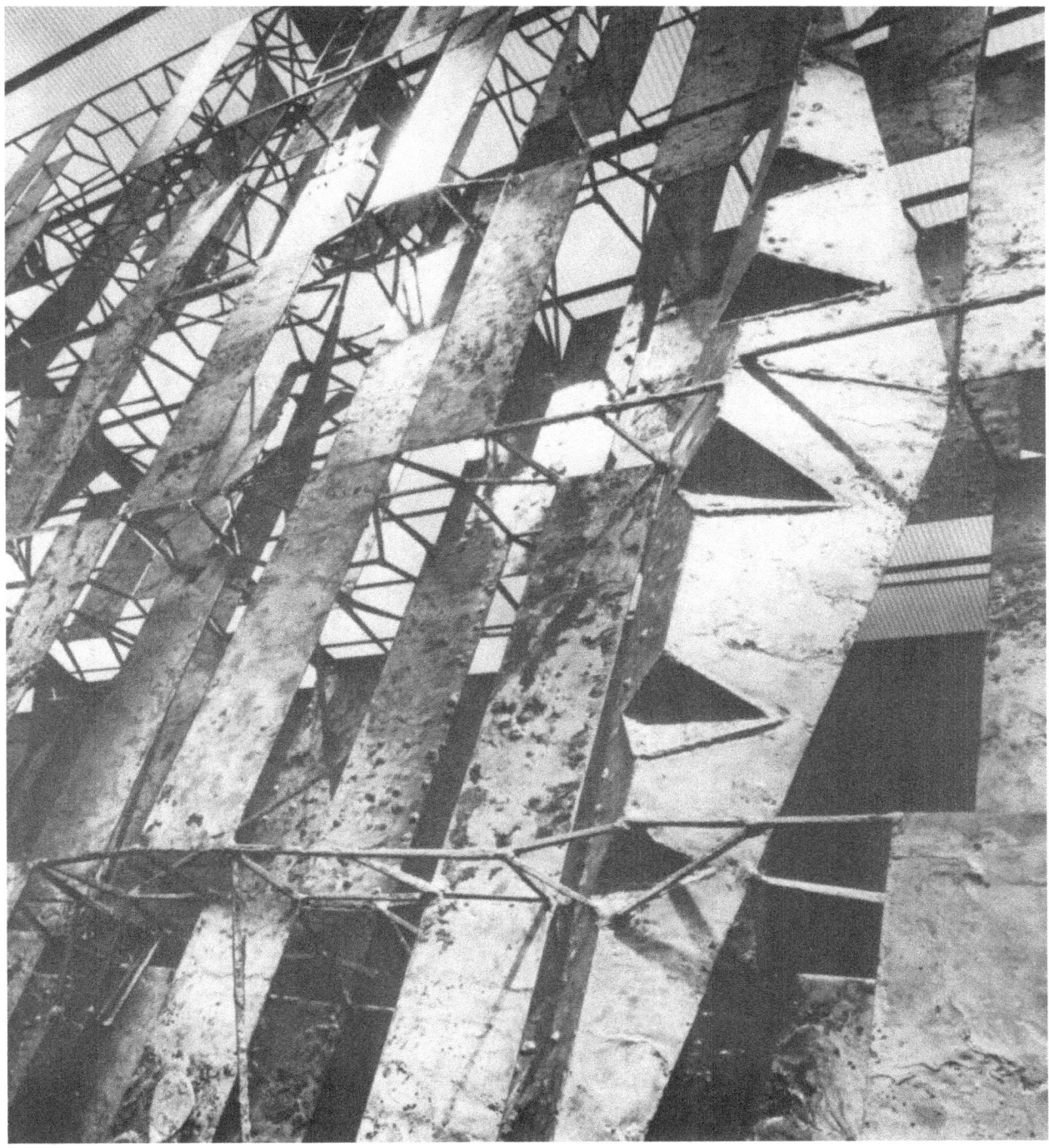

23. Detail of Manufacturers Hanover Trust Co. screen.

25. Reredos (1955), welded metal, about 24 x 12 ft. x 4 in.
Massachusetts Institute of Technology.

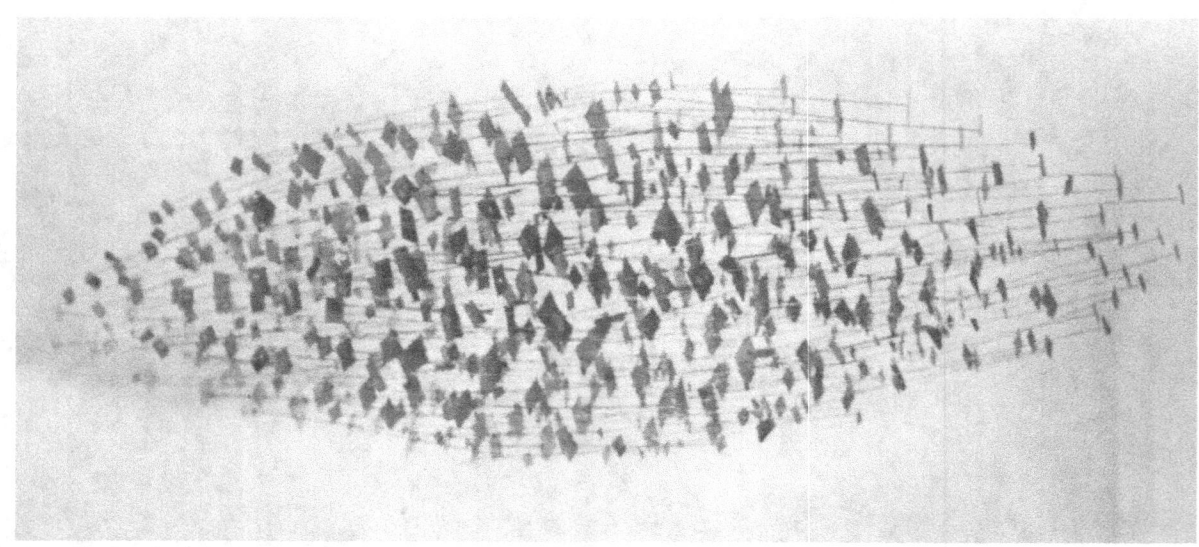

24. Wall-hung sculpture (1954), welded metal, about 13 x 27 in. German Mancini.

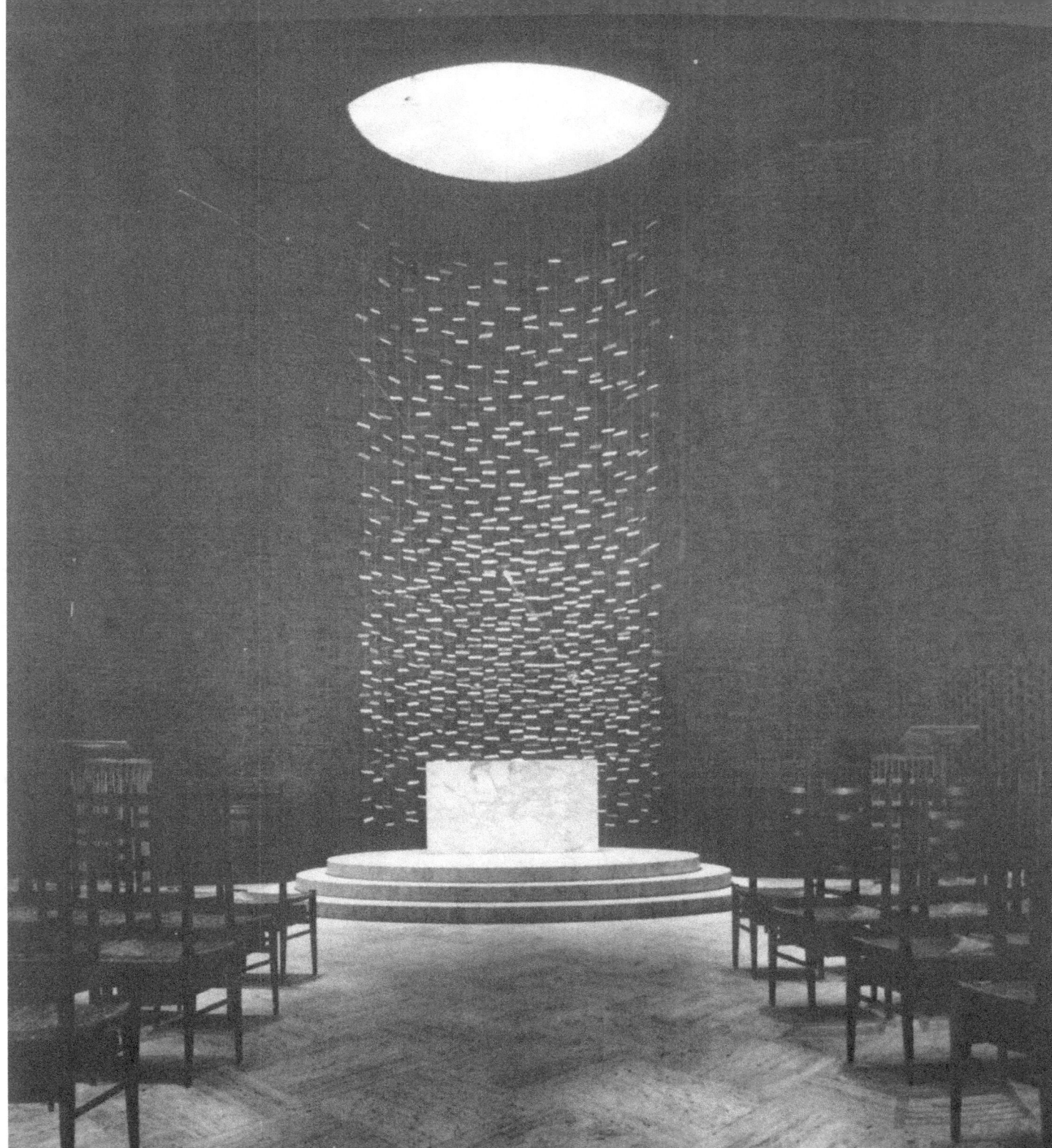

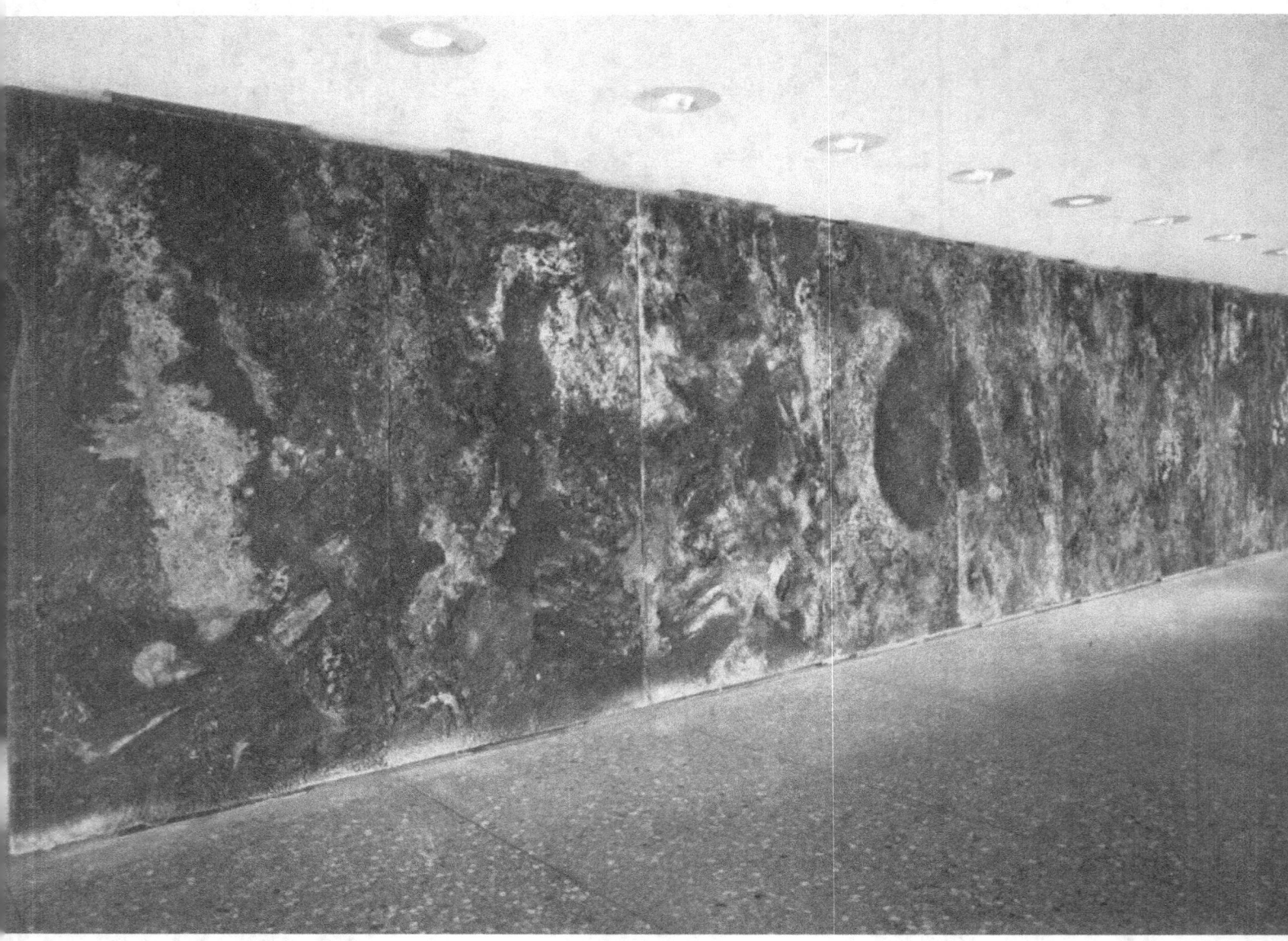

26. Mural (1963), poured bronze panels, about 8 x 36 ft. x 4 in. Dulles International Airport.

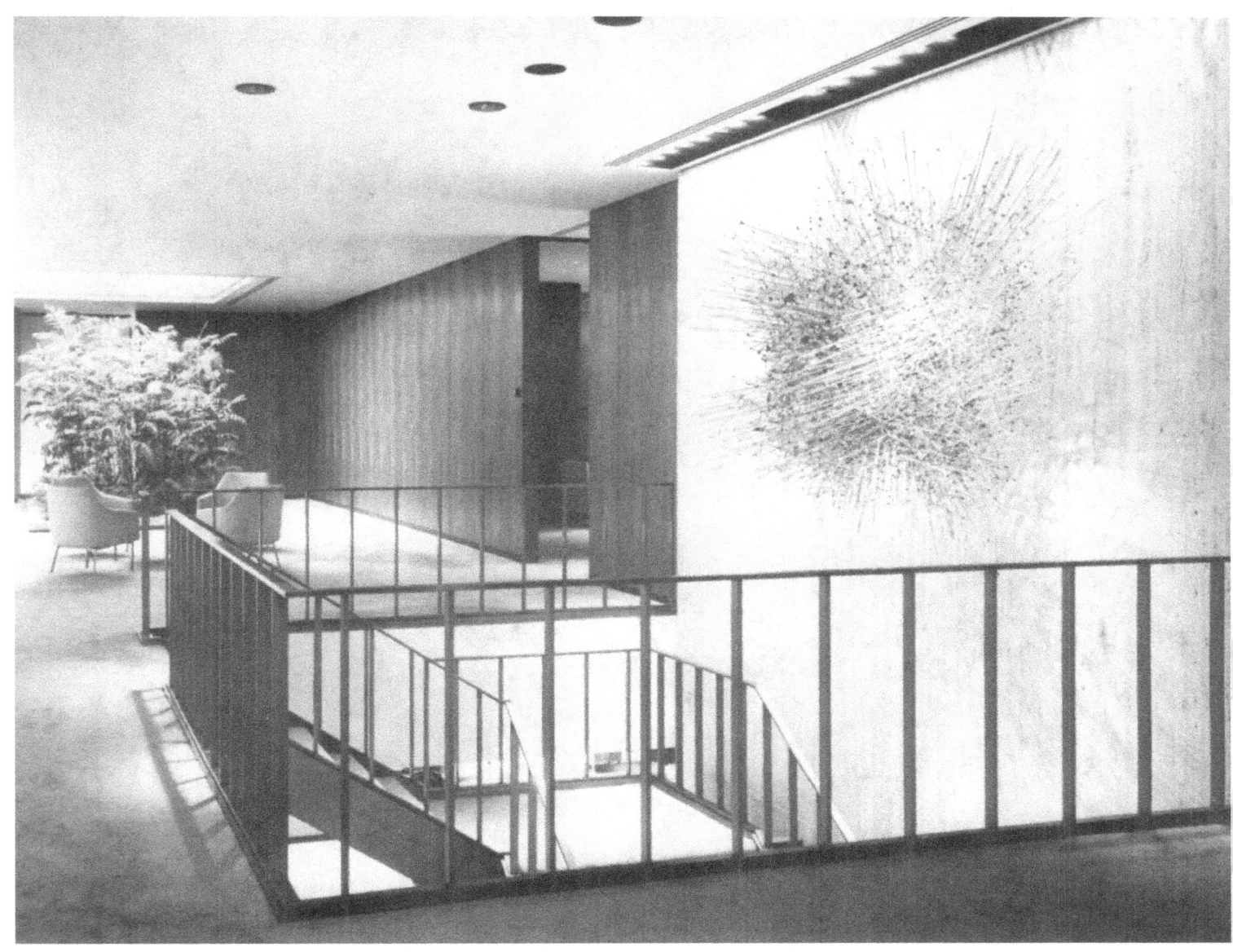

27. Wall hanging (1962), welded metal, about 6½ ft. wide. Bankers Trust Co.

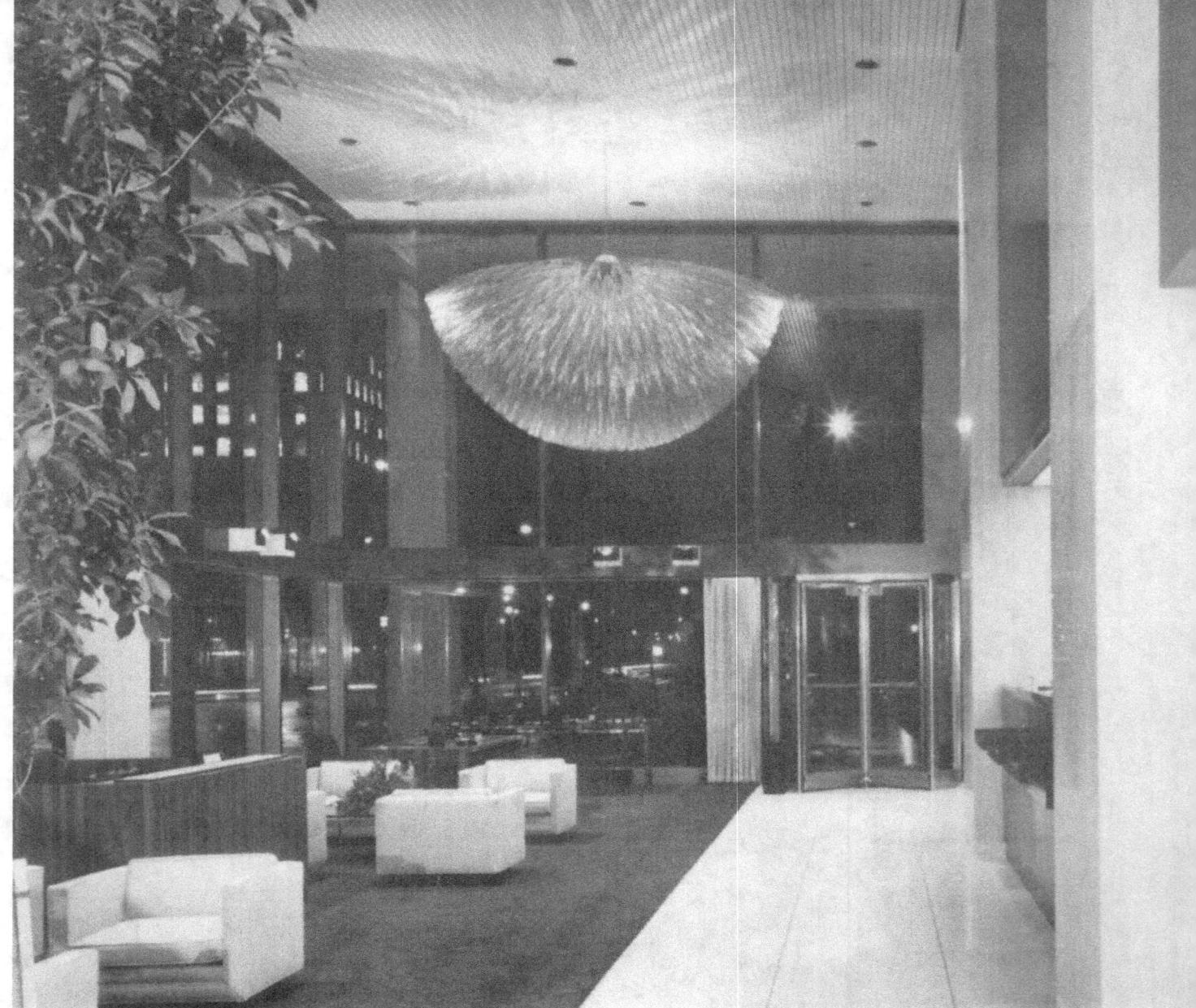

28. Hanging hemisphere (1965), stainless steel, about 6 ft. high, 12 ft. diam. Cuyahoga Savings Association.

29. Globe (1964), bronze, about 50 in. diam. Princeton University.

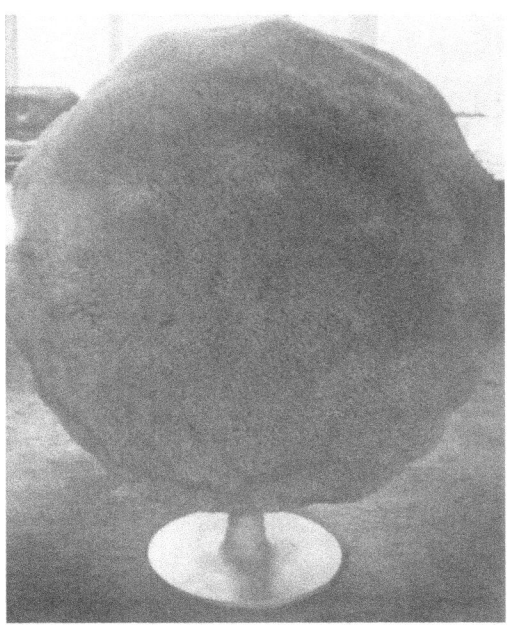

30. Another view of Princeton University globe.

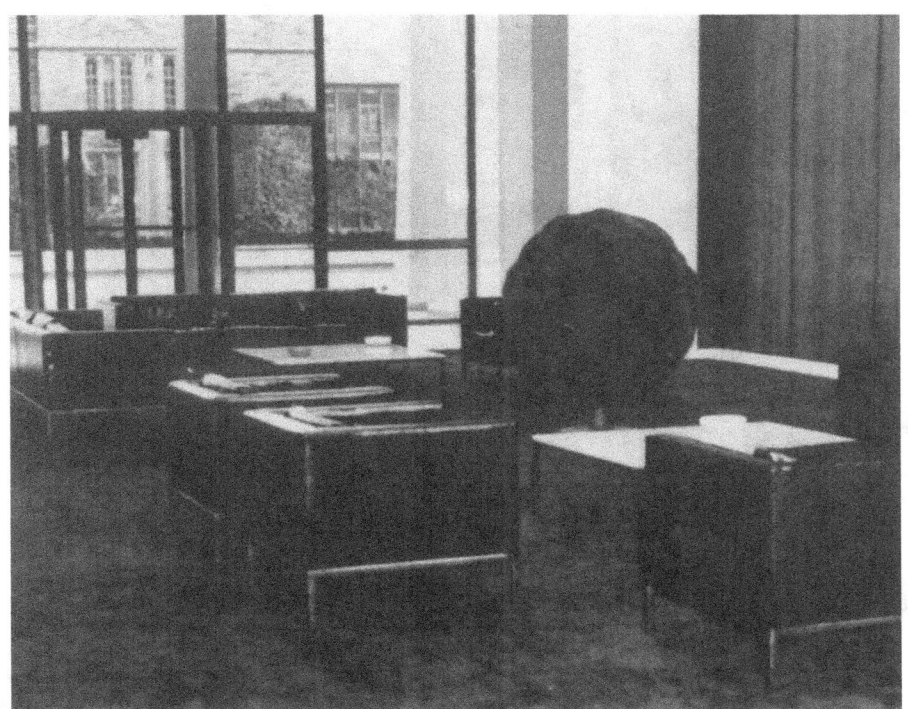

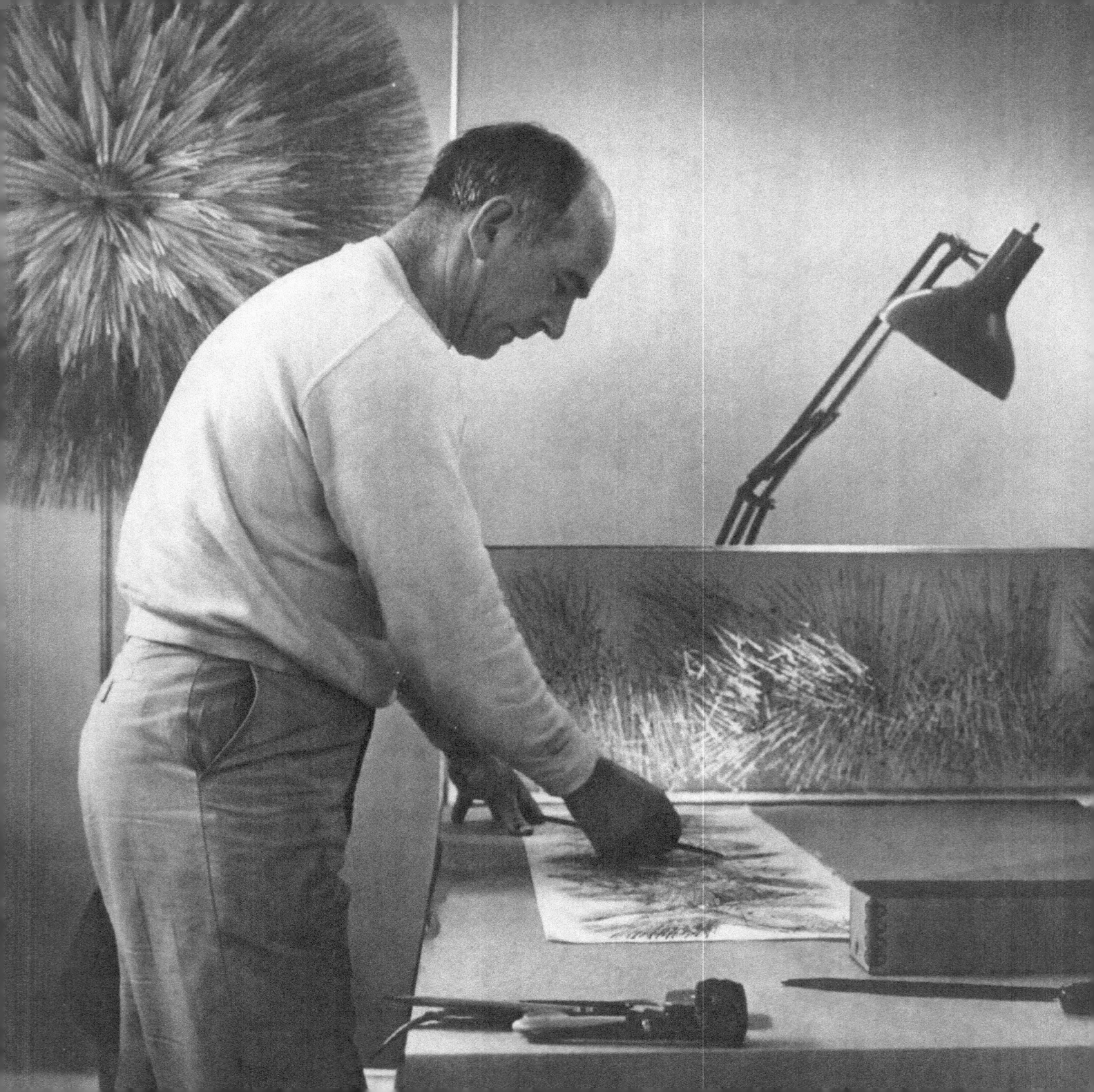

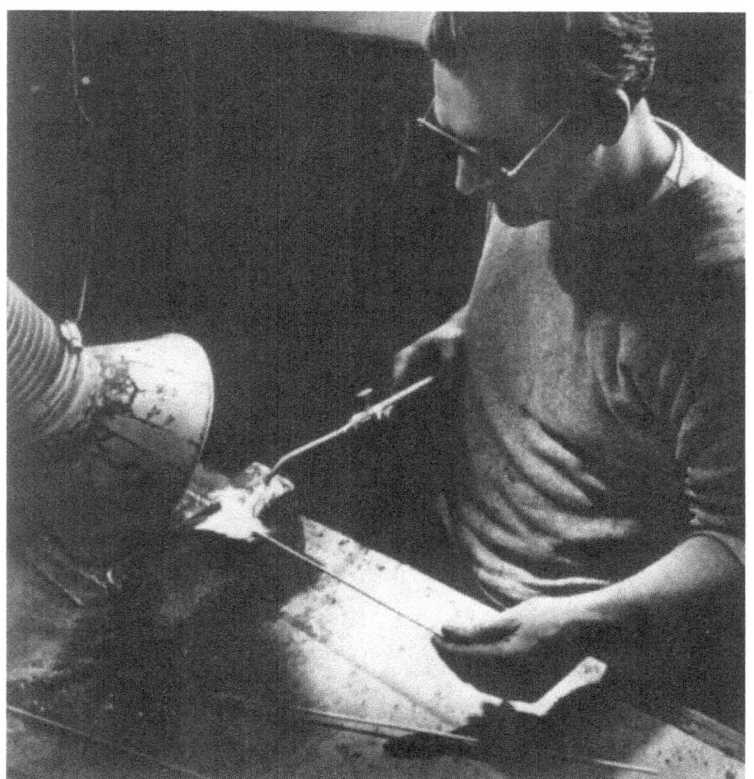

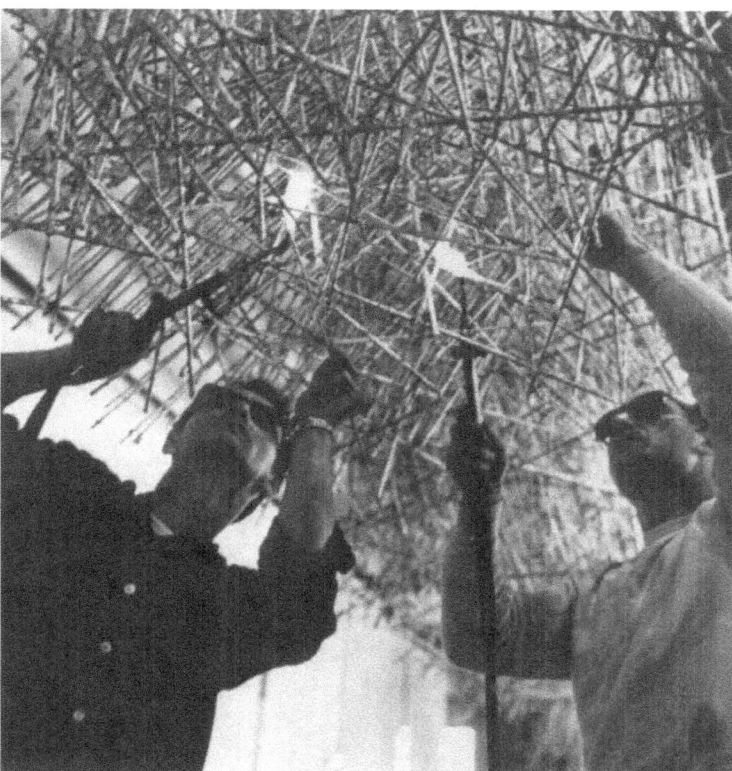

32. Assistant Jim Flanagan feeds a steel rod through a puddle of molten brass to create a textured surface.

33. Bertoia and Jim Flanagan weld a rod at the desired angle for "Sunlit Straw."

31. Bertoia in his studio working on drawing for "Sunlit Straw," model for which is in background; to left, a "dandelion" of stainless steel wire.

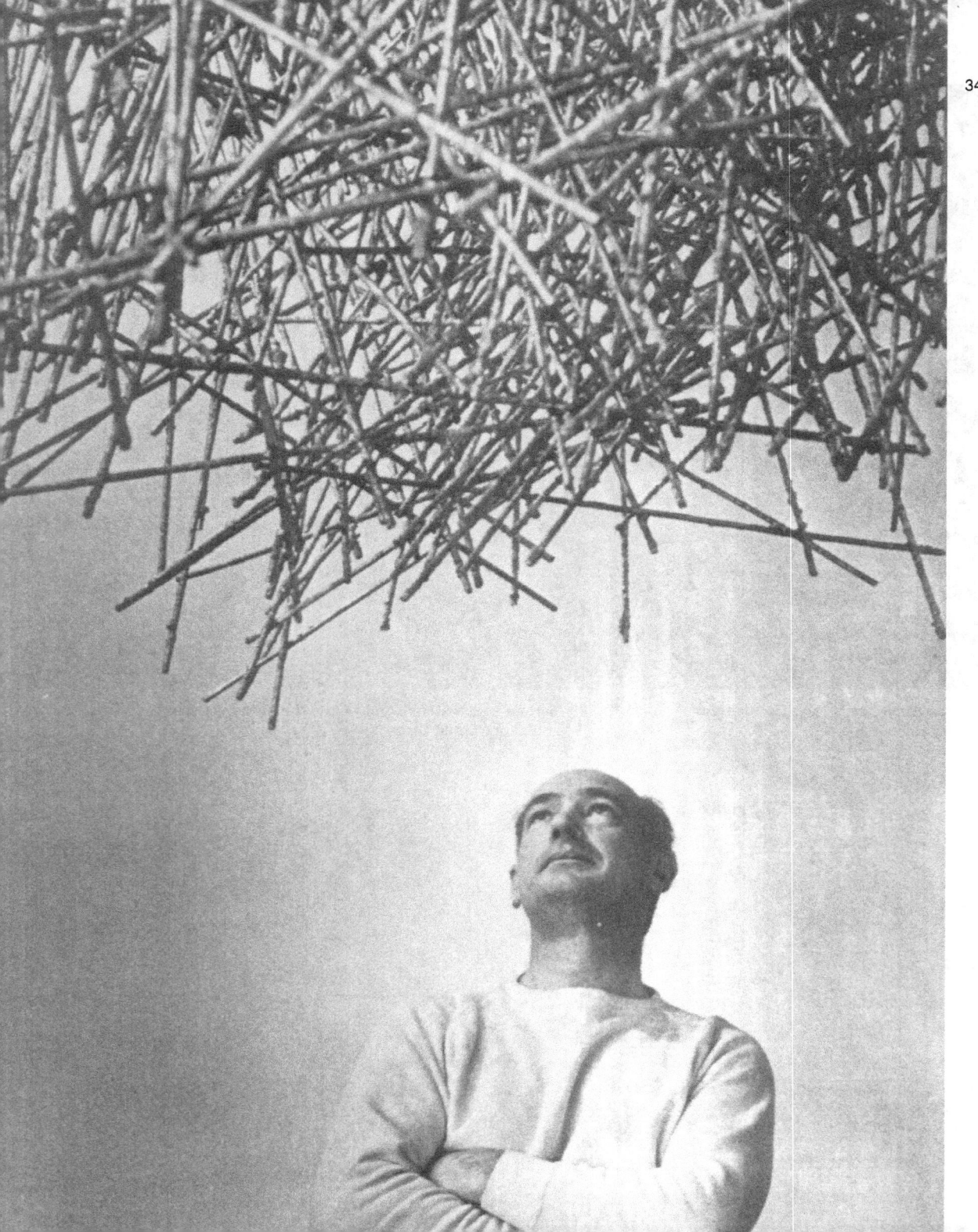

34. Bertoia examines half completed panel of "Sunlit Straw" suspended from studio ceiling; the maze of rods was eventually extended to the floor to reach its full 14-ft. height.

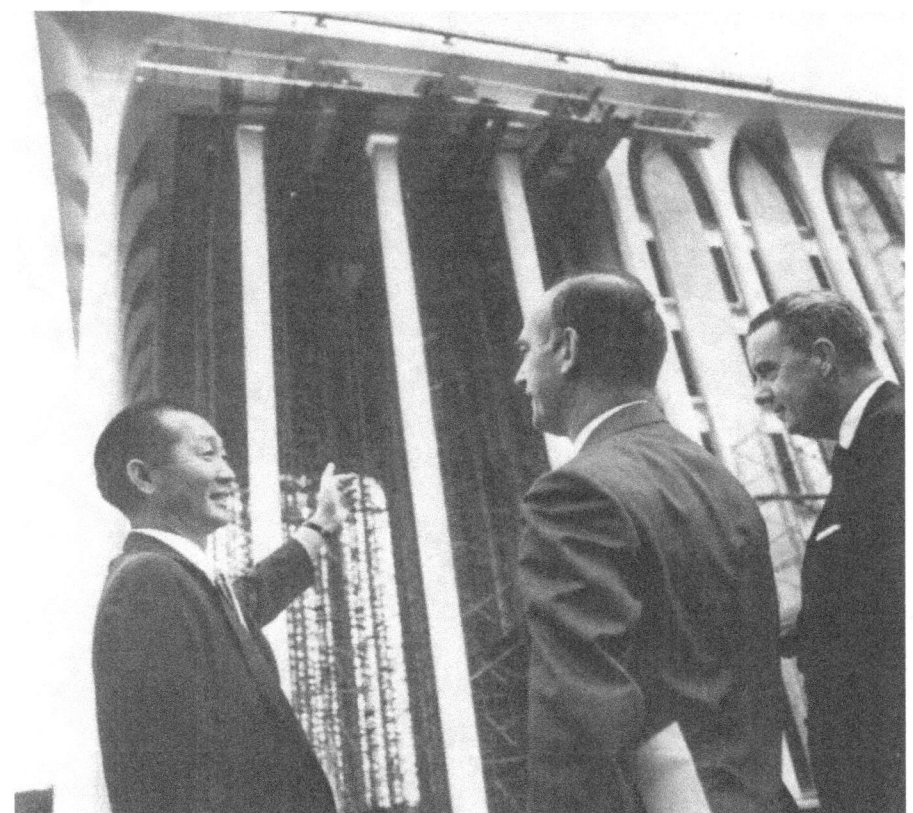

35. Minoru Yamasaki directs Bertoia's attention to the arched entry plaza which will lead to the lobby housing "Sunlit Straw."

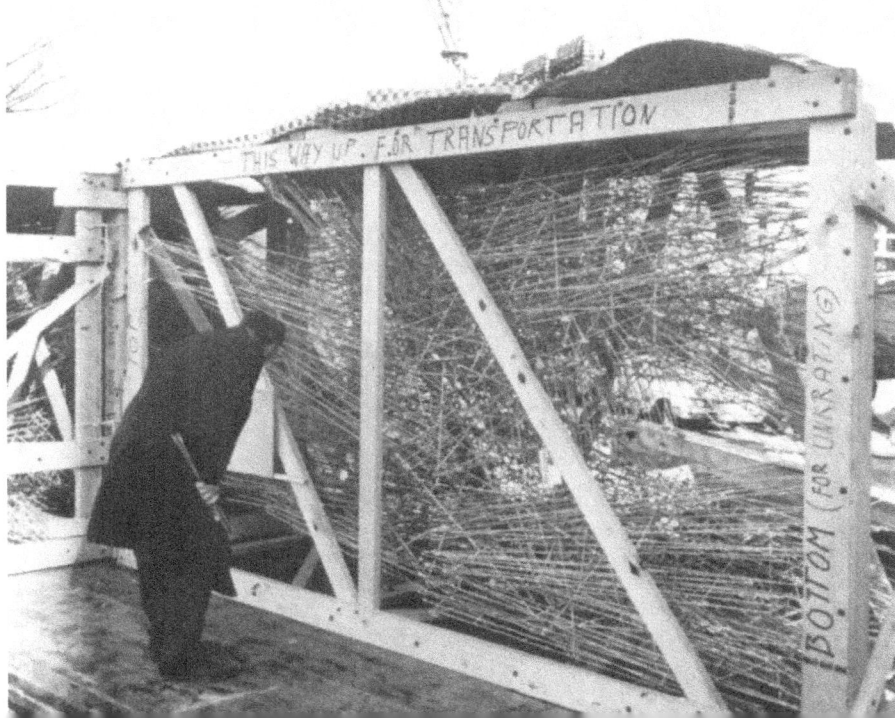

36. Sections of the crated sculpture as they arrived in Minneapolis on a flatbed truck; Bertoia was there to inspect for damage in transit.

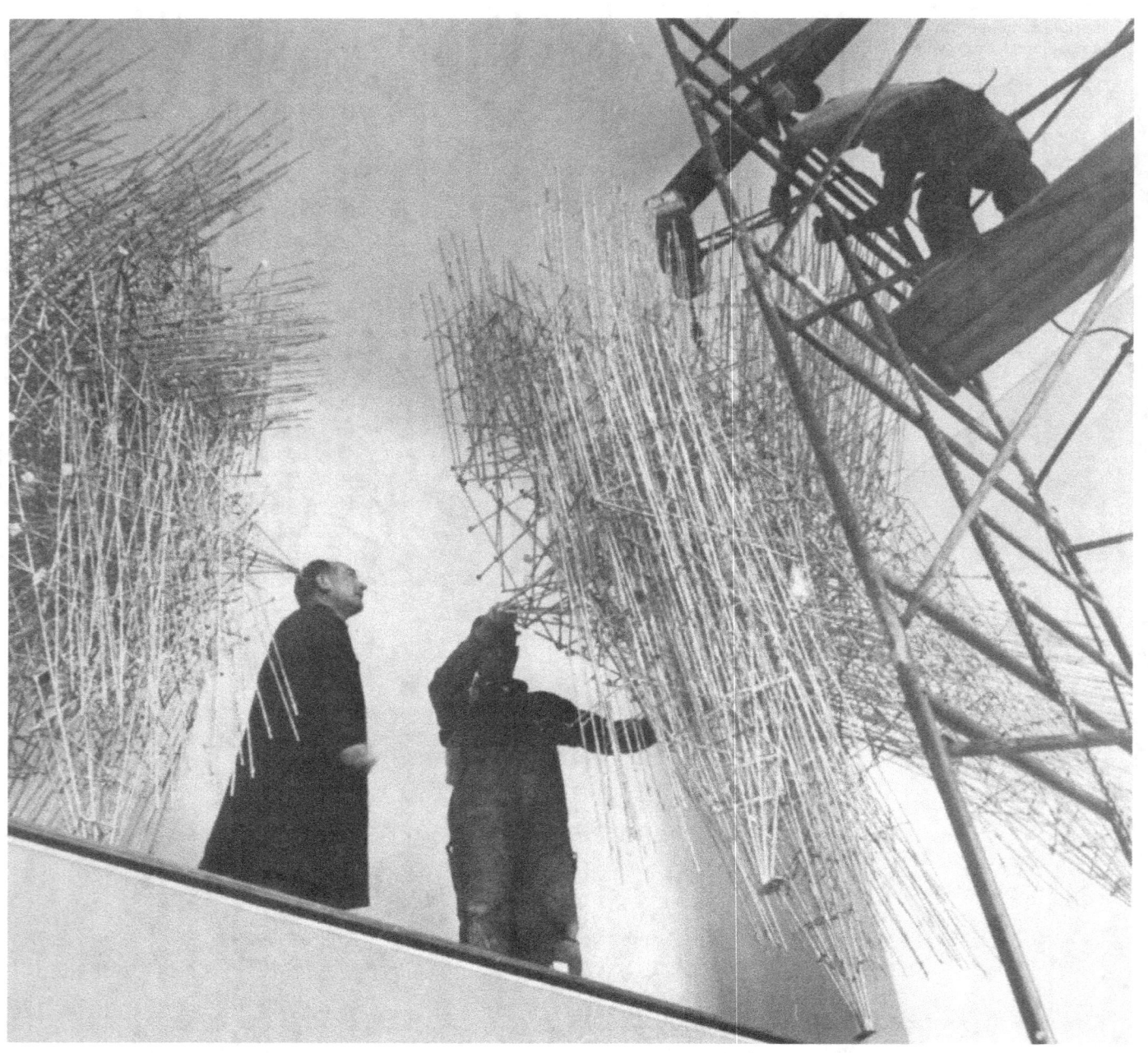

37. Section of "Sunlit Straw" being hoisted into position on ledge of the lobby wall.

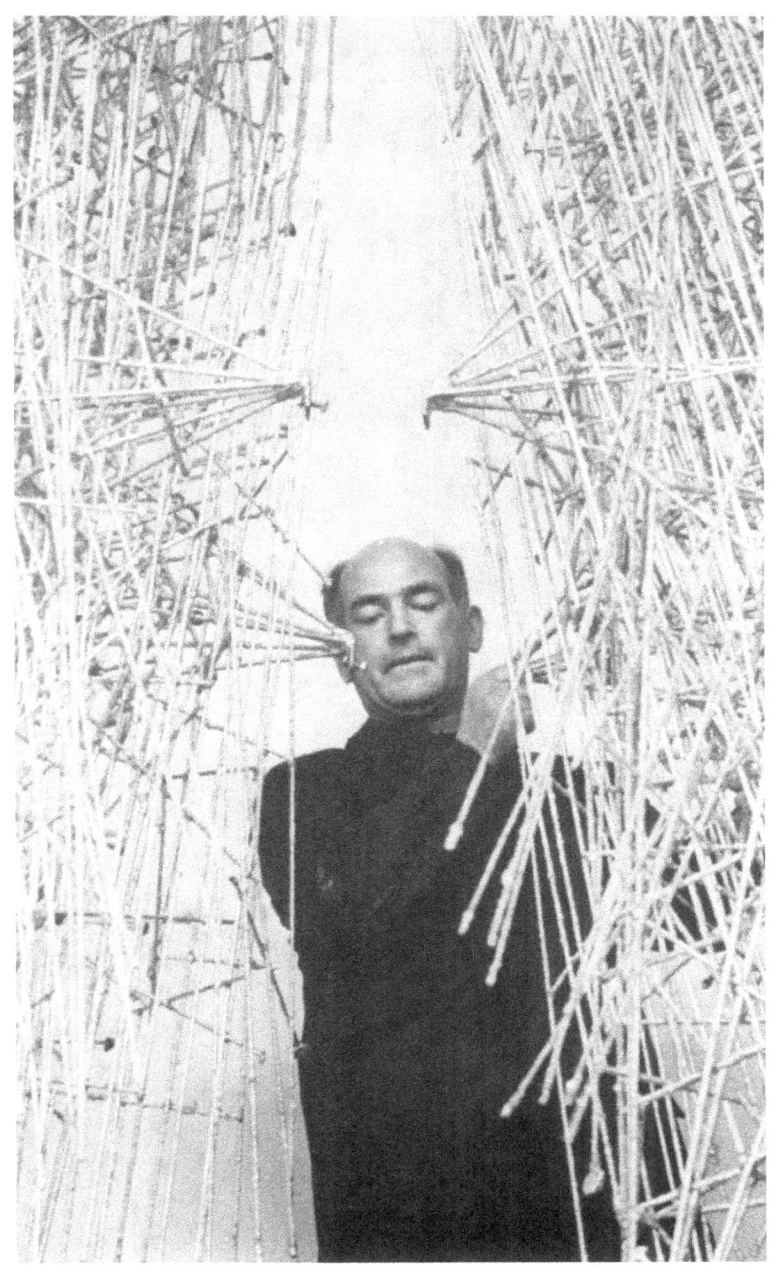

38. Bertoia matches the joining positions of two sections of ''Sunlit Straw.''

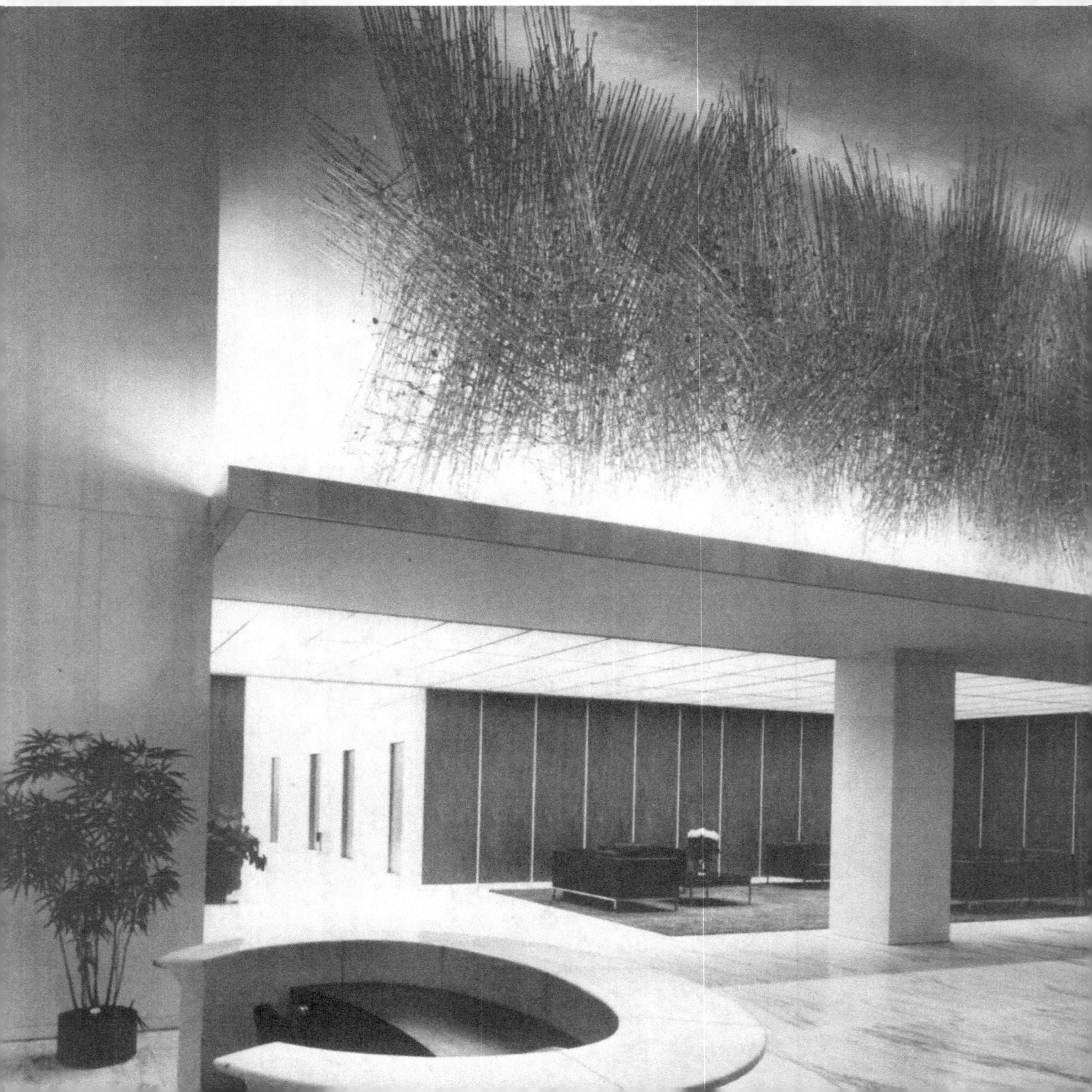

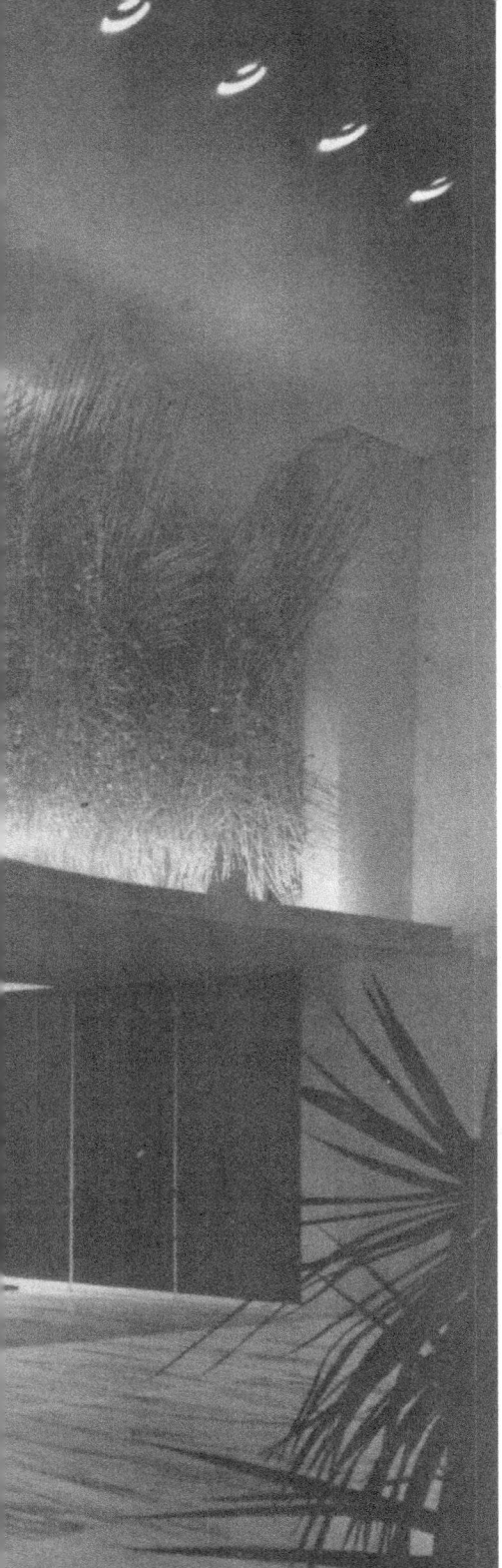

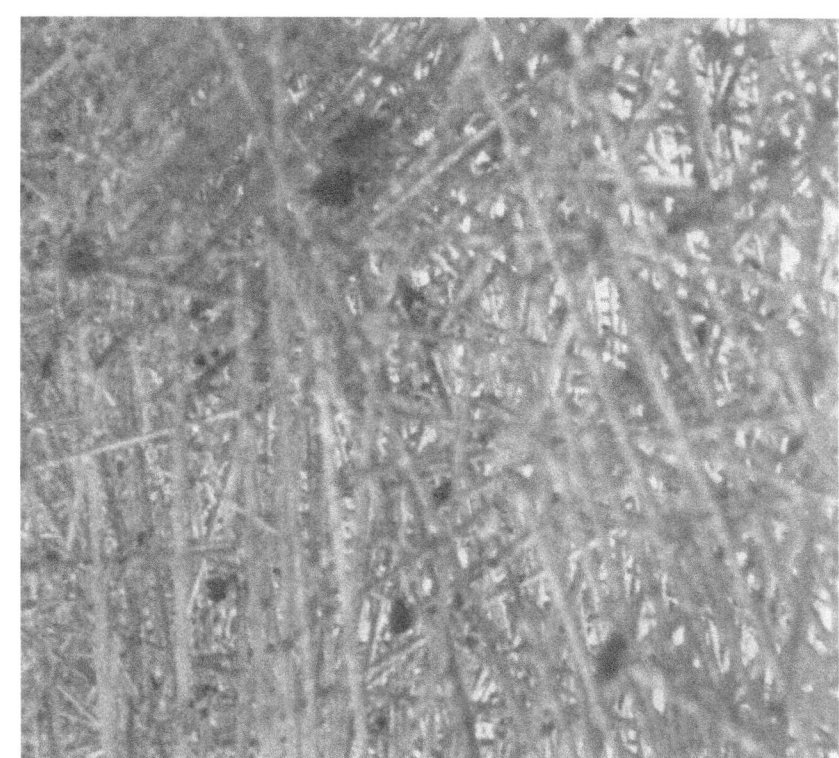

40. Detail of "Sunlit Straw," from the back.

39. "Sunlit Straw" (1964), brass-coated steel rods, about 14 x 46 x 4 ft.
Northwestern National Life Insurance Co.

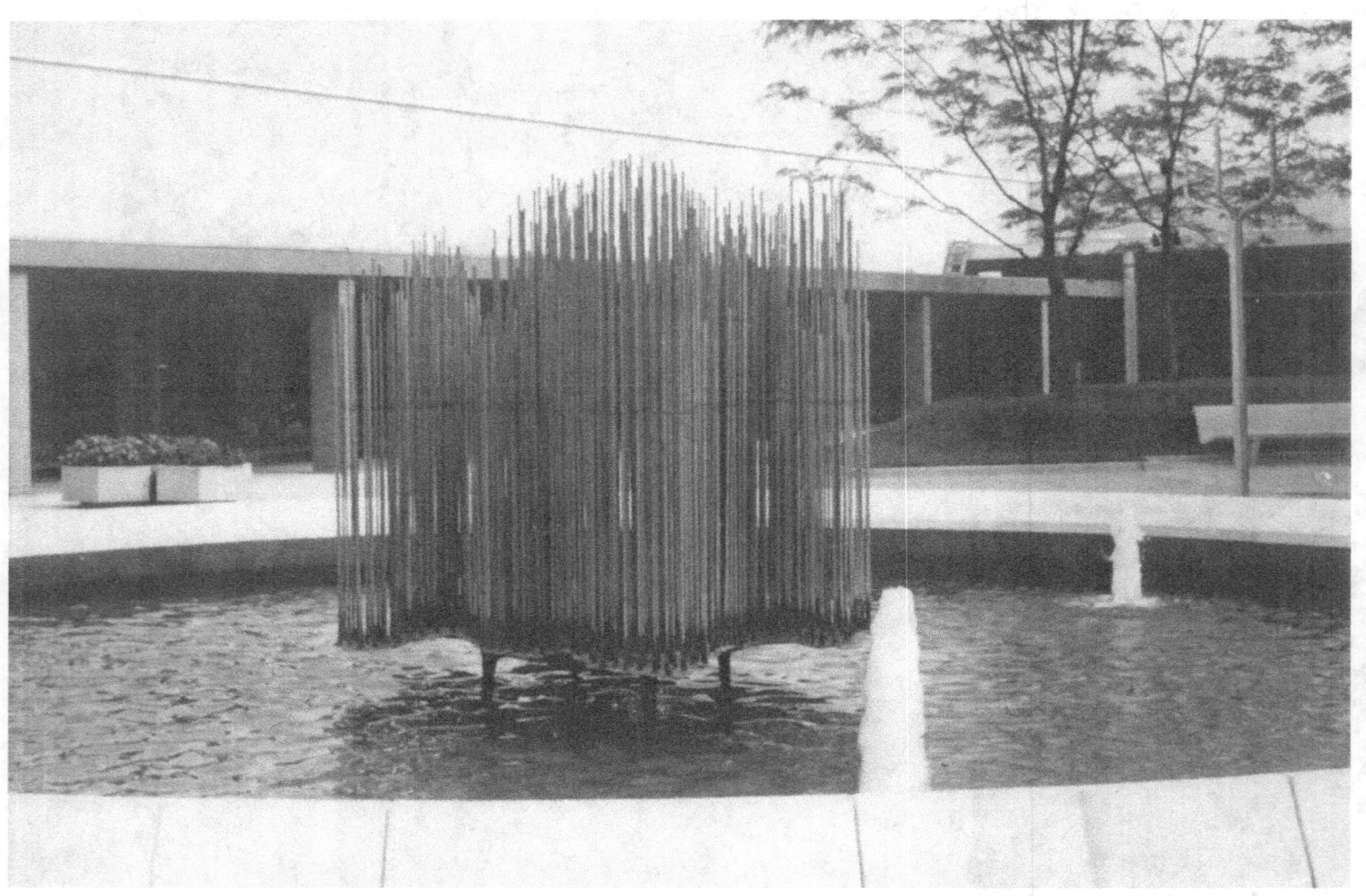

41. Musical fountain sculpture (1966), Tobin bronze rods, about 9 x 10 x 8 ft. River Oaks Shopping Center.

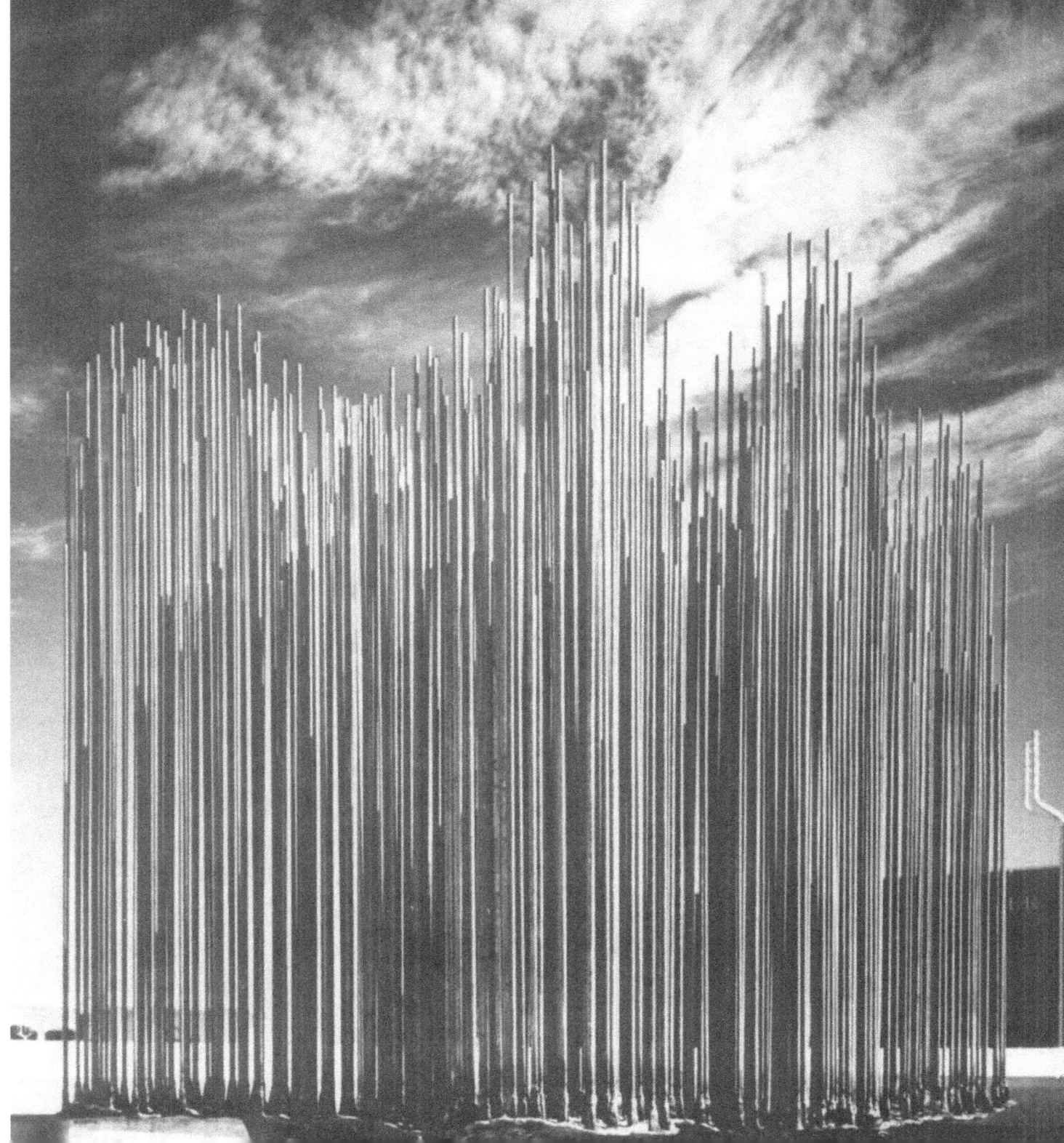

43. Sculpture screen (1967), laminated asbestos squares, textured and painted, about 24 x 36 x 3 ft. Brooklyn Federal Court Building.

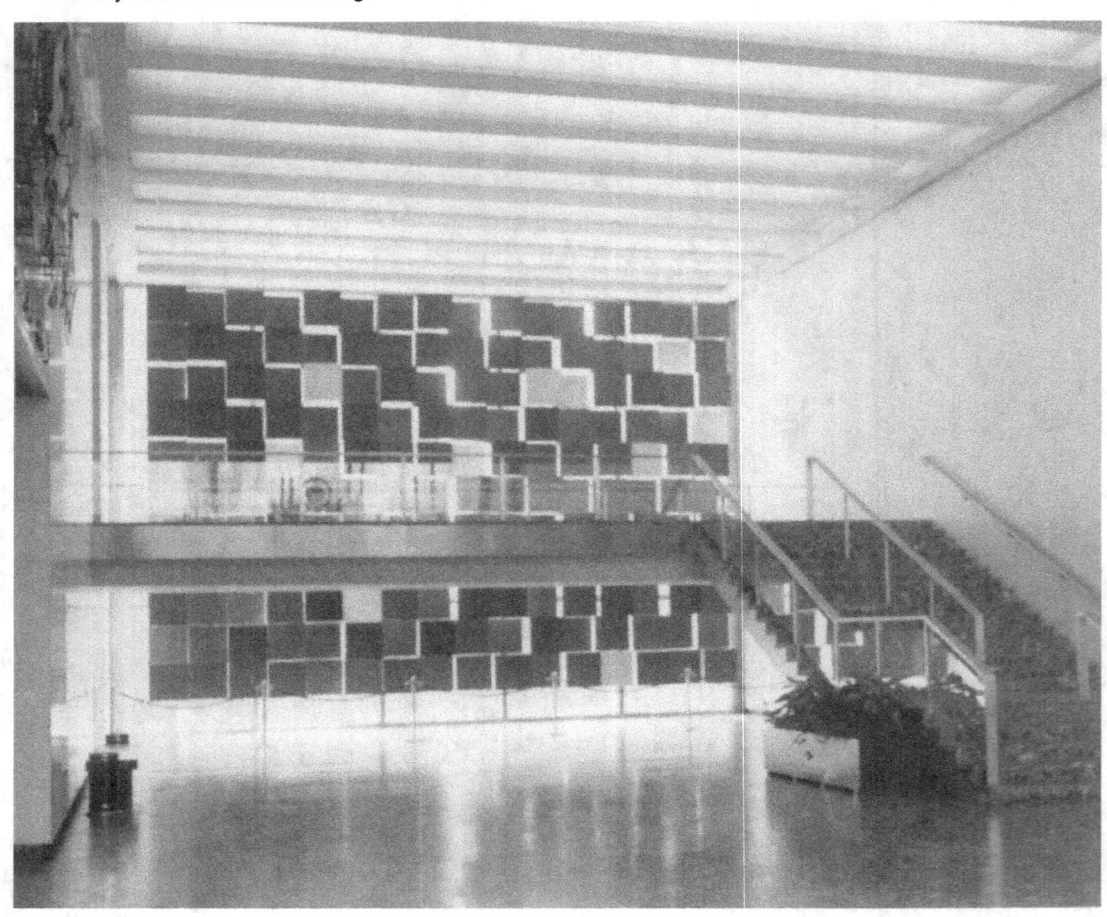

44. Detail of Brooklyn screen.

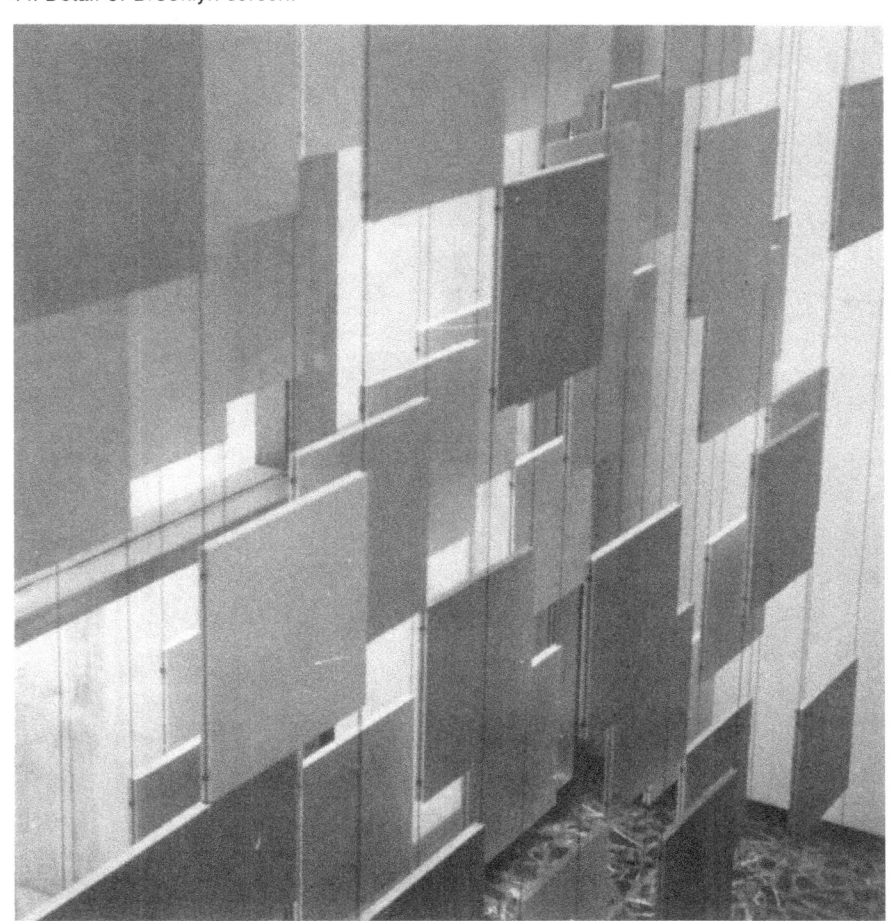

45. Fountain sculpture (1967), copper
    tubes, bronze-welded, about 14 ft.
    high, 16 ft. diam. Philadelphia
    Civic Center.

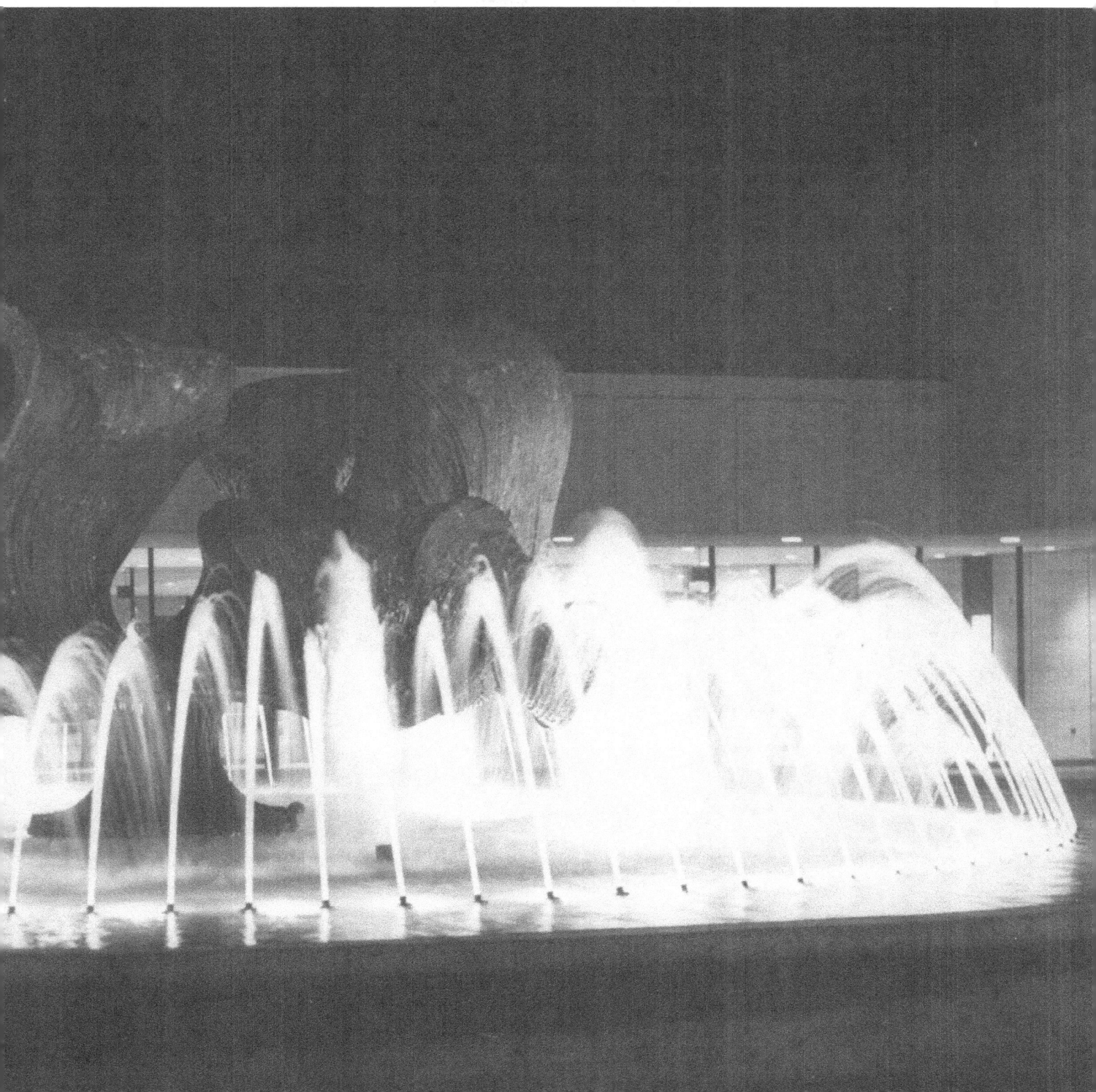

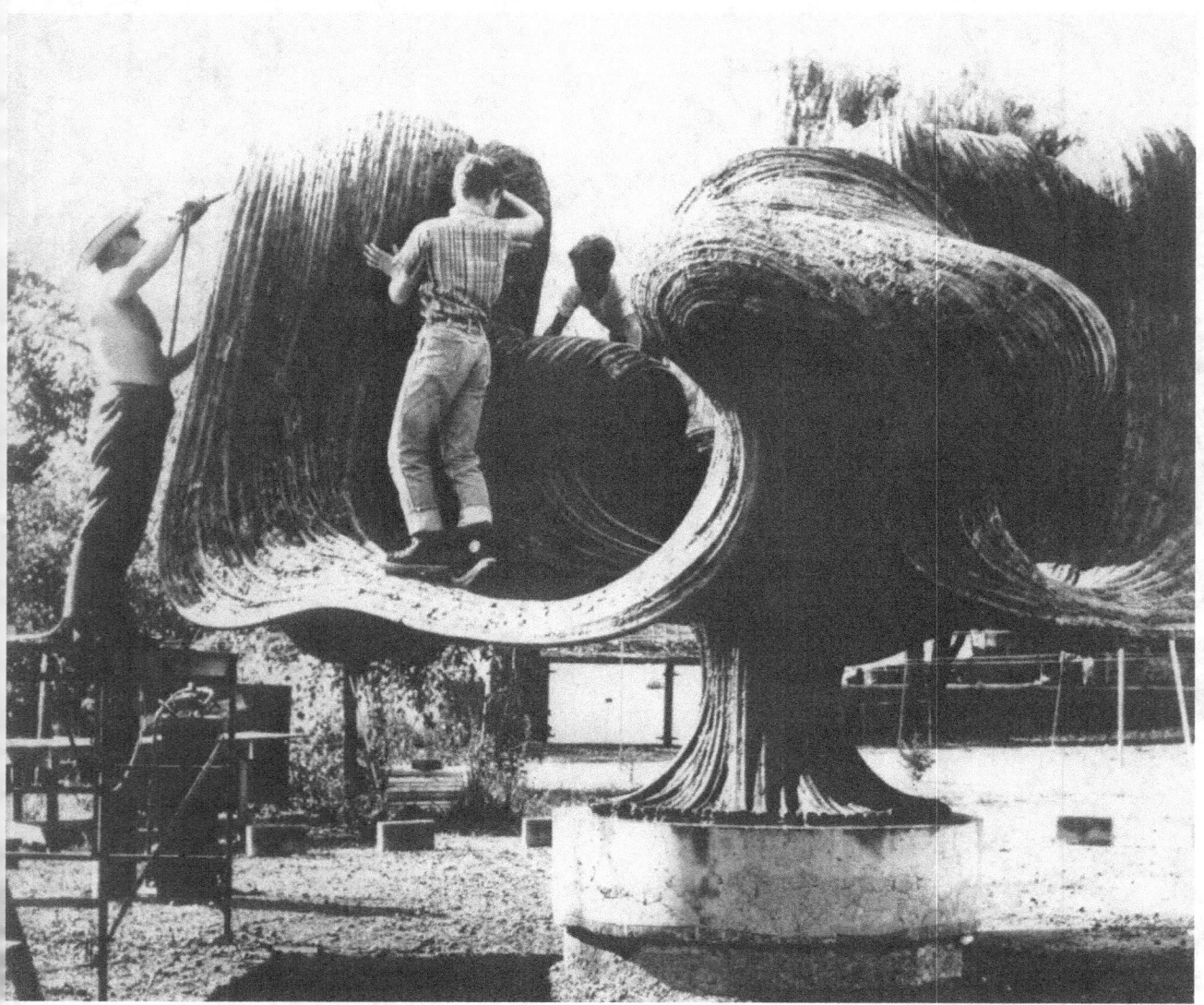

46. Philadelphia fountain under construction in backyard of Bertoia's studio.

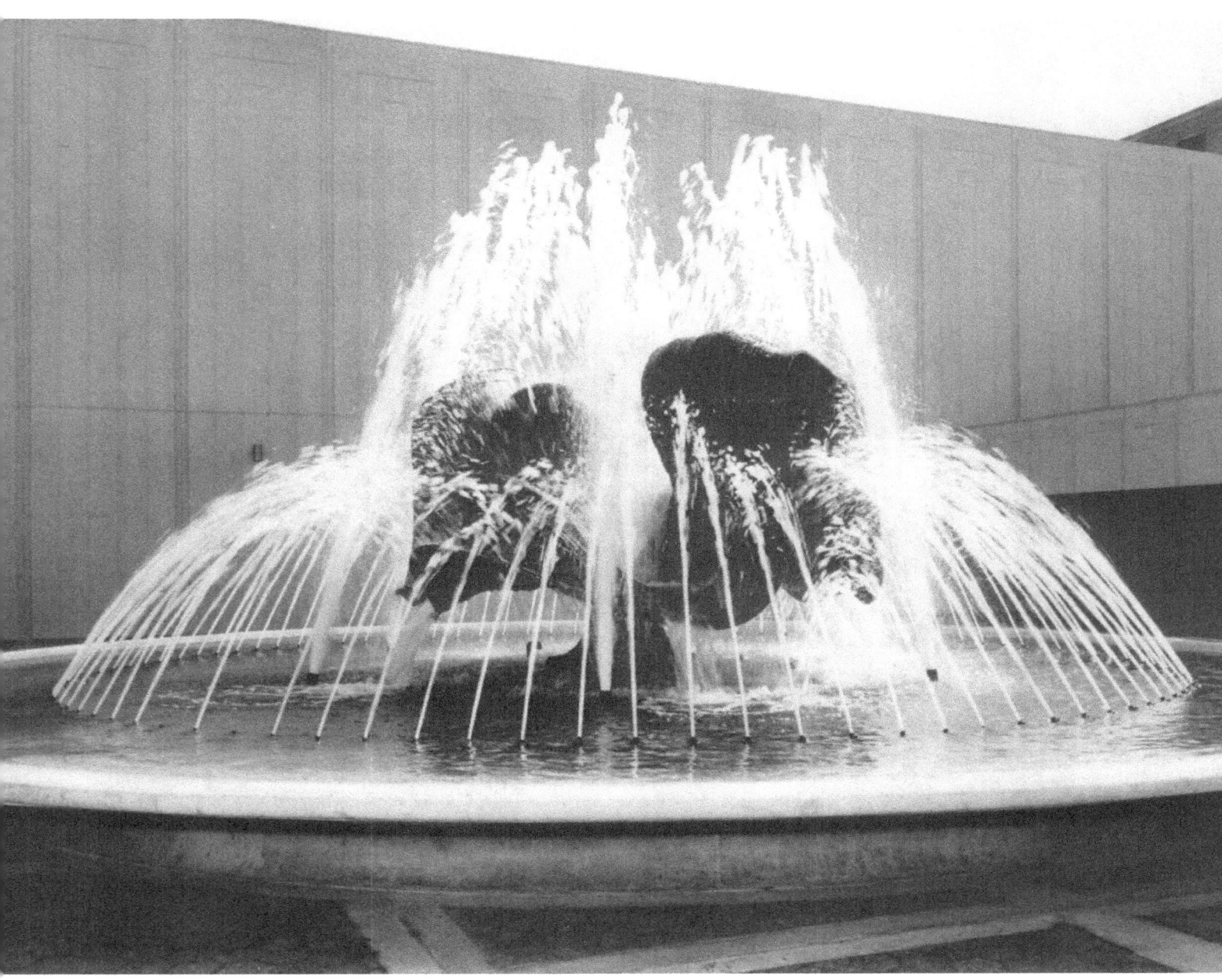

47. View of no. 45 with water jets at highest level.

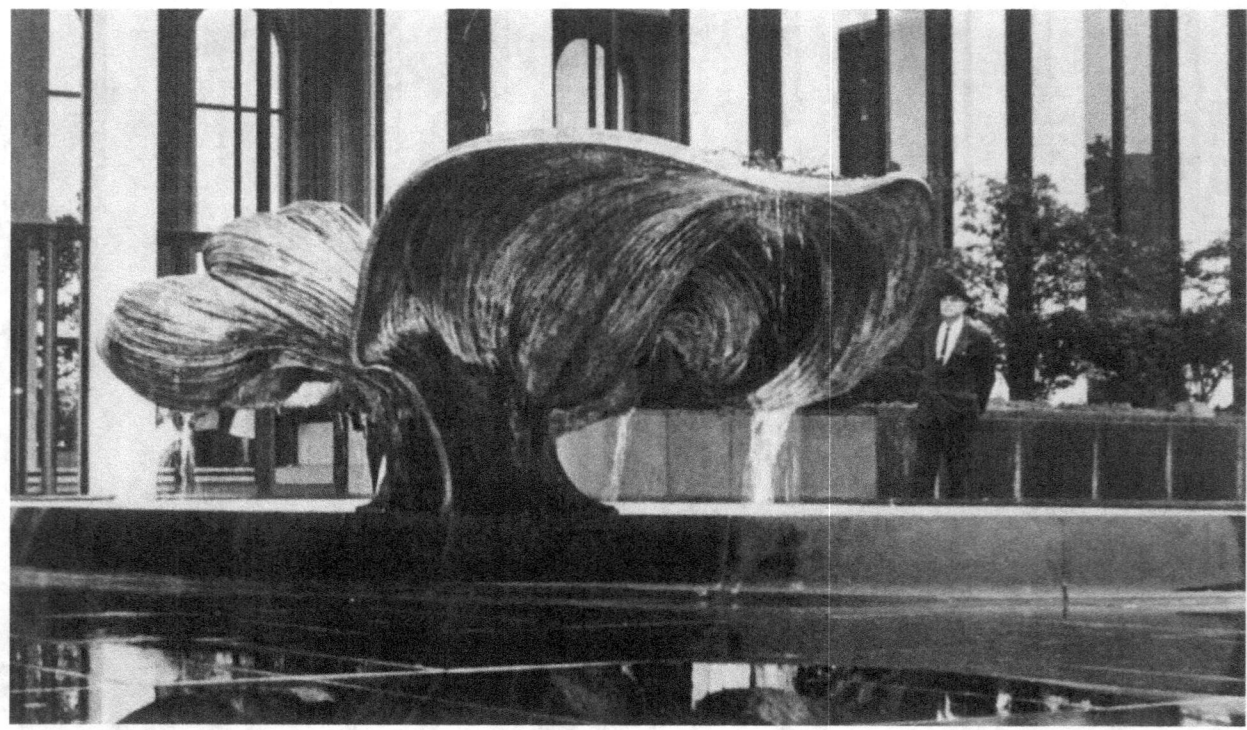

48. Fountain sculpture (1968), copper tubes, bronze-welded, about 7 x 18 x 12 ft. Manufacturers & Traders Trust.

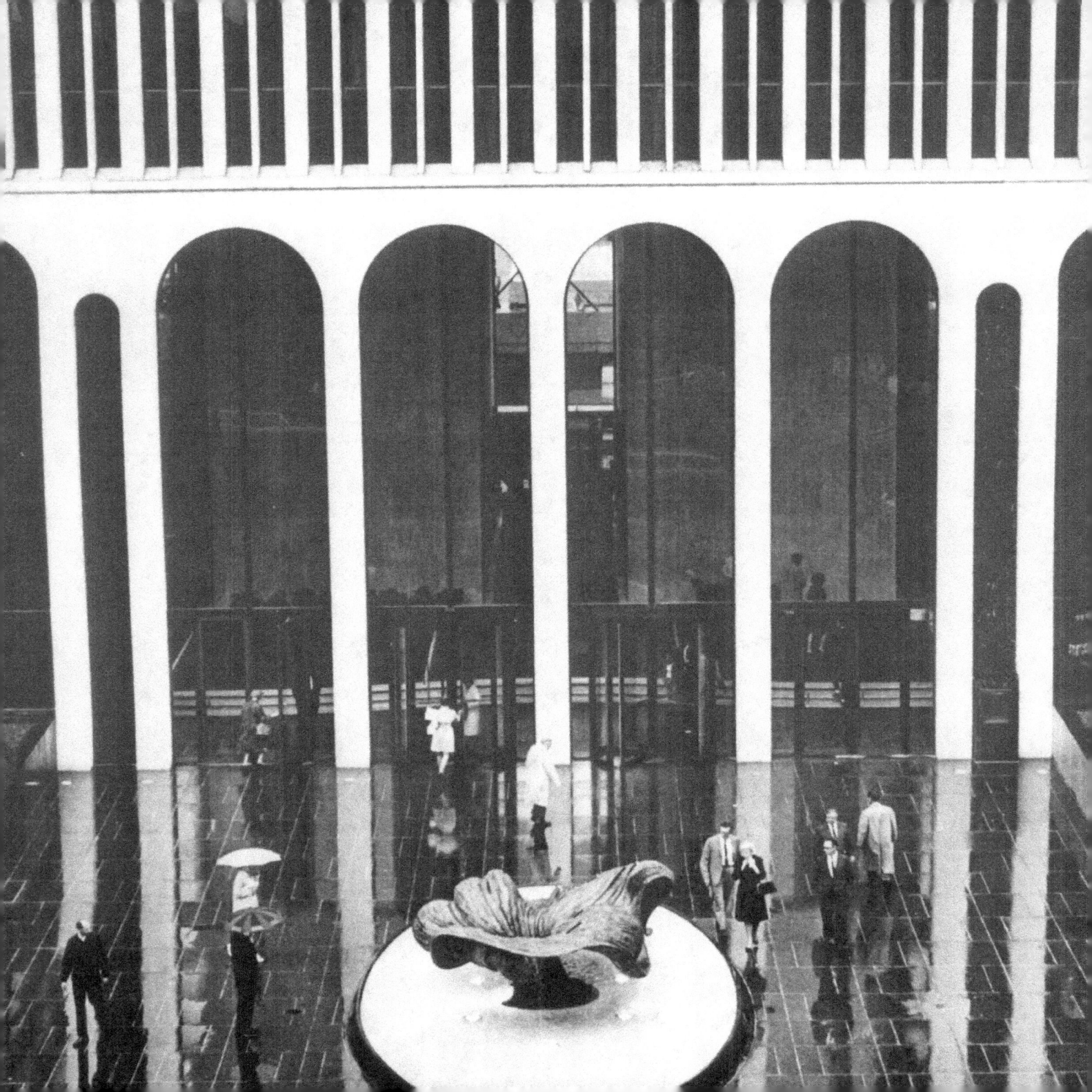

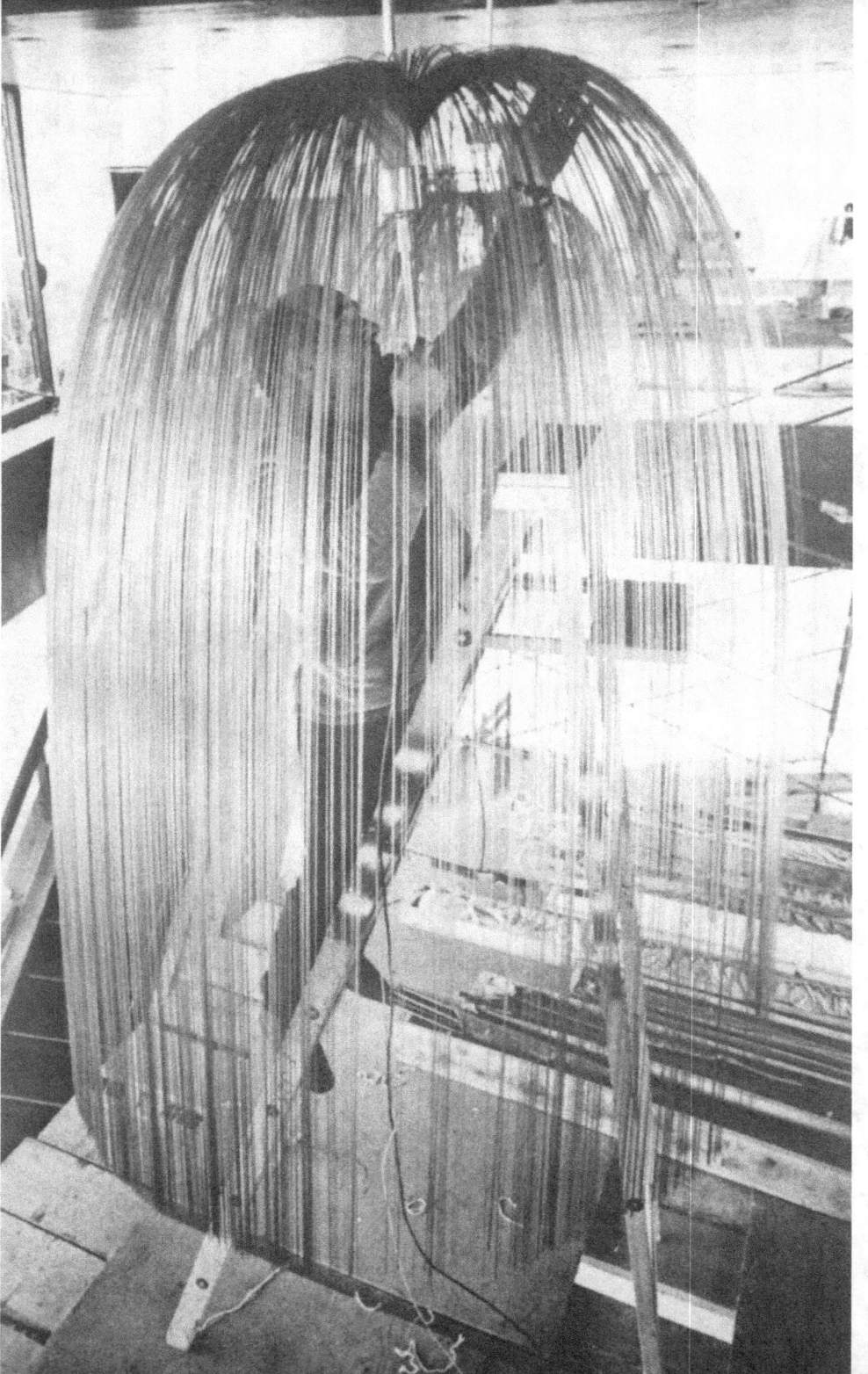

50. Bertoia installing a segment of ceiling sculpture (1968), stainless steel, 32 ft. diam. overall. Seattle-First National Bank.

51. "Comet" (1964), brass-coated steel rods, about 14 ft. high, 3 ft. diam. W. Hawkins Ferry.

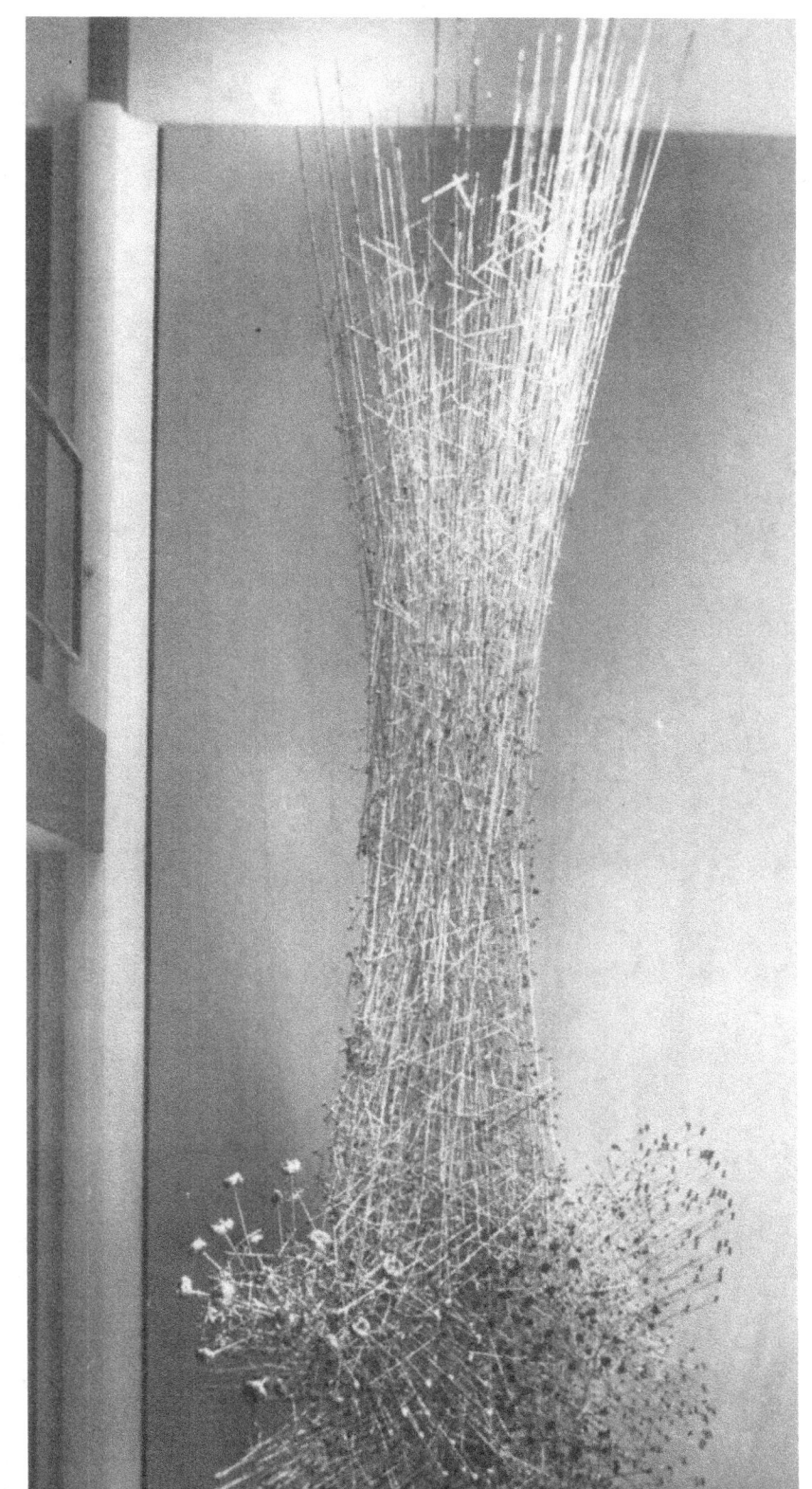

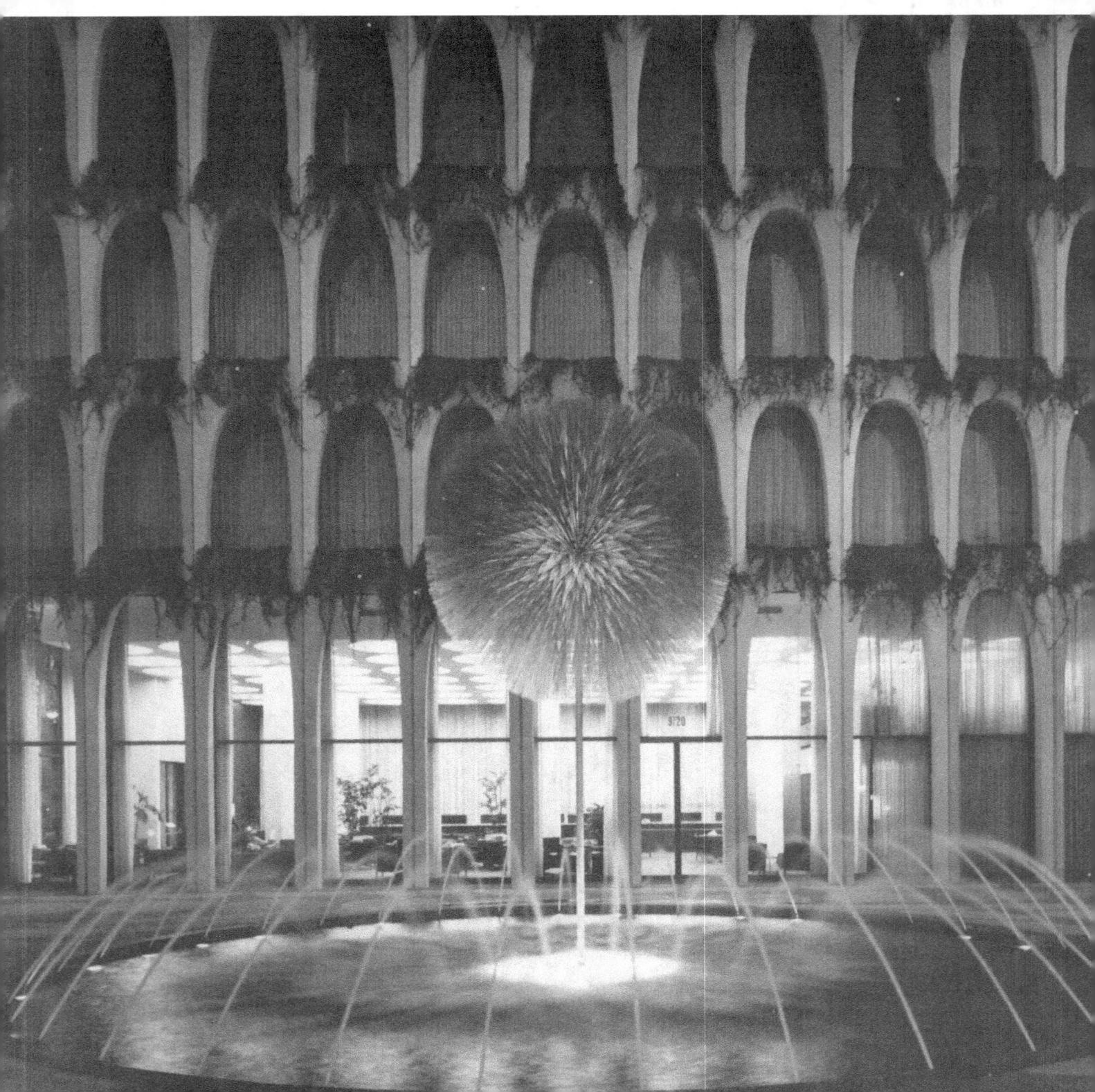

52. Fountain sculpture (1963), gilded wire, 20 ft. high, 10 ft. diam. Collection, the artist.

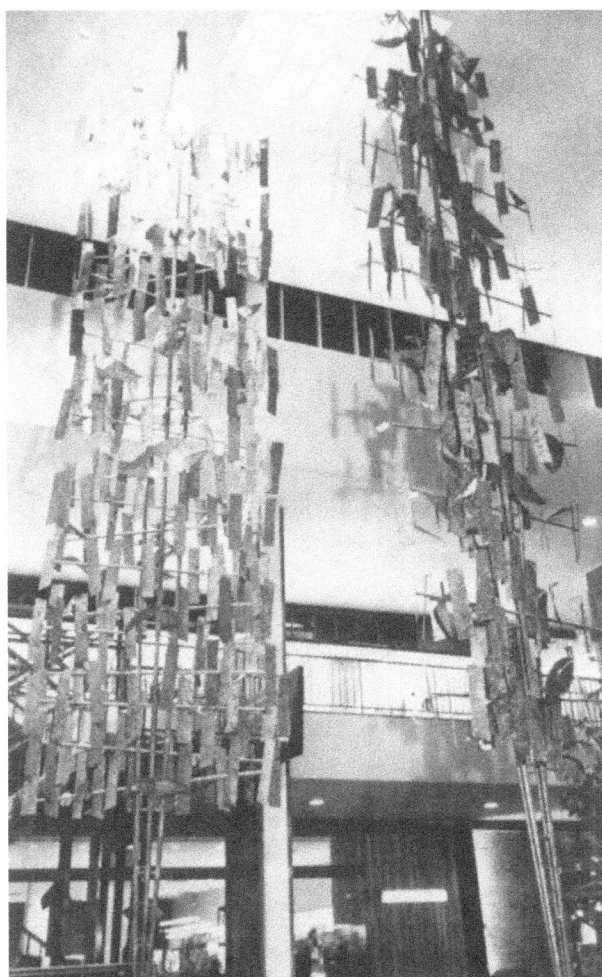

53. "Golden Trees" (1956), two welded metal screens, each about 48 ft. high. Dayton Store, Southdale Center.

54. Sculpture screen (1955), welded metal, about 10 x 24 ft. Dallas Public Library.

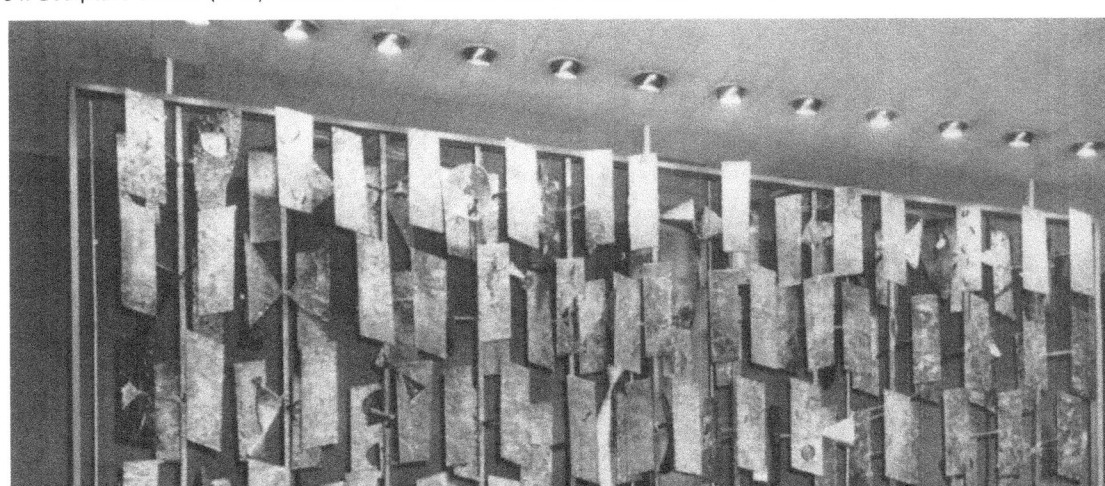

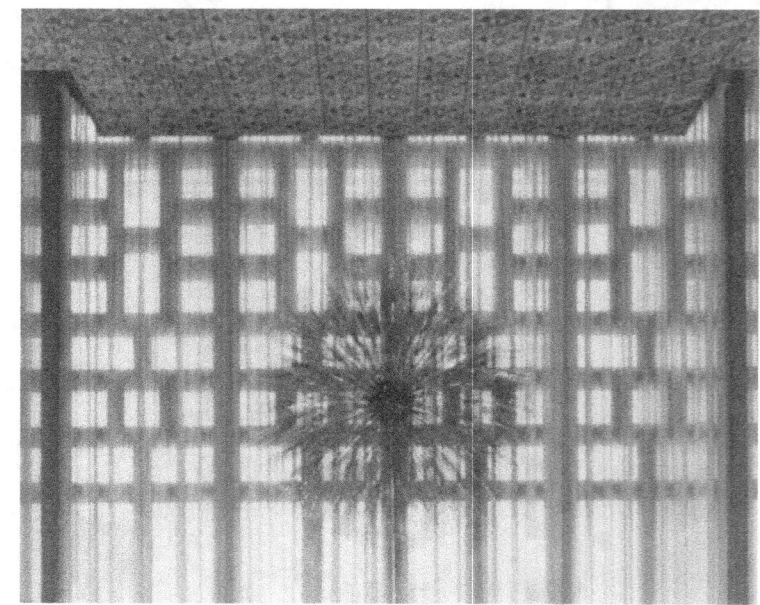

55. Balanced sphere (1961), chrome-plated wire, about 8 ft. high. Denver Hilton Hotel.

56. Sculpture screen (1961), welded metal, about 8 x 12 x 4 ft. Denver Hilton Hotel.

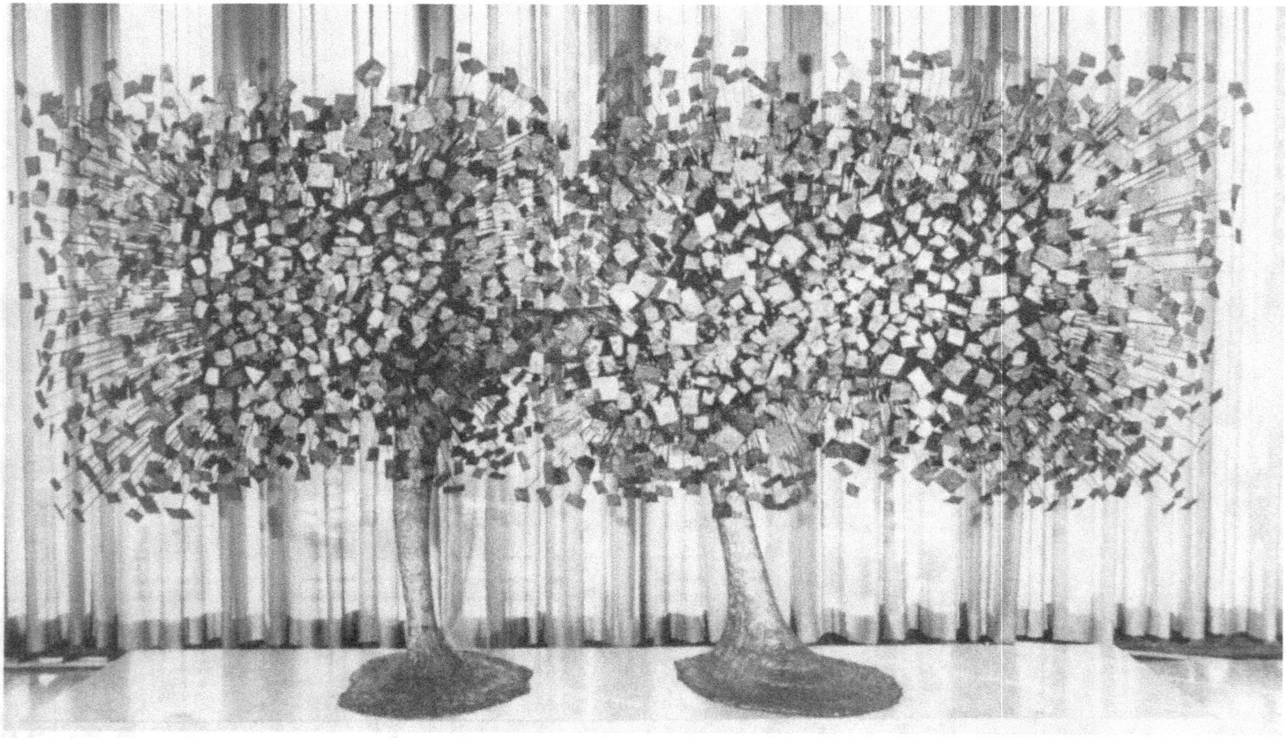

57. "Hollow Forms" (date uncertain), gilded bronze, 27 in. wide. Staempfli Gallery.

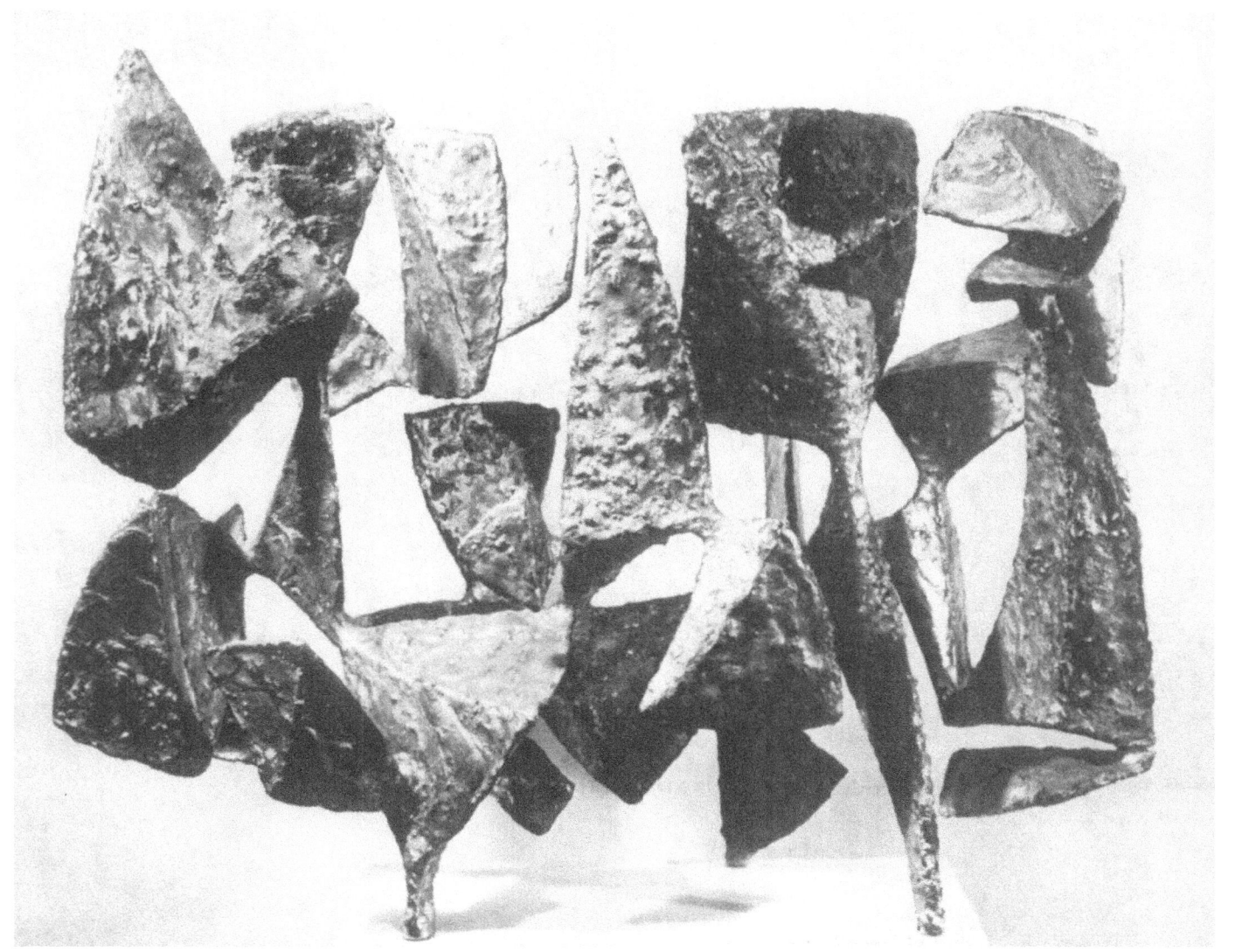

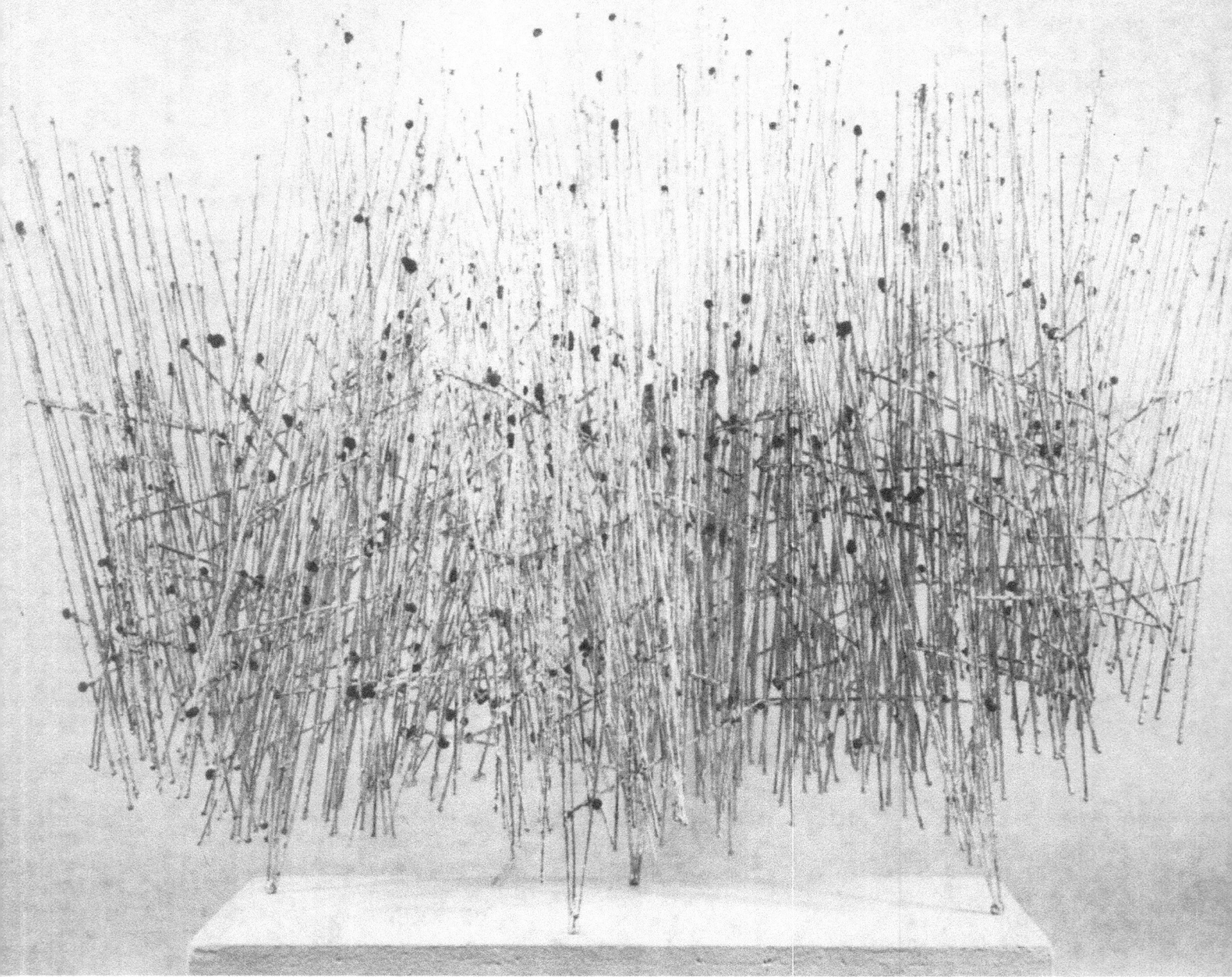

58. ''Golden Screen'' (1964), welded brass rods, 19 x 27 in. Mr. and Mrs. Robert W. Sarnoff.

59. Musical sculpture (1960-64),
    welded bronze, 41 x 16 x 7 in.
    Mr. and Mrs. Irving Castle.

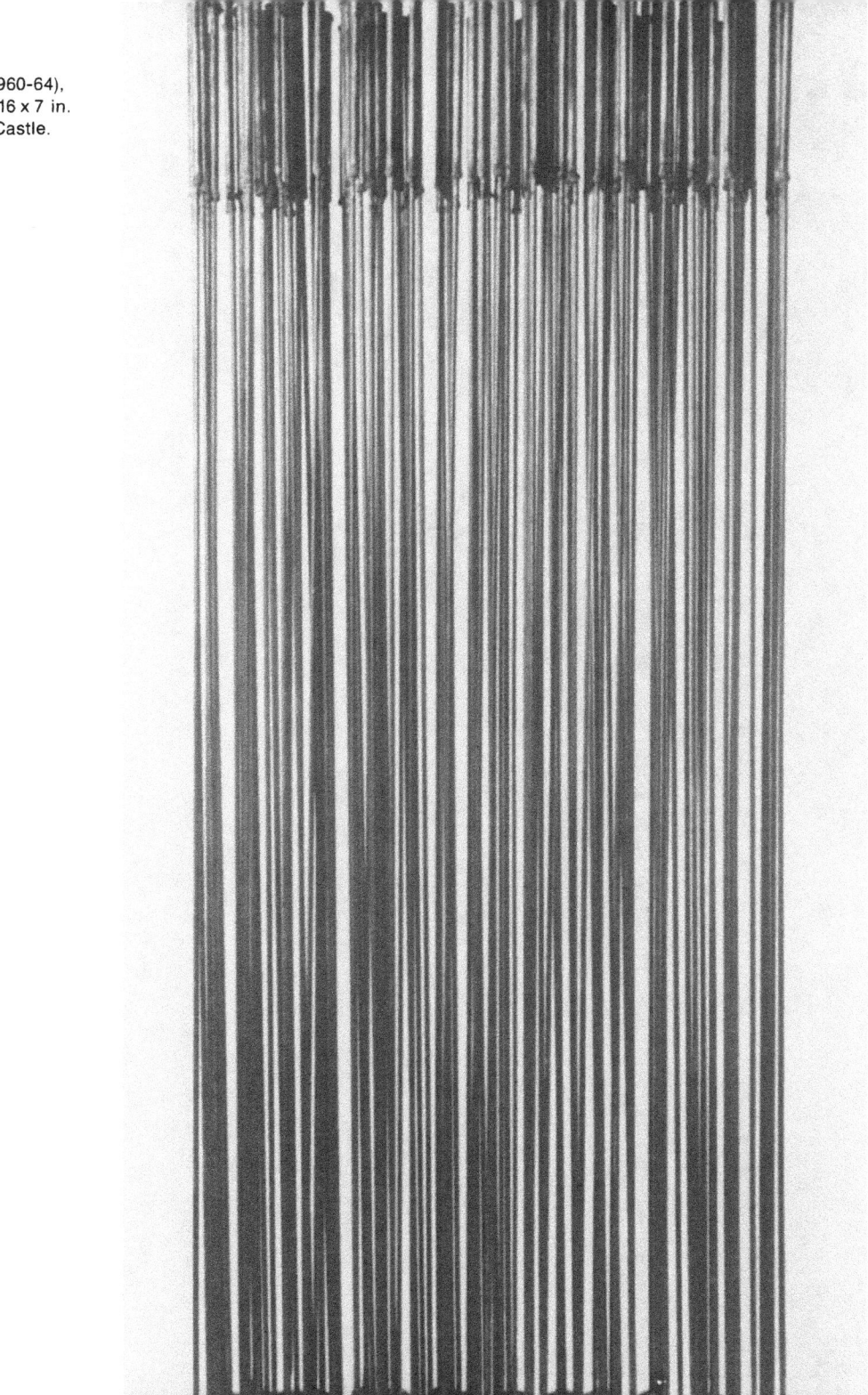

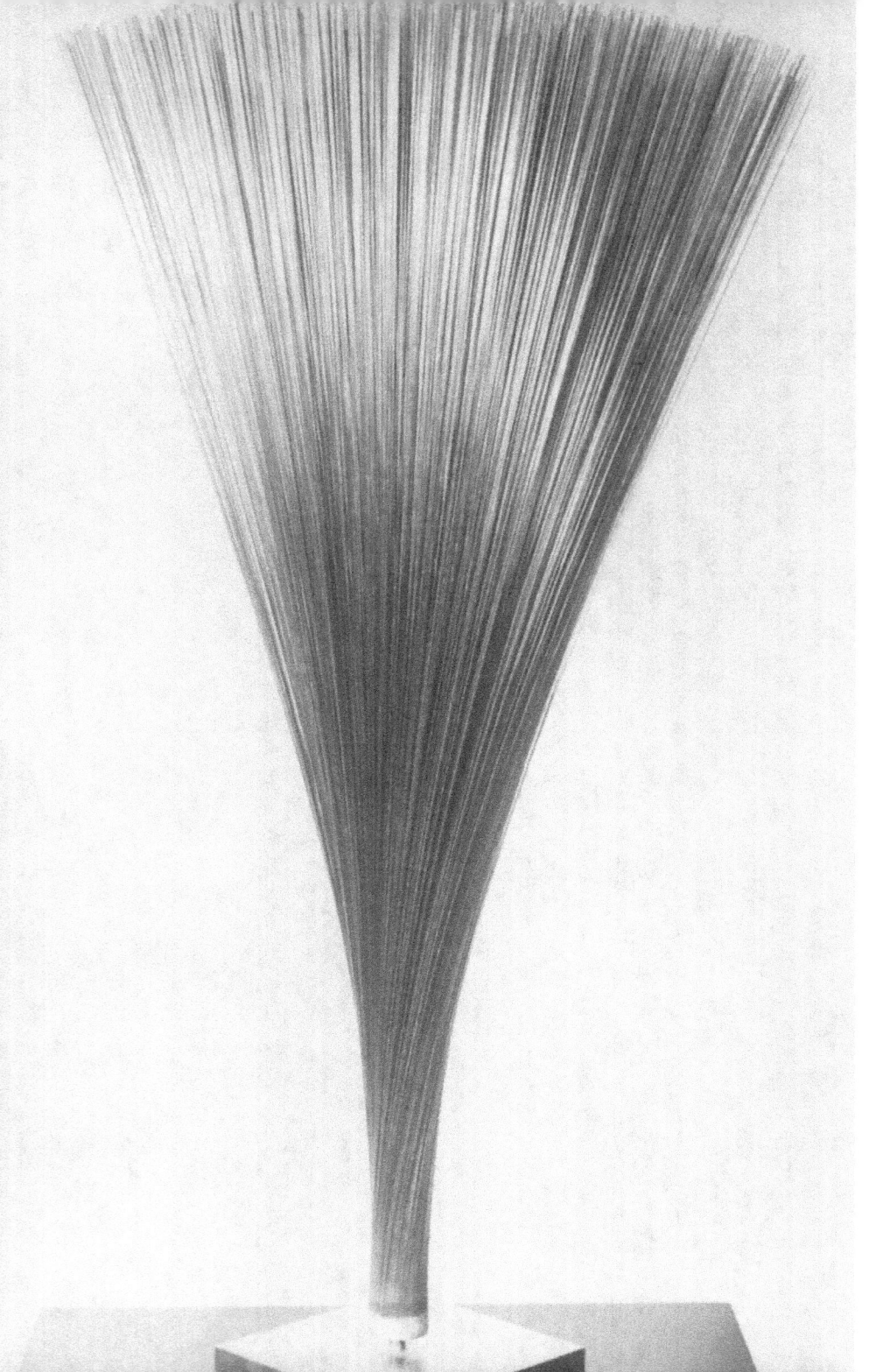

61. Musical sculptures (1968), welded
    bronze, heights from 3 to 6 ft.
    Staempfli Gallery exhibition.

60. Sculpture (1967), stainless steel,
    37 in. high. Mr. and Mrs. Martin
    Roaman.

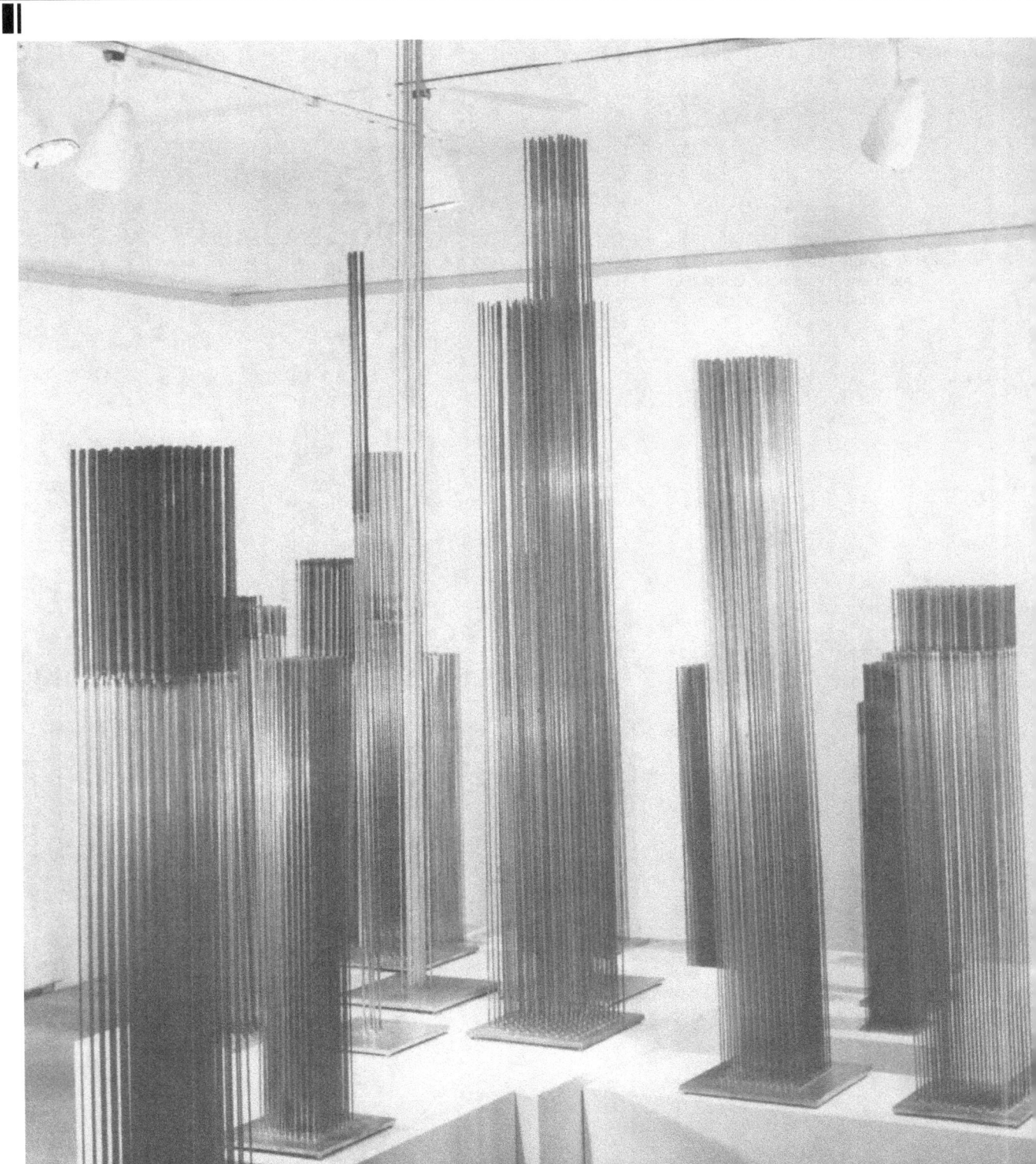

62. Sculpture (1967), stainless steel, each about 4 ft. high. Collection, the artist.

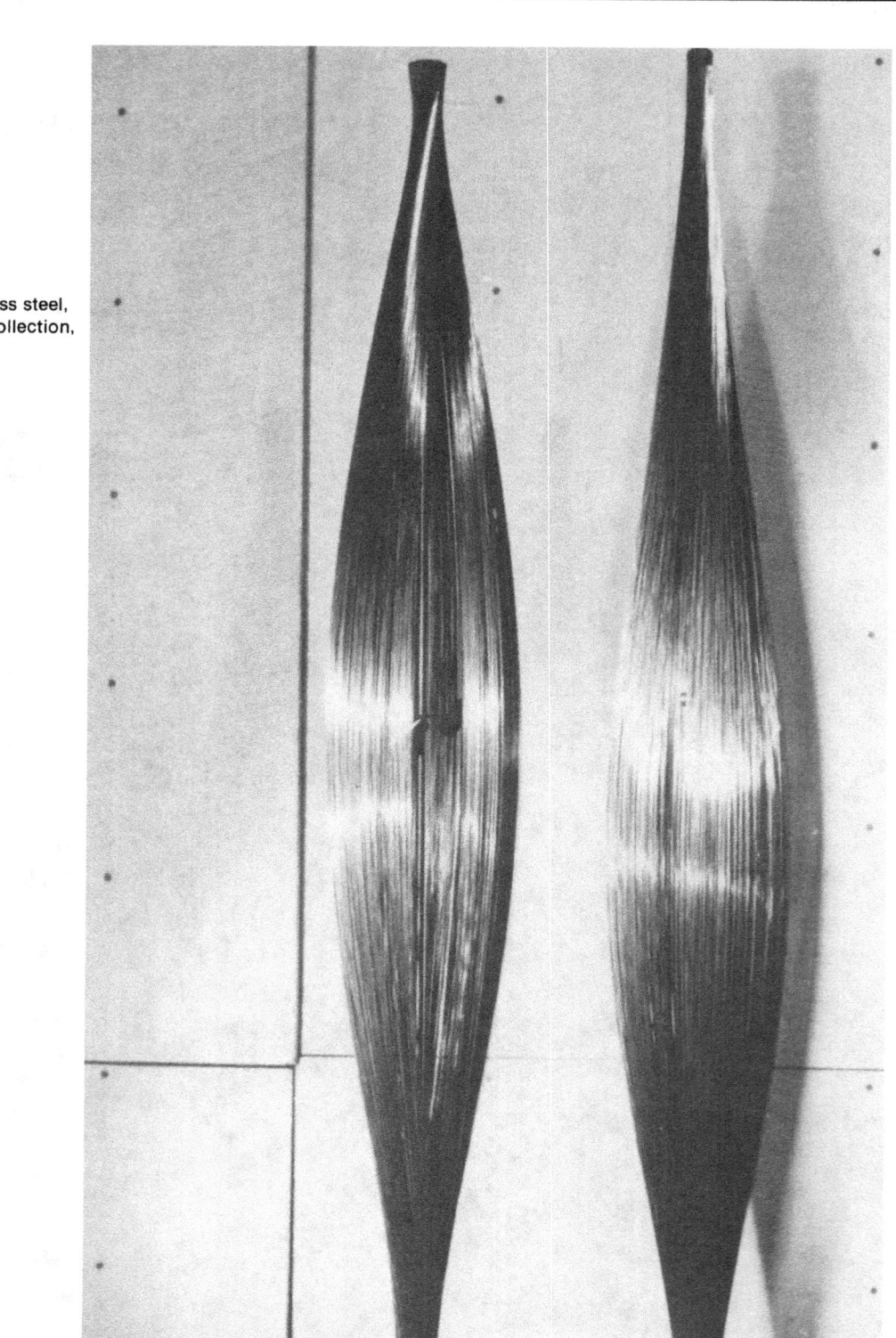

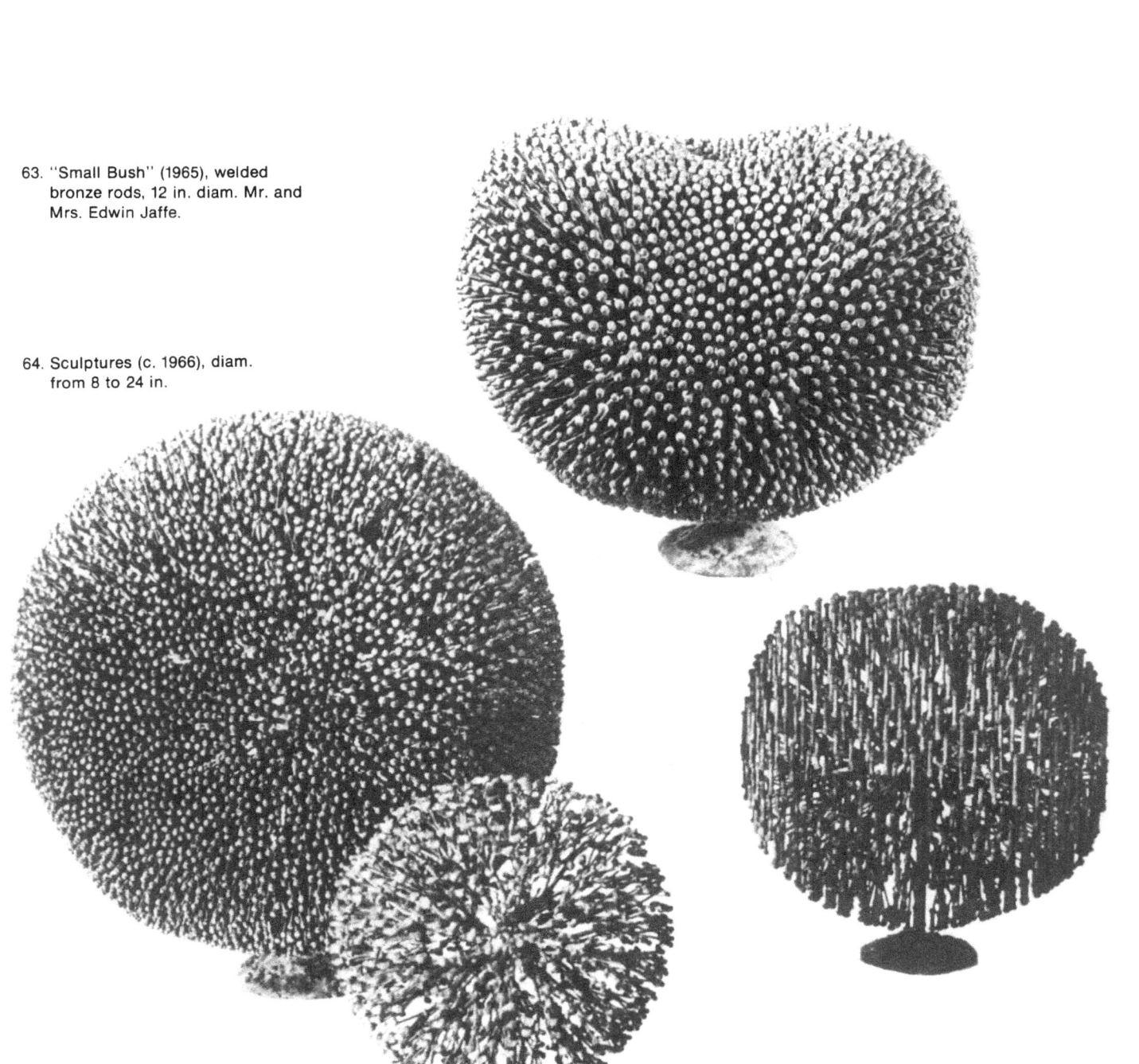

63. "Small Bush" (1965), welded
    bronze rods, 12 in. diam. Mr. and
    Mrs. Edwin Jaffe.

64. Sculptures (c. 1966), diam.
    from 8 to 24 in.

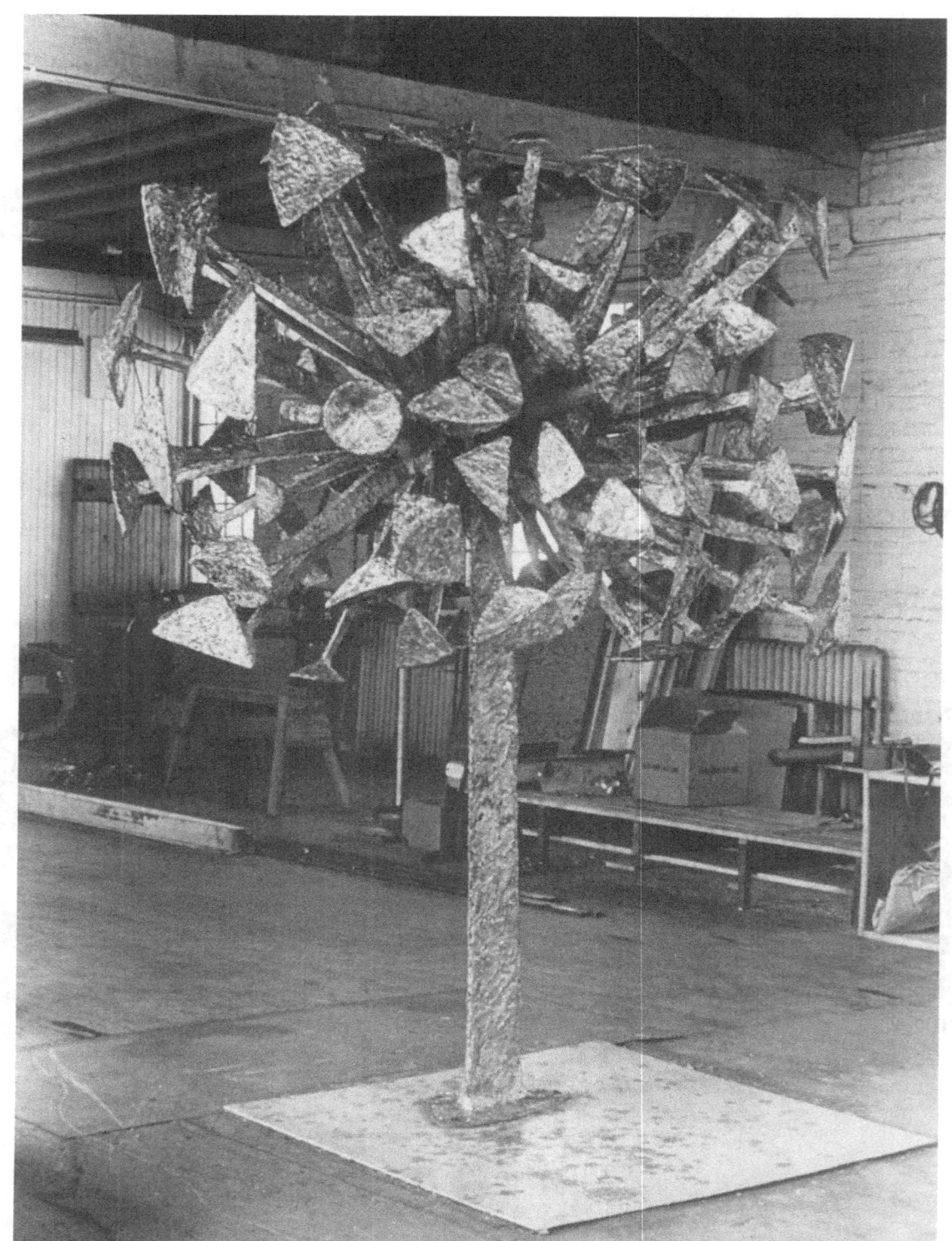

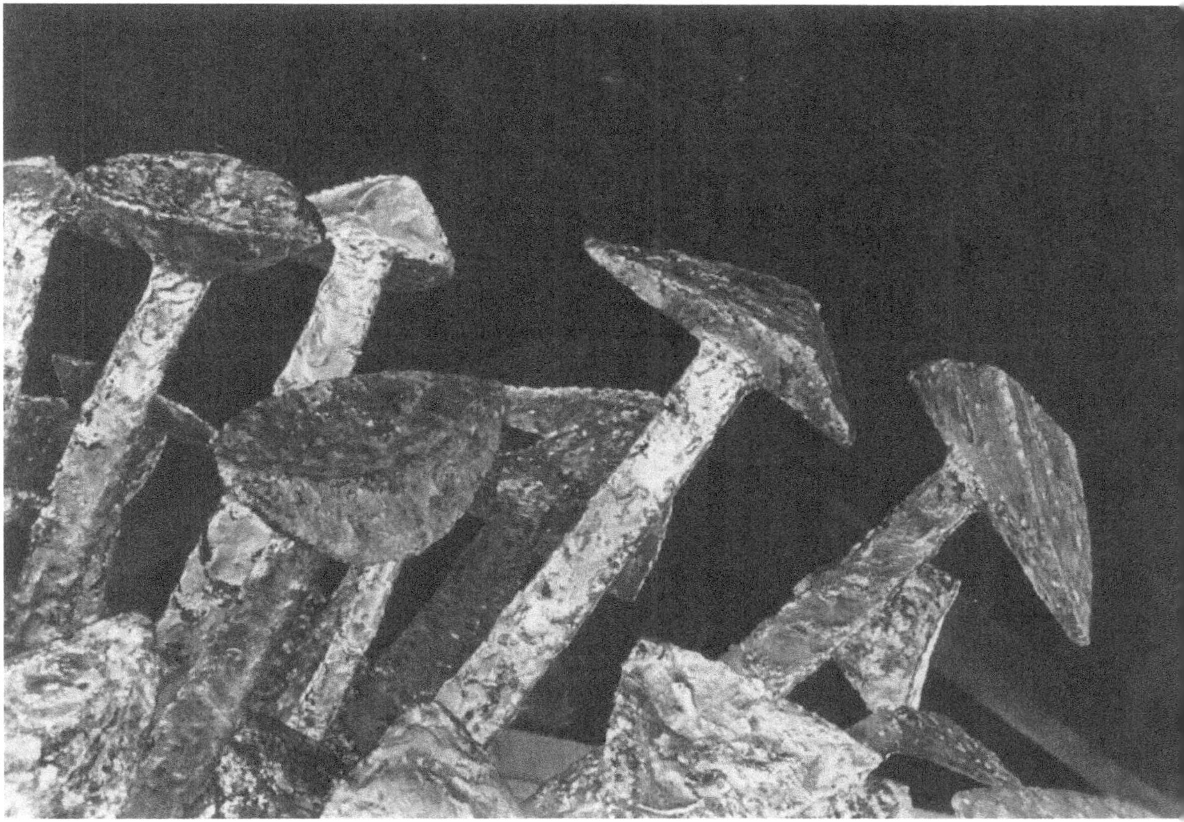

66. Detail of ''Gold Tree.''

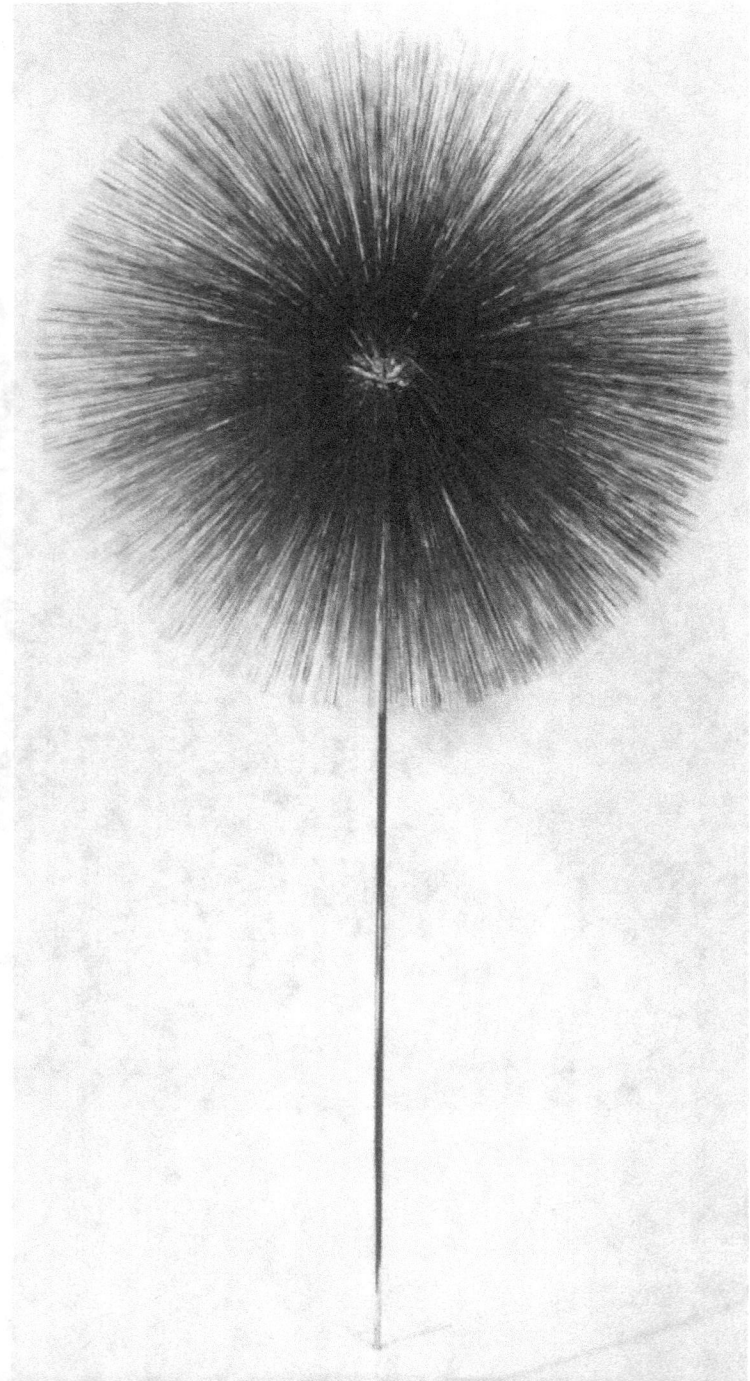

68. Drawing for proposed fountain
    sculpture (c. 1962). Collection,
    the artist.

69. Sculpture (c. 1956), about 7 ft.
    high. Florence Knoll Bassett.

67. Sculpture (1960), stainless steel,

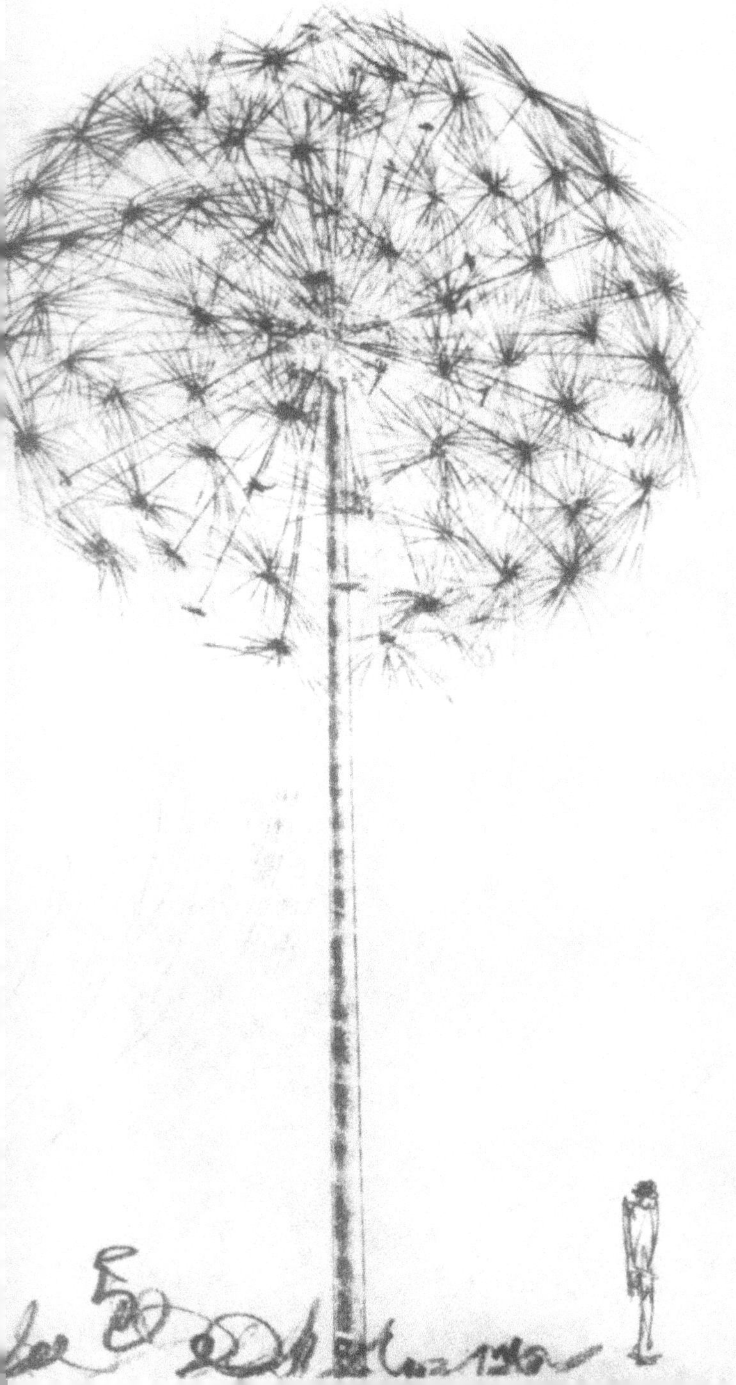

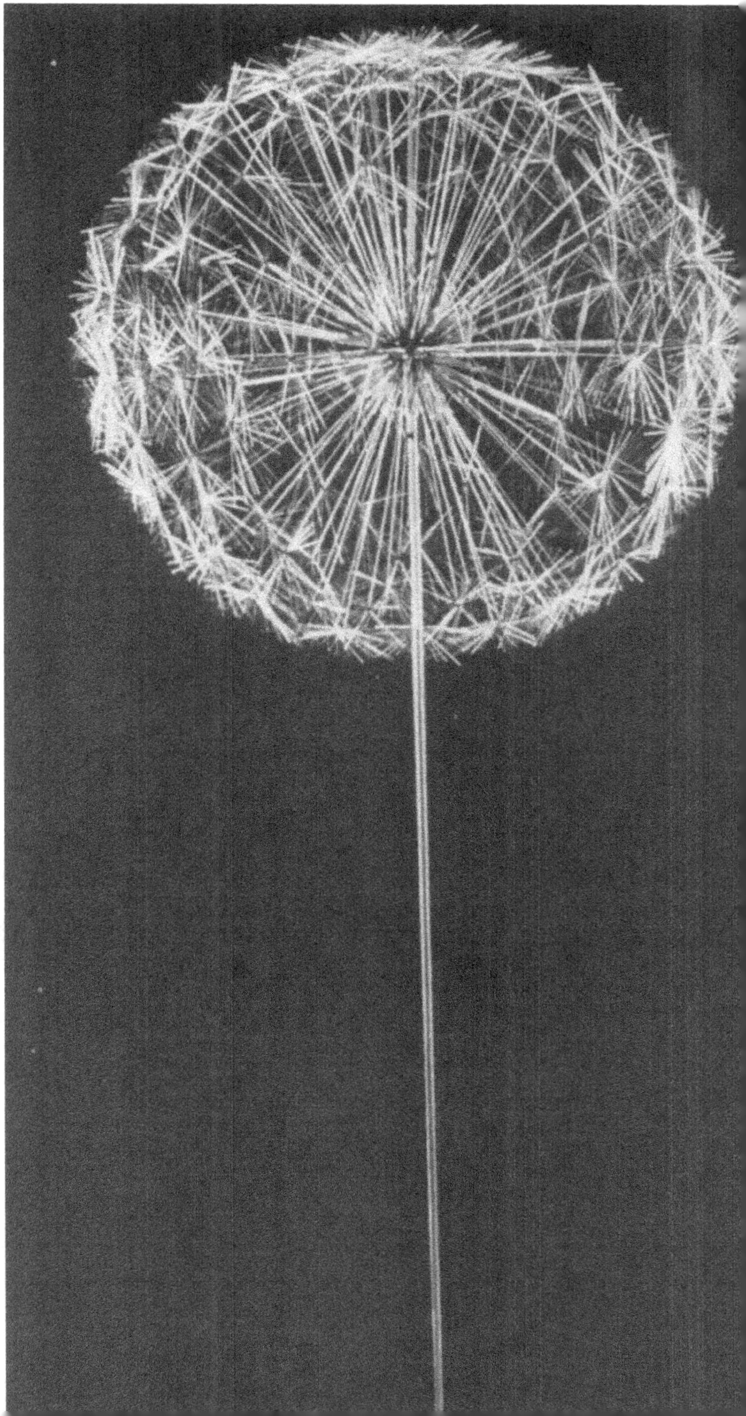

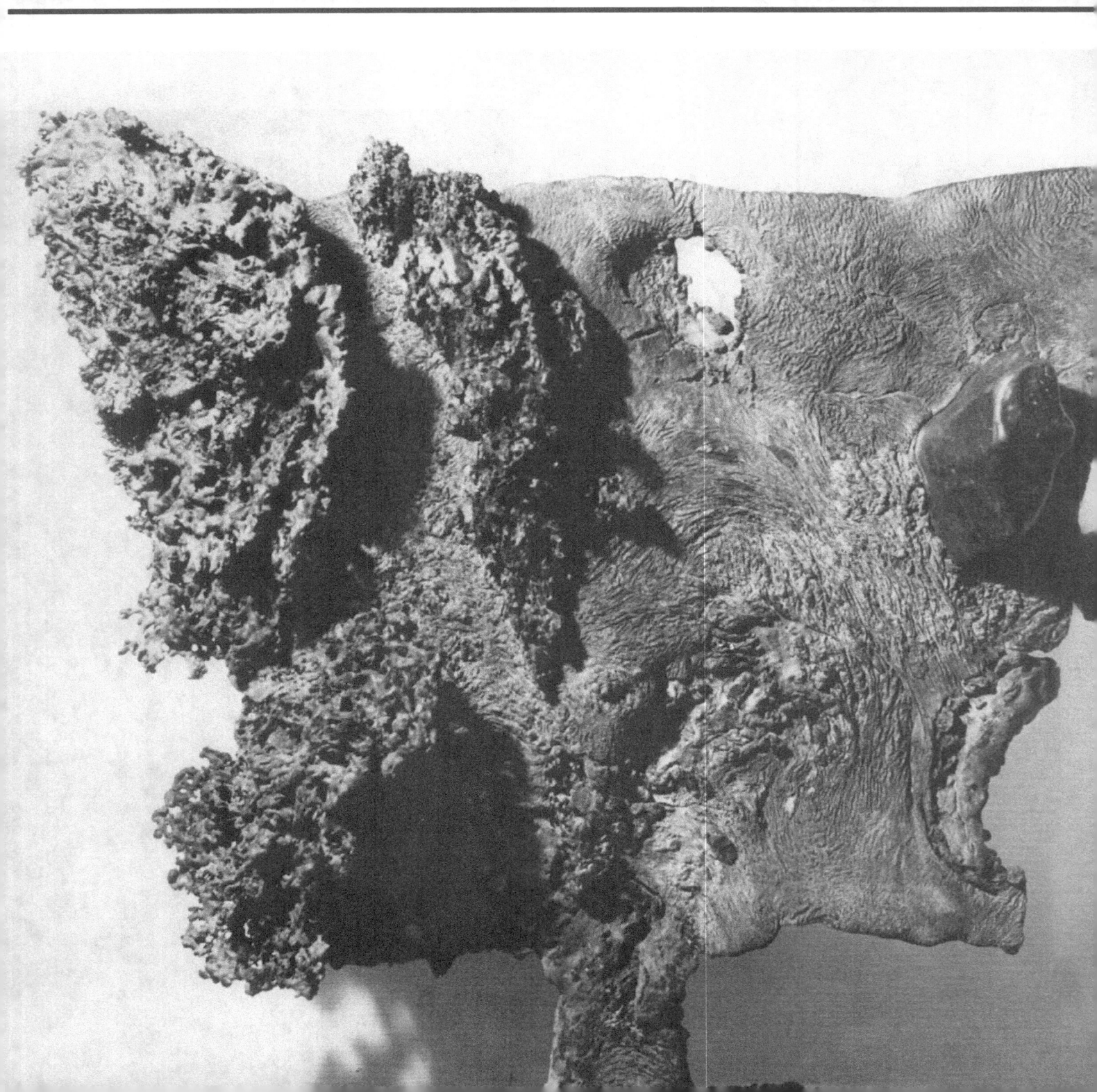

70. "Spring" (1965), bronze,
    33 x 33 x 9 in. Chase Manhattan
    Bank, N.A.

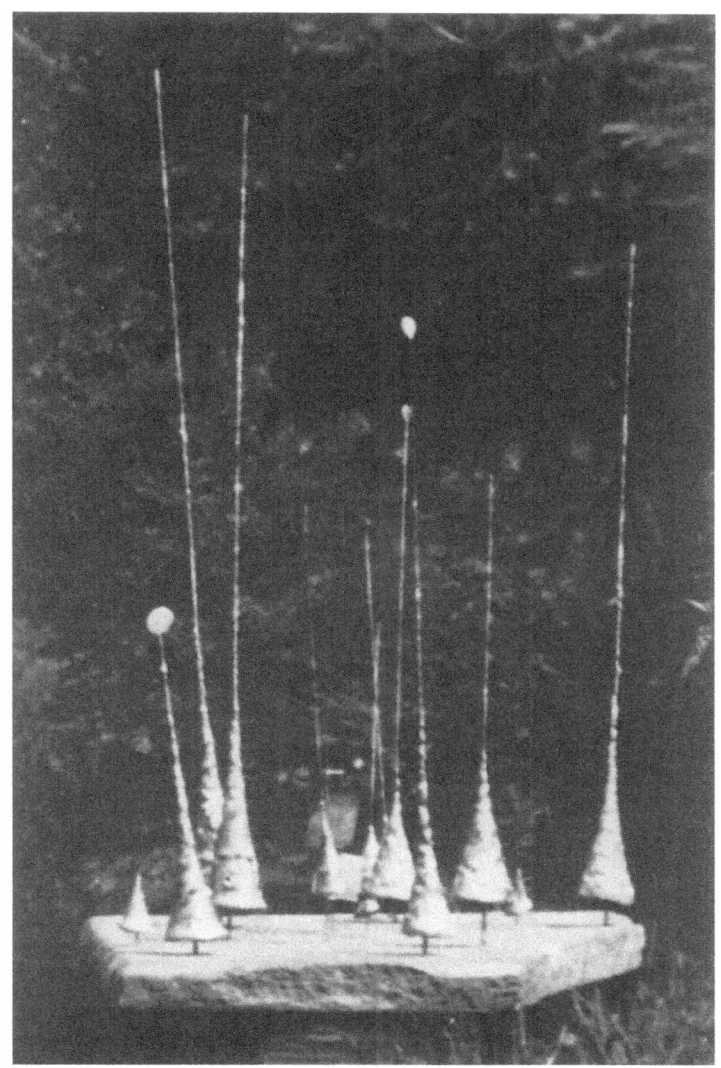

71. Model for bells (c. 1955), bronze, about 12 in. high. Collection,
    the artist.

72. Musical sculptures (1968-69), various metals, heights from
3 to 9 ft. Collection, the artist.

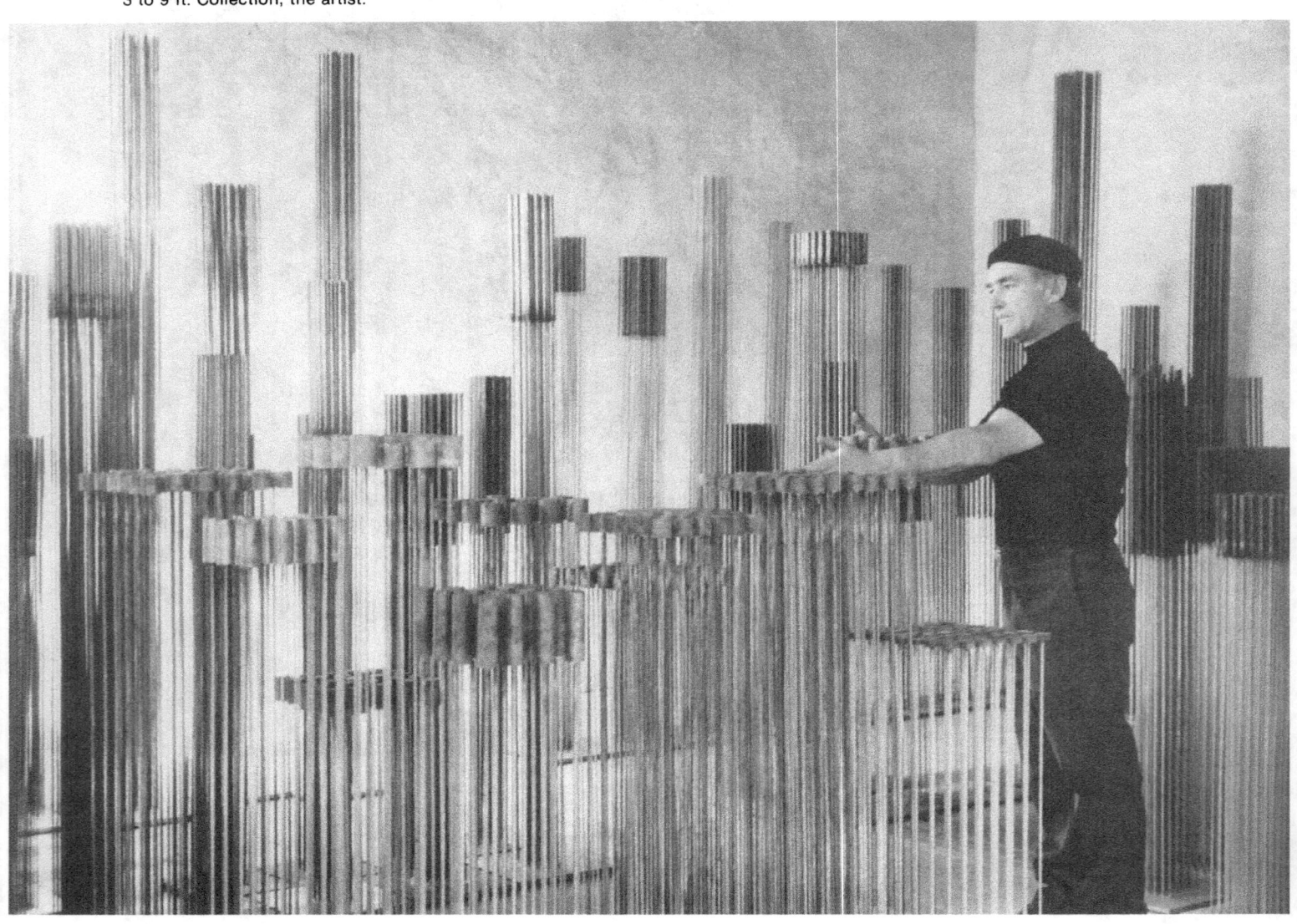

73. Head of a woman (c. 1958), welded metal rods, brass-coated, about 2 ft. high. Mr. and Mrs. Matthew Leibowitz.

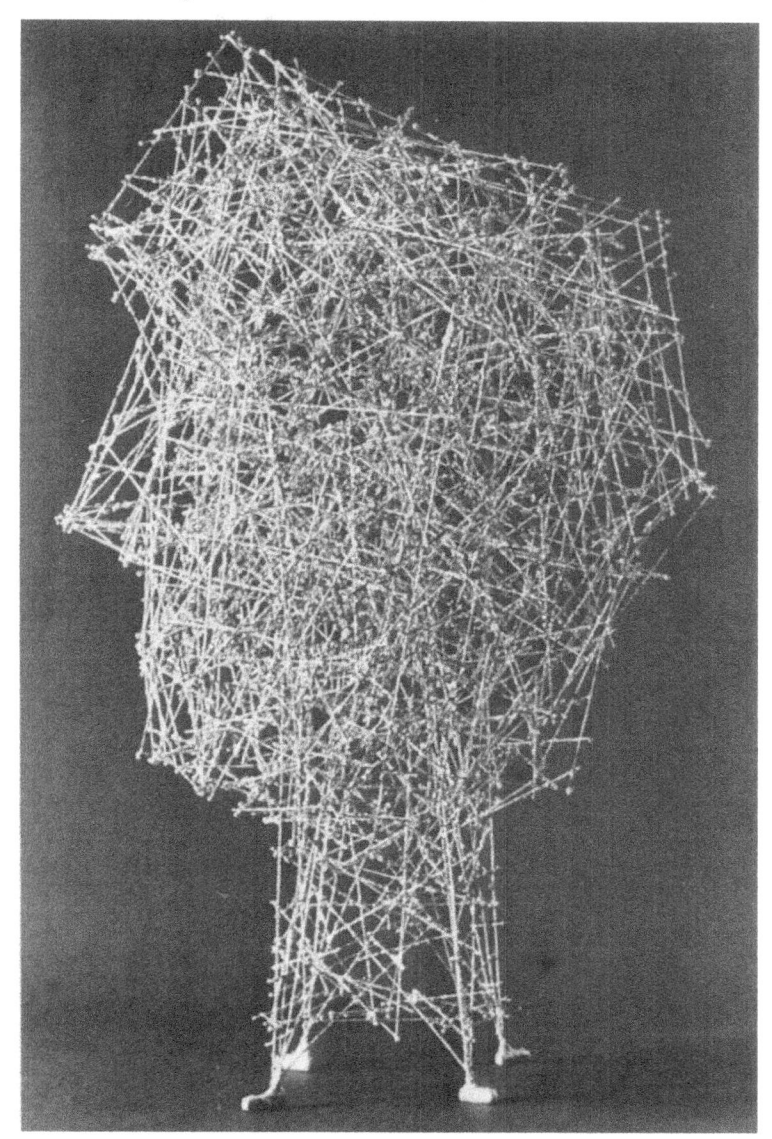

74. Ceiling sculpture (1954), welded metal, about 3 x 18 x 12 ft. Manufacturers Hanover Trust Co.

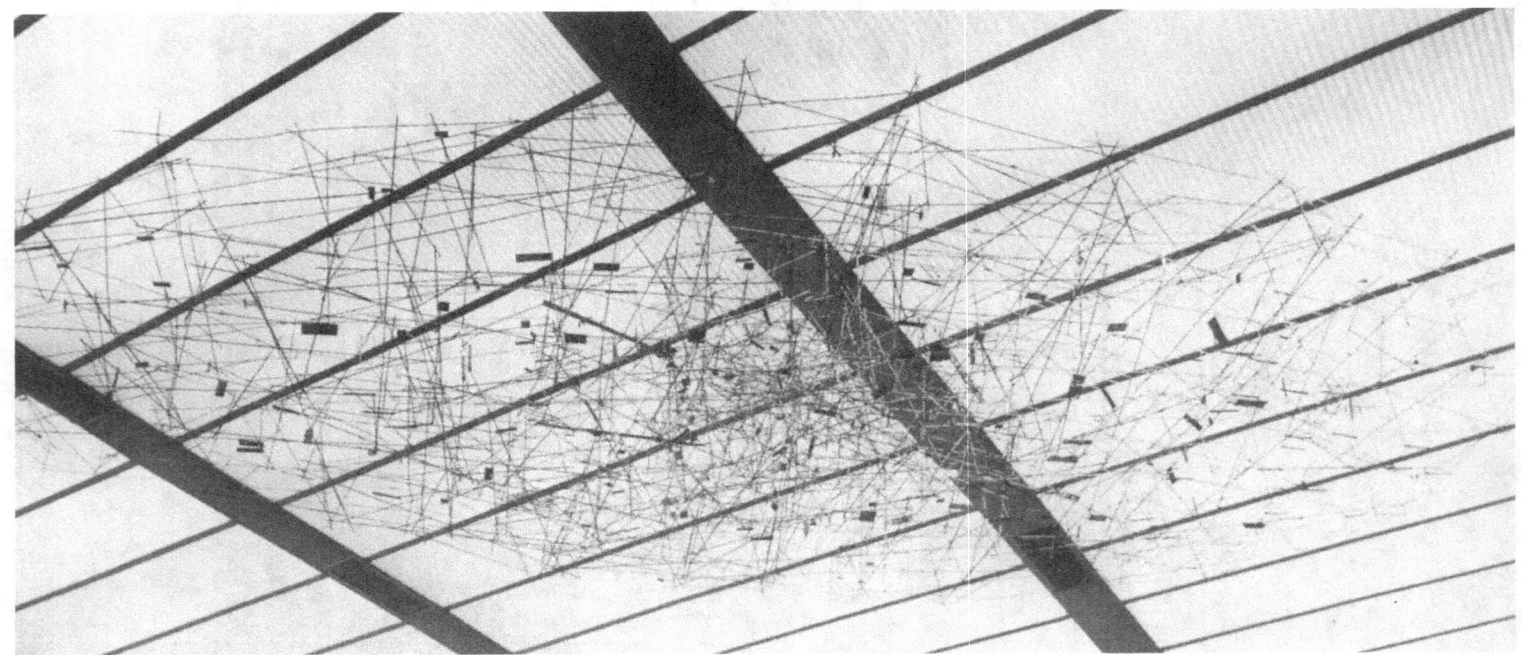

75. Sculpture screen (1954), welded metal, about 9 x 5 ft. Cincinnati Public Library.

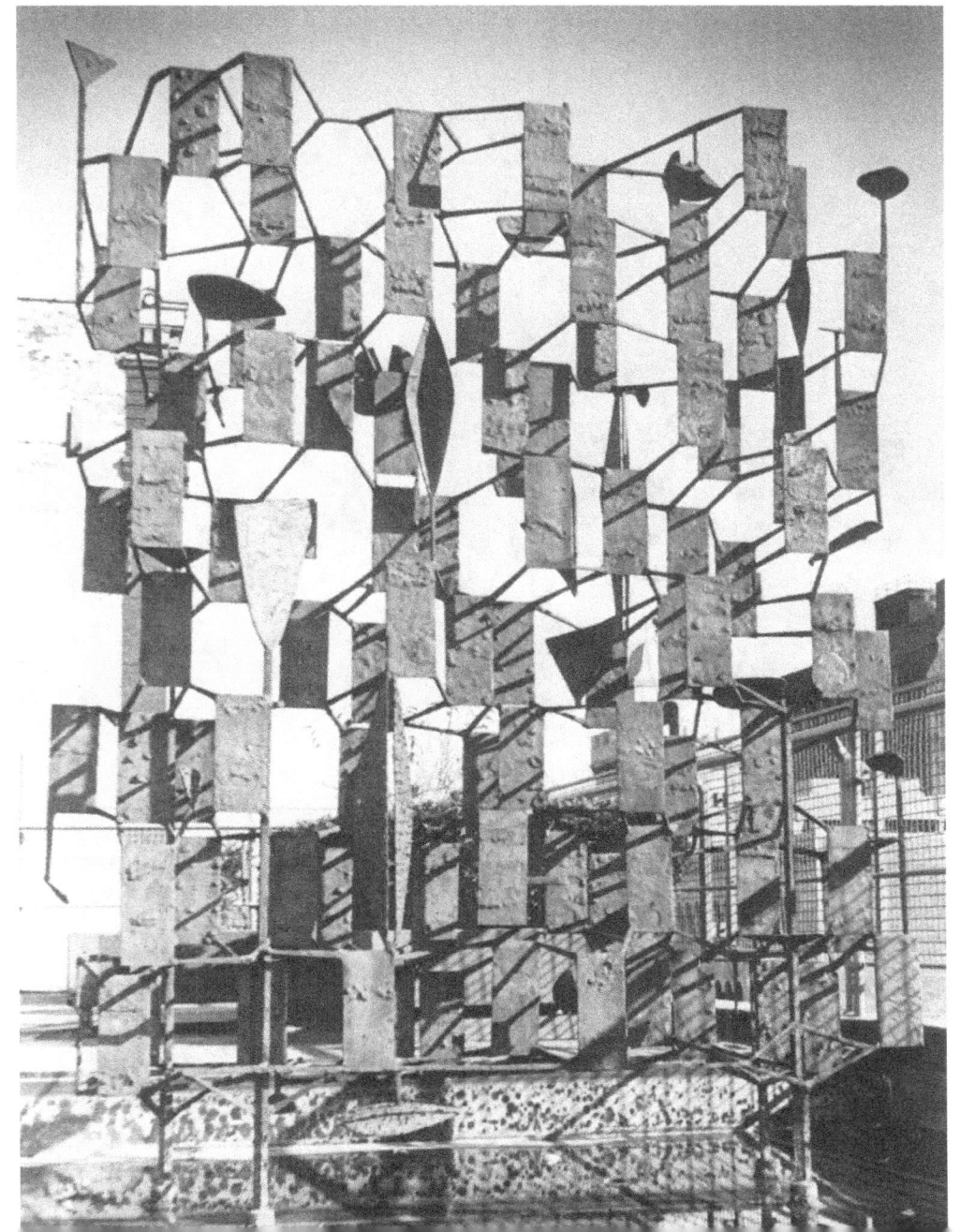

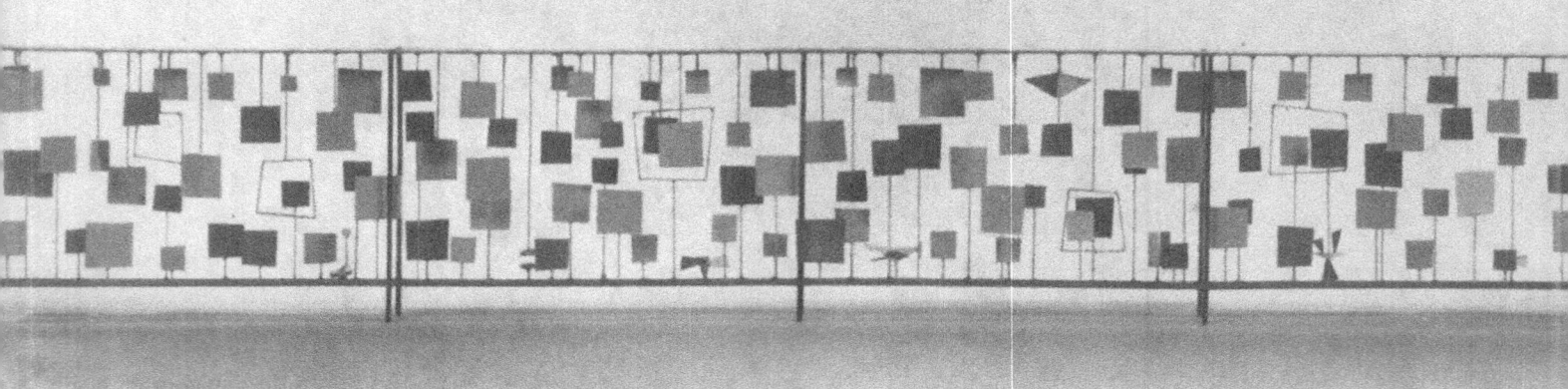

76. Sculpture screen (1955), welded and painted metal, 8 x 40 x 2 ft. Lambert-St. Louis Airport.

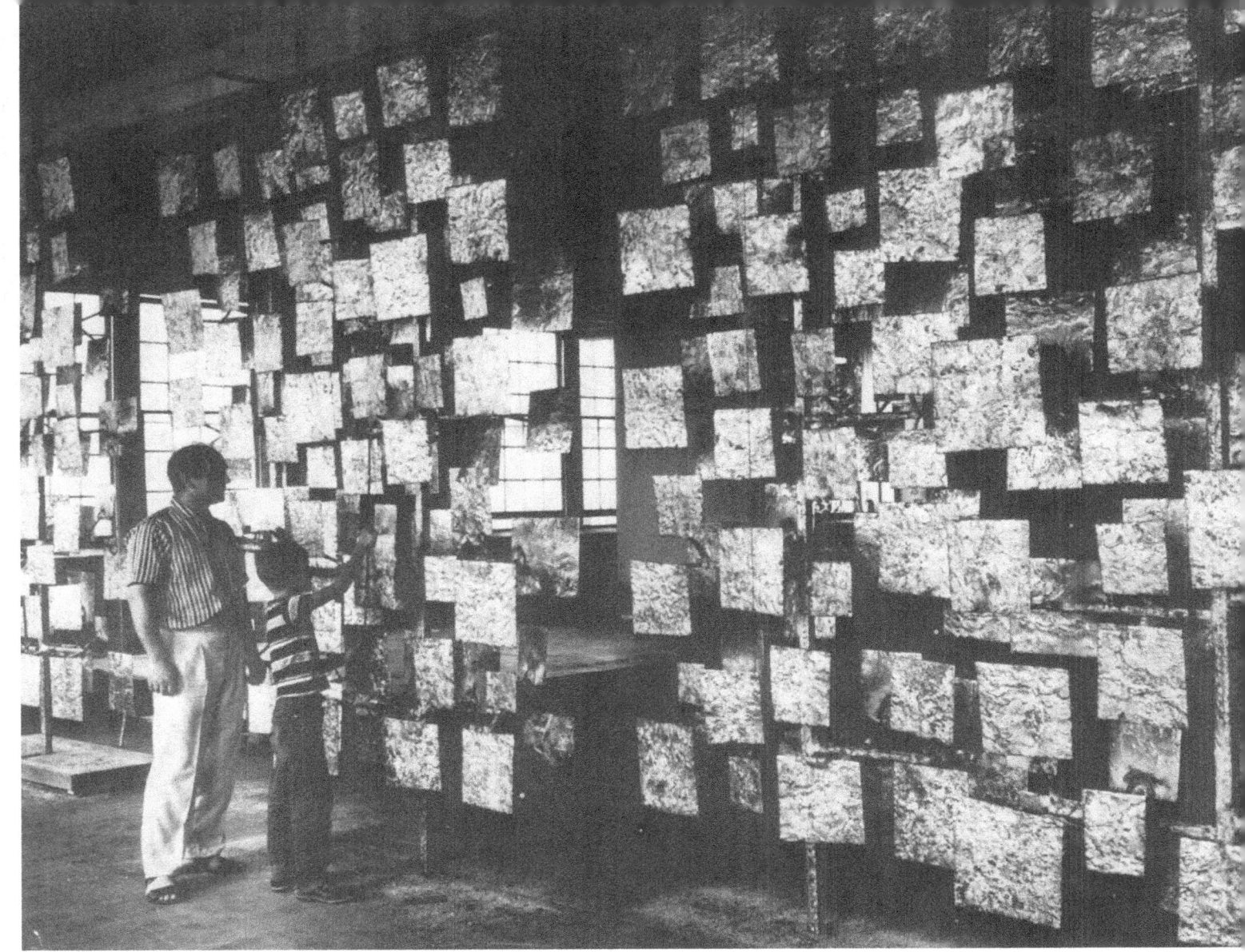

77. Sculpture screens (1956), welded metal, each about 12 x 4 x 2 ft. First National Bank of Miami.

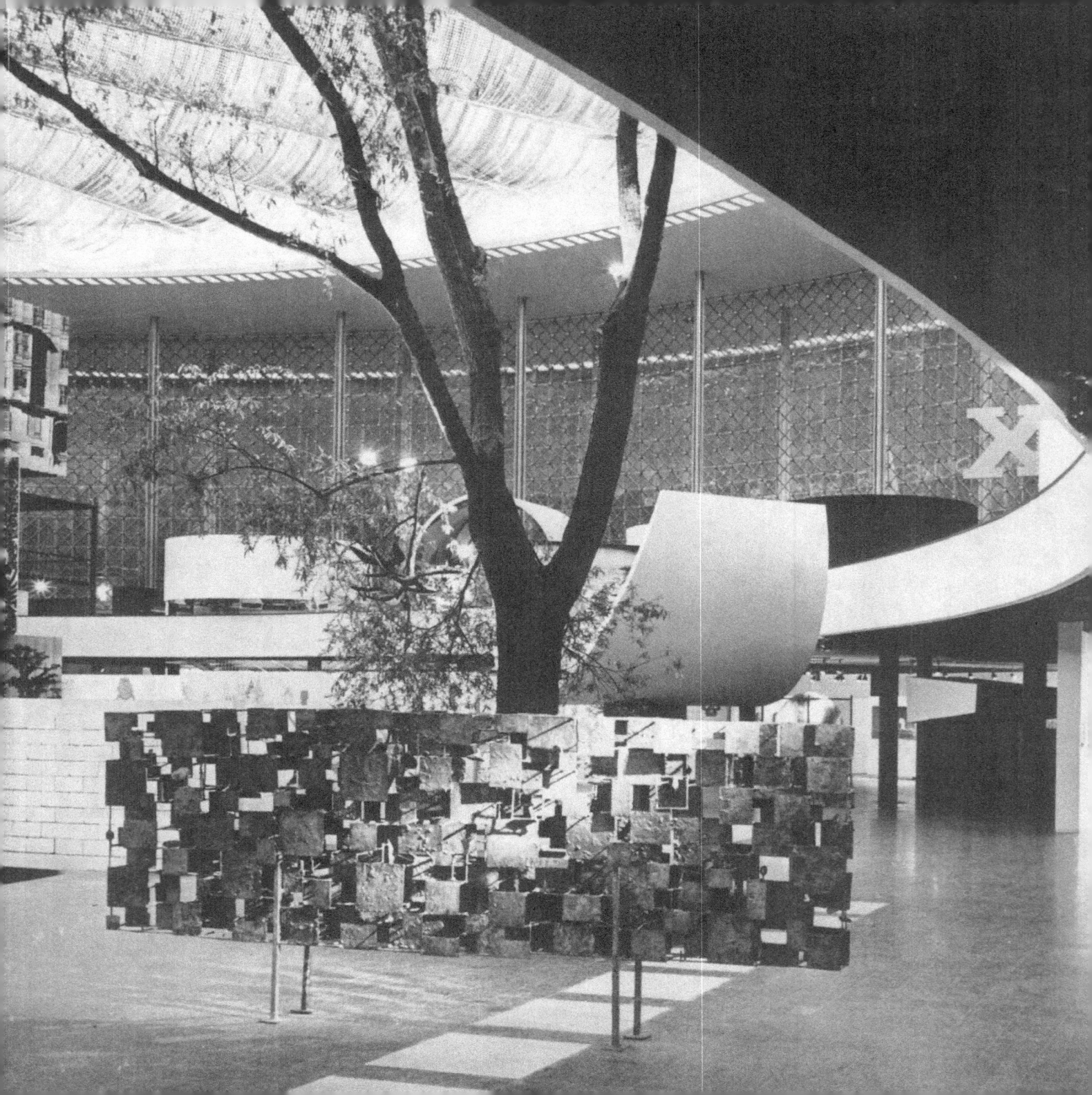

78. Sculpture screen (1956), welded metal, about 10 x 18 ft. U.S. Department of State.

79. Rectangular frame with gong (1956), welded metal, about 8 x 16 ft. U.S. Department of State.

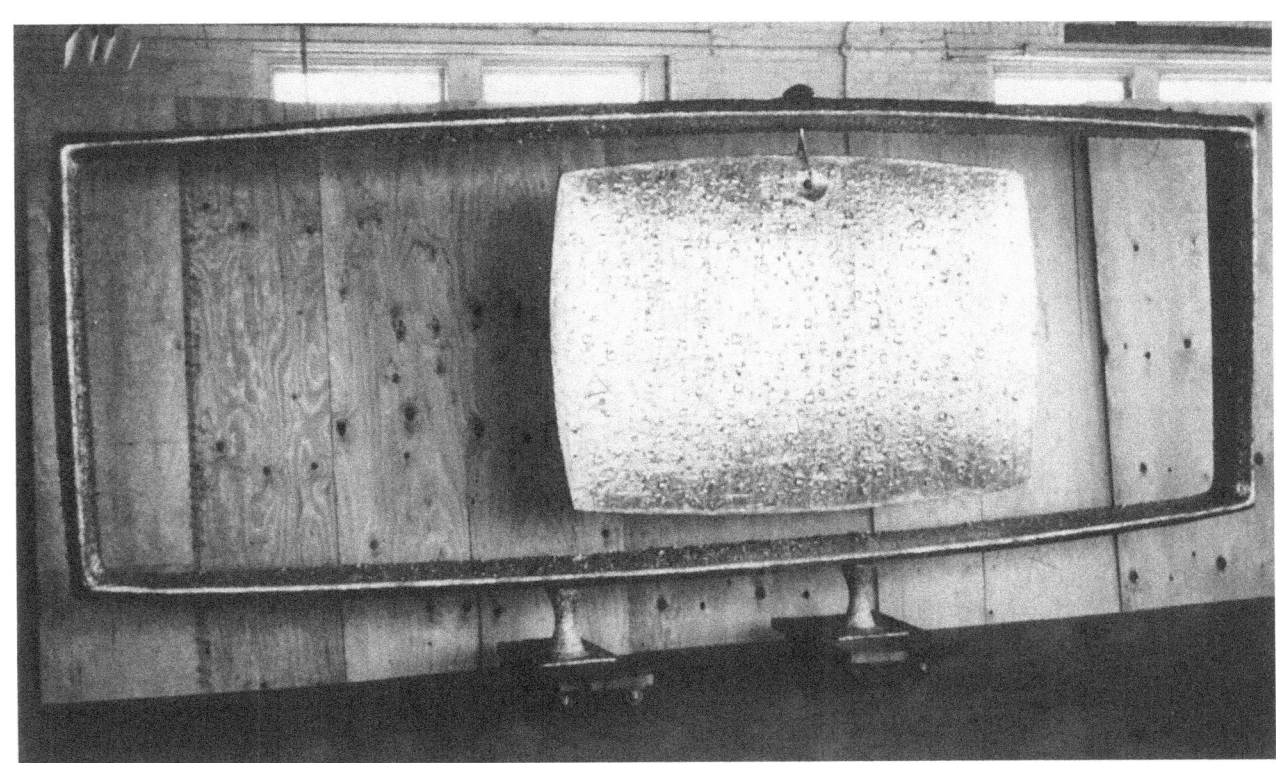

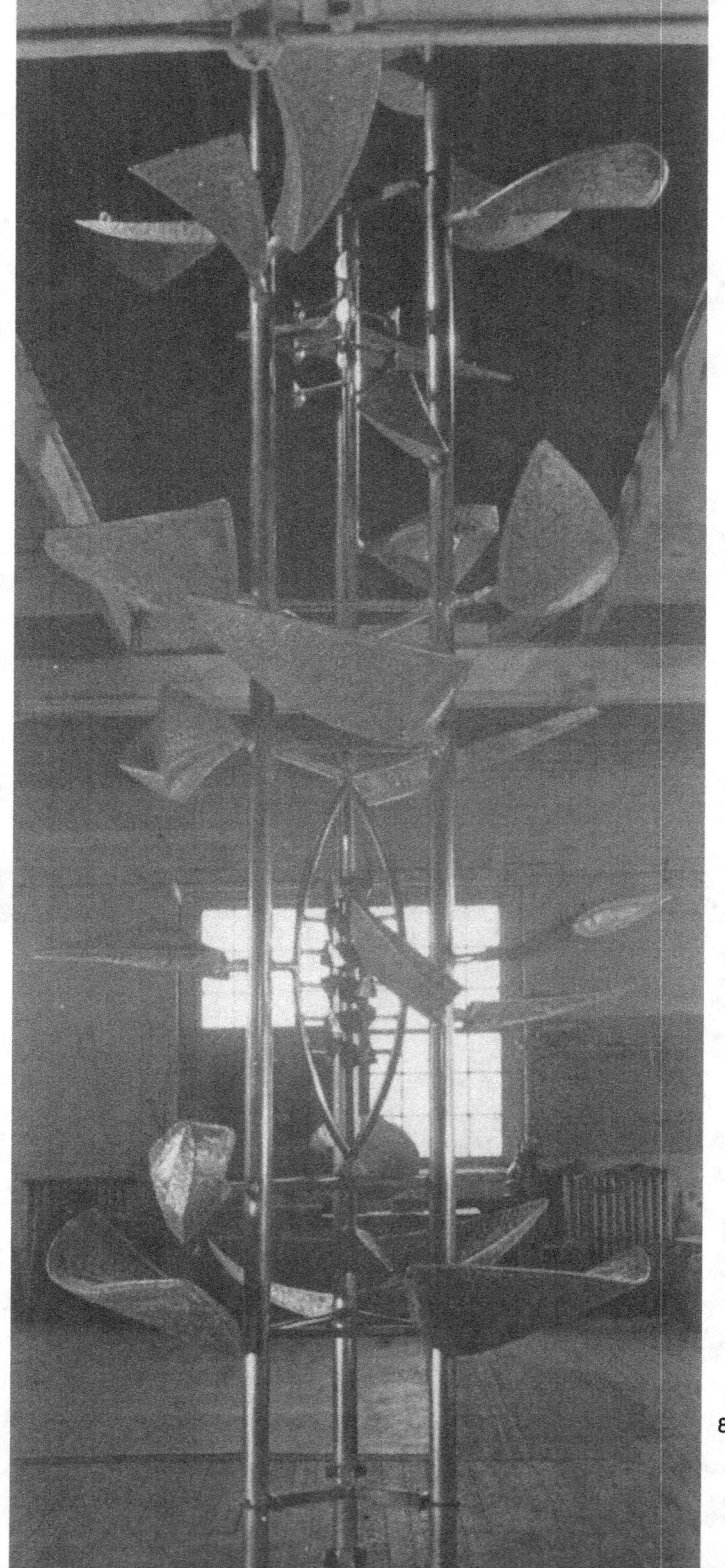

80. Fountain sculpture (1957), welded metal, about 15 ft. high, 7 ft. diam. First National Bank & Trust Co. of Tulsa.

81. Sculpture screen (1961), welded steel and brass, about 8 x 13 x 2 ft. Albright-Knox Art Gallery.

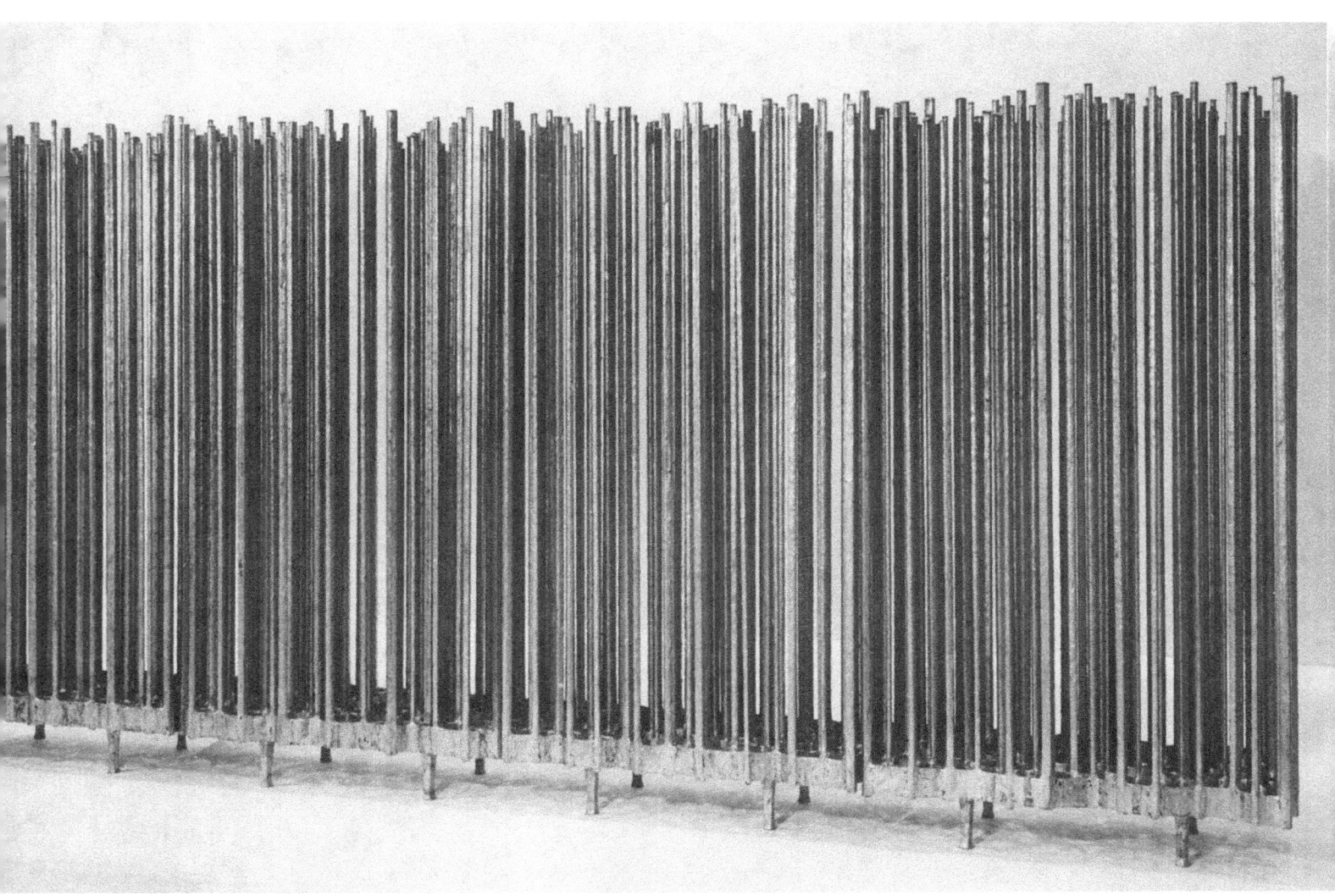

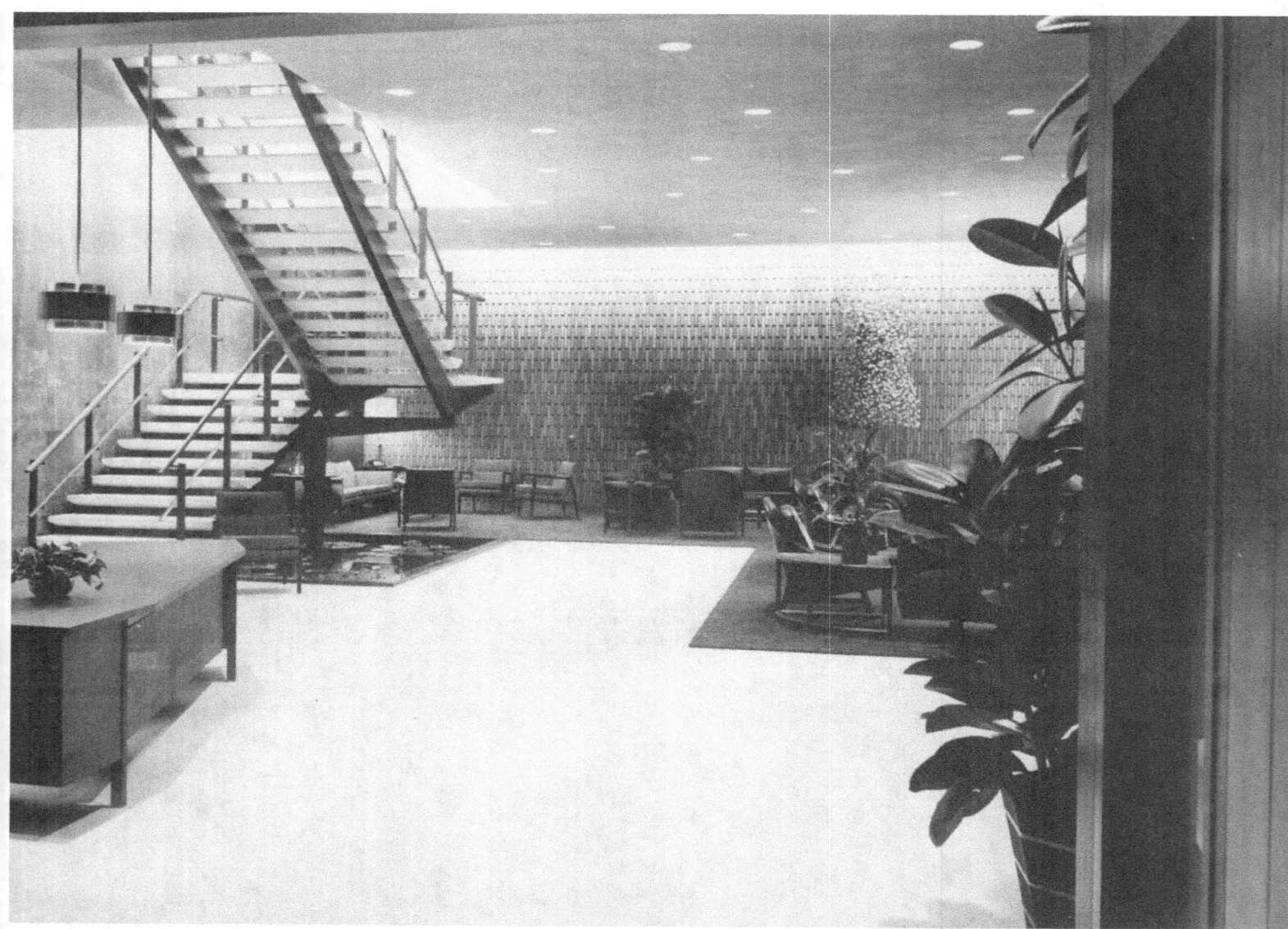

82. Wall-hung sculpture (1961), brass, about 5 x 2 ft. Eastman Kodak Company.

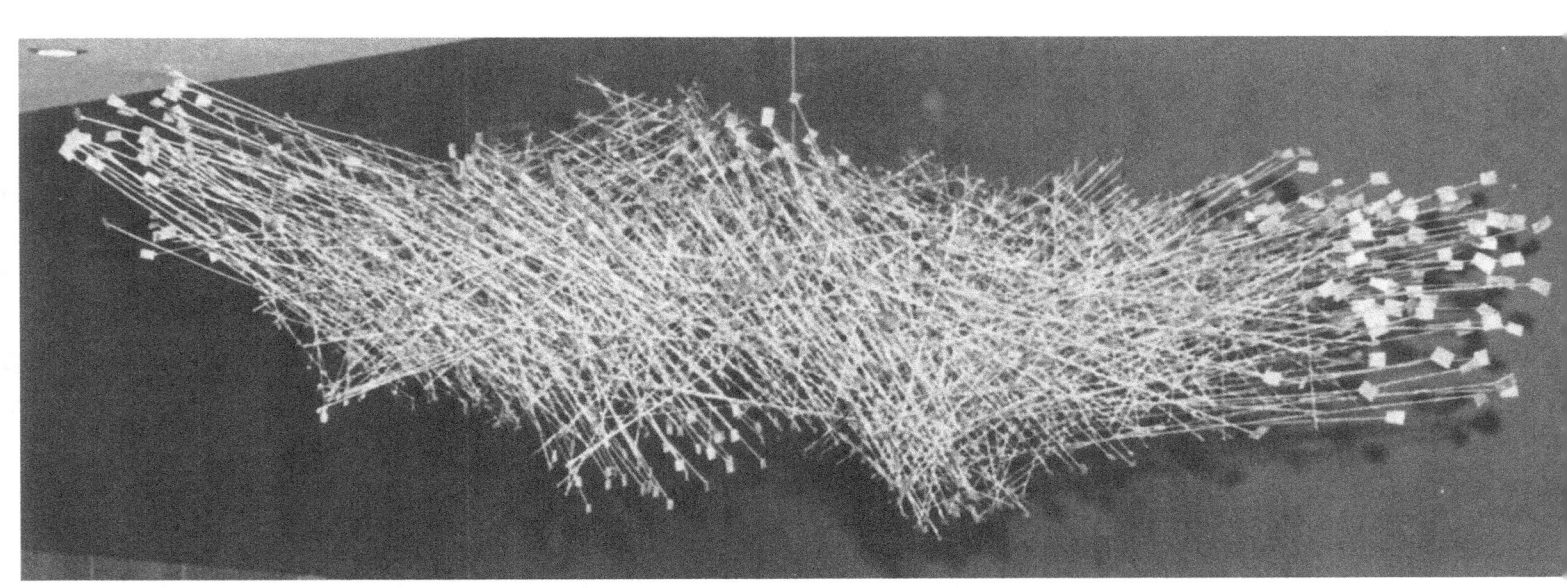

83. ''Nova'' (1961), bronze, copper, and steel, about 3 x 10 x 6 ft. Syracuse University.

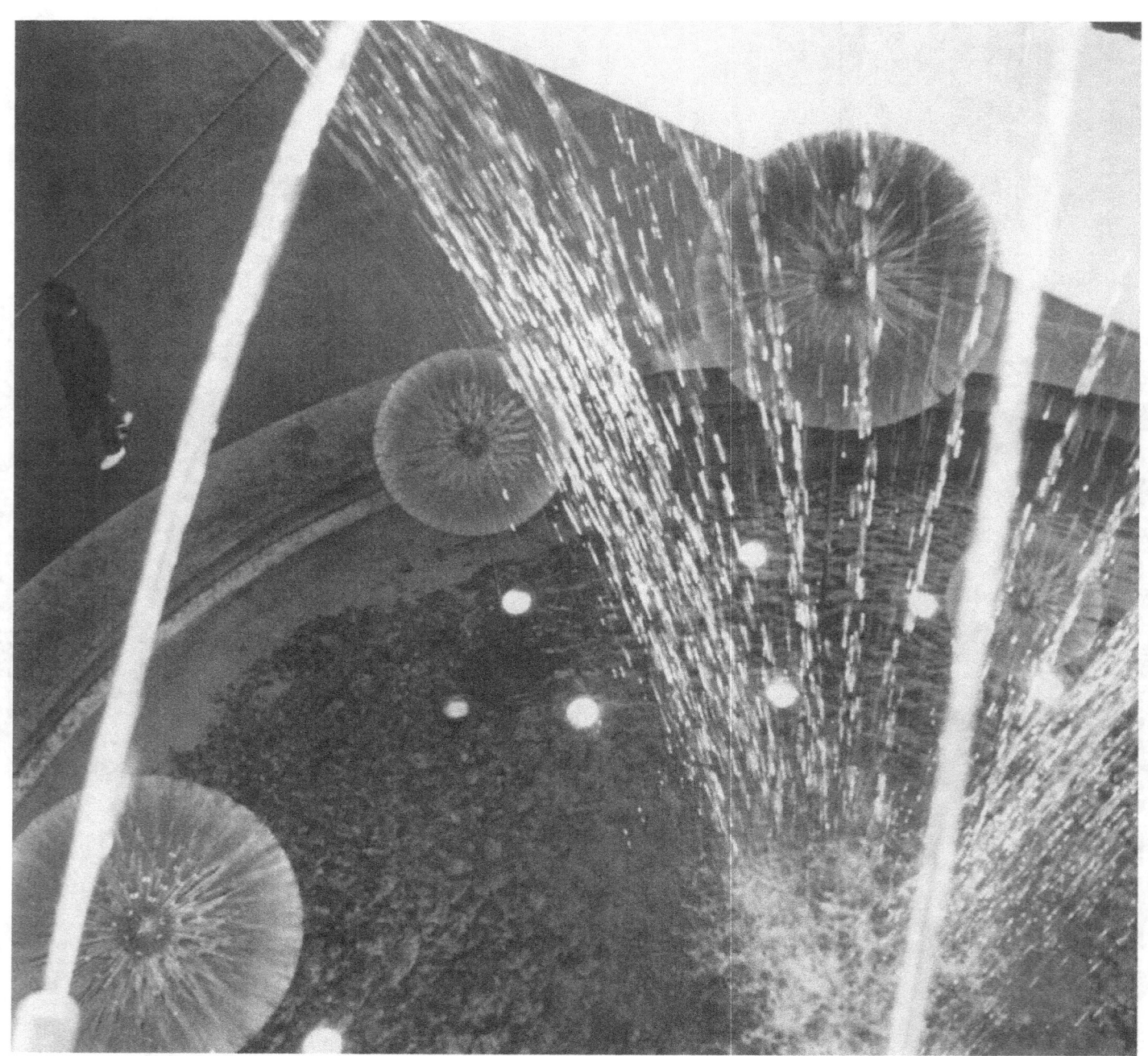

84. Sculptures for fountain (1964), gilded stainless steel, diam. from about 2½ to 5½ ft. Eastman Kodak Company.

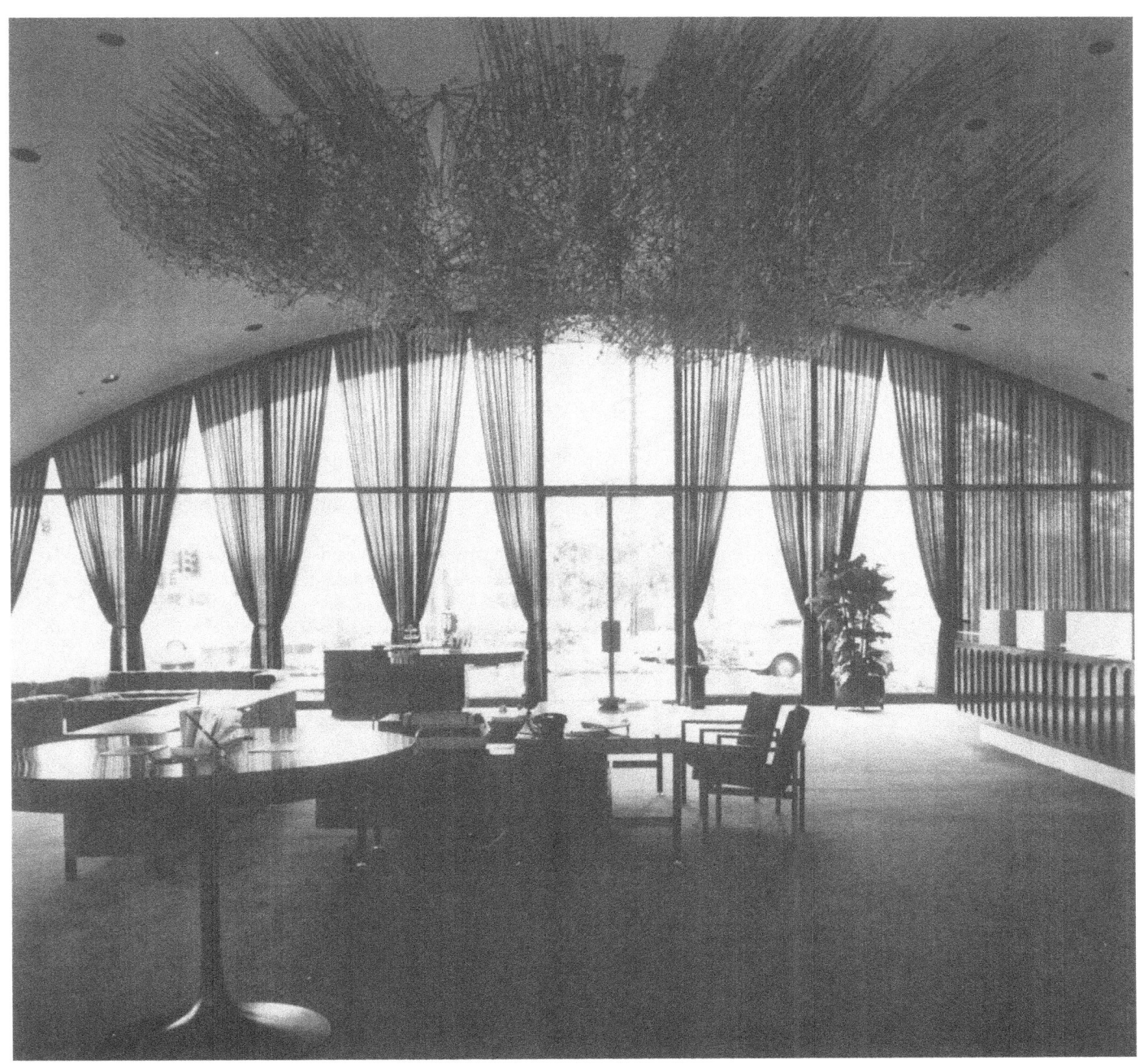

85. "Galaxy" (1964), welded metal, about 20 ft. diam. Golden West Savings and Loan Assn.

Appendix I
Chronology

1915	Born at San Lorenzo (Udine), Italy.
1930	To America with his father.
1936	Graduated from Cass Technical High School, Detroit.
1936	Scholarship to Detroit Society of Arts and Crafts.
1937	Scholarship to Cranbrook Academy of Art, Bloomfield Hills, Mich.
1939	Set up metal shop at Cranbrook and began teaching metalworking.
1943	Nineteen monoprints exhibited, non-objective painting show, Solomon R. Guggenheim Foundation, New York.
1943	Marriage to Brigitta Valentiner.
1943	Left Cranbrook for California to do warplant work and work on Eames chair.
1943	First showing of monoprints and jewelry at Nierendorf Gallery, New York.
1945	Show of monoprints, San Francisco Museum of Art.
1946	American citizenship obtained.
1947	Last exhibition of monoprints and jewelry at Nierendorf Gallery.
1947-49	Graphic work at Point Loma Naval Electronics Laboratory.
1950	Set up studio in Pennsylvania under auspices of Knoll Associates.
1950	Fairweather Hardin Gallery, Chicago representative.
1951	First exhibition of sculpture at Knoll Associates, New York.

1952	Bertoia chair introduced by Knoll.
1953	First architectural sculpture commission (General Motors Technical Center screen).
1956	First sculpture show at Fairweather Hardin Gallery, Chicago.
1956	Awarded Craftsmanship Medal by American Institute of Architects.
1957	Awarded $10,000 Fellowship by Graham Foundation for Advanced Studies in the Fine Arts.
1957	First European trip.
1958	Two sculptures exhibited, U.S. Pavilion, Brussels World's Fair.
1958	Represented, "Sculpture 1950-1958," Allen Memorial Art Museum, Oberlin College.
1959	Represented, "Recent Sculpture, USA," Museum of Modern Art traveling exhibition.
1959	Staempfli Gallery, New York representative.
1959	First sculpture show at Staempfli Gallery.
1961	Show of sculpture, Fairweather Hardin Gallery, Chicago.
1961	Show of sculpture, Staempfli Gallery, New York.
1963	Represented, London Triennial Exhibition of Sculpture in the Open Air, Battersea Park.
1963	Show of sculpture, Staempfli Gallery, New York.
1964	Show of sculpture and graphics, Knoll International, Paris.
1967	Show of sculpture and chairs under auspices of Knoll International, Amsterdam.
1968	Show of sculpture, Fairweather Hardin Gallery, Chicago.
1968	Show of sculpture, Staempfli Gallery, New York.
1968	Show of sculpture and chairs under auspices of Knoll International, Zurich.

Appendix II
Checklist of Commissioned Works 1953-1968

Dimensions (in order, height, width, depth) are in feet (approximate).
*Since removed. † Building not constructed.

Date	Description	Commissioned by	Architect or other factor	Plate
1953	Welded metal screen 10 x 36 x ⅔	General Motors Technical Center, Warren, Mich.	Eero Saarinen	21
1954	Welded metal screen 16 x 70 x 2	Manufacturers Hanover Trust Co., New York	Skidmore, Owings & Merrill (Gordon Bunshaft)	22
1954	Oval welded metal ceiling piece 3 x 18 x 12	Manufacturers Hanover Trust Co.	same as above	74
1954	Metal screen 9 x 5	Cincinnati Public Library	Woodie Garber & Assoc.	75
1955	Metal reredos 24 x 12 x ⅓	Massachusetts Institute of Technology, Cambridge	Eero Saarinen	25
1955	Welded metal screen 10 x 24	Dallas Public Library	George L. Dahl	54
1955	Painted metal screen 8 x 40 x 2	Lambert Airport, St. Louis*	Hellmuth, Yamasaki & Leinweber	76
1956	*Golden Trees* (2 vertical metal screens) ea. 48 h.	Dayton Store, Edina, Minn.	Victor Gruen Assoc. (Herman Guttman)	53
1956	10 free-standing metal screens, ea. 12 x 4 x 2	First National Bank, Miami, Fla.	Florence Knoll	77
1956	Free-standing metal screen 10 x 18	U.S. Dept. of State for America House, Bremen, Ger.†	Skidmore, Owings & Merrill (Bunshaft)	78
1956	Rectangular metal frame with gong 8 x 16	U.S. Dept. of State for American Consulate, Düsseldorf, Ger.†	same as above	79

1965	Hanging hemisphere (stainless steel wire) 6 h., 12 dia.	Cuyahoga Savings Assn., Cleveland	Lawrence & Assoc.	28
1966	Fountain (Tobin bronze rods) 9 x 10 x 8	River Oaks Shopping Center, Calumet City, Ill.	Loebl, Schlossman, Bennett & Dart	41
1967	Screen (laminated asbestos squares, textured and painted) 24 x 36 x 3	General Services Admin. for Federal Court Building, Brooklyn, N.Y.	Carson, Lundin & Shaw, and Lorimer Rich	43
1967	Fountain (copper tubes, bronze welded) 14 h., 16 dia.	Civic Center, Philadelphia, Pa.	Davis, Pool & Sloan; E. D. Stone, consultant	45
1968	3 molten bronze cube planters, ea. 4	Rochester Institute of Technology, Rochester, N.Y.	Kevin Roche, John Dinkeloo & Assoc.	
1968	Oval fountain (copper tubes, bronze welded) 7 x 18 x 12	Manufacturers & Traders Trust, Buffalo, N.Y.	Minoru Yamasaki	48
1968	36-piece ceiling-suspended sculpture (stainless steel wire) 32 dia.	Seattle-First National Bank, Seattle, Wash.	Naramore, Bain, Brady & Johanson	50

Notes

Names followed by full dates denote letters to the author.

Life and Personality

1. Augusta G. Quintavalle, *Il Bertoja* (Milano: "Silvana" Editoriale d'Arte, 1963).
2. Gino Damerini, *Scenografi veneziani dell'ottocento* (Venezia: Neri Pozza Editore, 1962).
3. Irving Berg, Department Head, Art, Cass Technical High School, Detroit, Mich. Apr. 18, 1967, quoting Mr. Schuholtz, Bertoia's drawing teacher.
4. Interview at Bally, Pa., Aug. 24, 1966. Subsequent Bertoia quotations, unless otherwise noted, are from this or later interviews.
5. Kevin Roche, Sept. 24, 1968.
6. John Garber, Sept. 25, 1968.
7. Aline B. Saarinen, *The Proud Possessors* (New York: Random House, 1958), p. 280.
8. Pipsan Saarinen Swanson, Apr. 4, 1967.
9. Eleanor T. West, script for soundtrack of film, *Harry Bertoia's Sculpture,* produced and directed by Clifford B. West, 1965.

Experiments and Techniques

1. Morris E. Guirl, *How Long the Night* (Grosse Pointe, Mich.: Golden Basket Bookshop, 1943).
2. "Drawing," *Arts and Architecture* LXI (Apr. 1944), 22-24.
3. "Five Drawings," *Arts and Architecture* LXII (May 1945), 22-23.
4. "Light and Structure" (transcription of speech, International Design Conference, Aspen, Colo.), *Print* IX (July 1955), 16.
5. July 24, 1943. Clipping in Bertoia file, Cranbrook Academy of Art, Bloomfield Hills, Mich.
6. M. R., "Review of Loan Exhibition on Third Floor of Museum of Non-Objective Painting," *Art Digest* XVIII (Nov. 1, 1943), 12.
7. Maude Riley, "Monoprints by Bertoia," *Art Digest* XIX (Feb. 1, 1945), 19.
8. *Art News* XLIII (Feb. 1, 1945), 25.
9. Ben Wolf, "At Nierendorf Gallery," *Art Digest* XX (Dec. 15, 1945), 10.
10. *Art News* XLIV (Oct. 1, 1945), 28.
11. "The Story of Knoll Associates," *American Artist* XV (Sept. 1951), 46.

12. "The Challenge of Contemporary Art," *Art in America* XLVIII (Summer 1960), 65.
13. O. G., "Bertoia: His Sculpture, His Kind of Wire Chair," *Interiors* CXII (Oct. 1952), 120.
14. *Print* IX (July 1955), 16.
15. Lawrence Campbell, "Creative Casting," *Craft Horizons* XXIII (Nov.-Dec. 1963), 11.

Large Scale Commissions
1. "Banker's Showcase," *Arts* XXIX (Dec. 1, 1954), 13.
2. Ruth Ullmann, Manufacturers Hanover Trust Co., New York, Jan. 25, 1967, quoting *Contract*, Dec. 1966.
3. See note 15, above.
4. Wunsch, Jan. 31, 1967.
5. Schmeckebier, Sept. 25, 1968.
6. Loebl, Jan. 18, 1967.
7. *Print* IX (July 1955), 16.
8. "My Motivations in Collecting," *The W. Hawkins Ferry Collection* (Detroit Institute of Arts, 1966), n.p.; cf. no. 4.
9. Interview with W. Hawkins Ferry, Grosse Pointe Shores, Mich., June 1, 1966.
10. The past tense is used here advisedly, as this sculpture has since been removed.
11. "Dandelion Fountain Sculpture," *Architectural Record* CXXXIII (April 1963), 310.

Investigations
1. "Sculpture 1950-1958," *Allen Memorial Art Museum Bulletin* XV (Winter 1958), 62.
2. *Print* IX (July 1955), 16.

Concepts and Critiques
1. "Bertoia Mural Returned to New Dallas Library after Dispute," *Architectural Forum* CIII (Nov. 1955), 29.
2. S.T., "Exhibition at Staempfli Gallery," *Arts* XXXV (May 1961), 96.
3. Thomas H. Creighton, "The Relationship of Sculpture and Architecture," *Progressive Architecture* XLII (Nov. 1961), 232.
4. J. K.'s review of exhibition at Staempfli Gallery, *Art News* LX (May 1961), 48. Bertoia's reaction was: "I am convinced the writer of that has never walked with his bare feet on wet grass nor has he heard the lapping of ocean breakers."
5. "Useful Objects by Artists," *Art in America* LII (Dec. 1964), 54.
6. John E. Burchard, "Alienated Affections in the Arts," *Daedalus* LXXXIX (Winter 1960), 52-61.
7. John E. Burchard (ed.), "Views on Art and Architecture: A Conversation," *Daedalus* LXXXIX (Winter 1960), 62.

Bibliography

Where the author's name is followed by a question mark and enclosed in parentheses, it is a suggested name based on initials signed to the article.

"Accessions of American and Canadian Museums," *Art Quarterly* XXII (Spring 1959), 90.

Albright-Knox Art Gallery. Illustration of acquisition. *Gallery Notes* XXVI (Jan. 1963), 48.

"The American Institute of Architects Awards Harry Bertoia the Craftsmanship Medal," *American Institute of Architects Journal* XXV (May 1956), 213.

"American Sculpture in Paris," *Art in America* XLVIII (Fall 1960), 96.

Bertoia, Harry. "Drawing," *Arts and Architecture* LXI (Apr. 1944), 22-24.

—"Five Drawings," *Arts and Architecture* LXII (May 1945), 22-23.

—"Light and Structure" (reprint of speech, International Design Conference, Aspen, Colo.), *Print* IX (July 1955), 16-17.

Bertoia jewelry illustrated. *Design Quarterly* No. 33 (1955), pp. 2 ff.

"Bertoia Mural Returned to New Dallas Library after Dispute," *Architectural Forum* CIII (Nov. 1955), 29.

Burchard, John E. "Alienated Affections in the Arts," *Daedalus* LXXXIX (Winter 1960), 52 ff.

—(ed.). "Views on Art and Architecture: A Conversation," *Daedalus* LXXXIX (Winter 1960), 62 ff.

Burrows, Carlyle. "Review of the Non-Objective Painting Show Sponsored by the Solomon R. Guggenheim Foundation," *Christian Science Monitor* (Boston), July 24, 1943.

"California Artists," *Art News* XLV (June 1946), 21.

Campbell, Lawrence. "Creative Casting," *Craft Horizons* XXIII (Nov.-Dec. 1963), 11 ff.

Canaday, John. "Sculpture Alive," *New York Times,* Mar. 19, 1961, Sect. II, p. 19.

Chermayeff, Serge. "Painting Toward Architecture," *Arts and Architecture* LXV (June 1948), 31.

"The Circle is Freed," *Art News Annual* XX (1950), 146.

Clute, Eugene. "Abstractions in Metal," *Progressive Architecture* XXXVI (Feb. 1955), 104 ff.

"The Creation of an Unusual Metal Sculpture," *Minneapolis Tribune,* Sunday Picture Magazine, Jan. 10, 1965, pp. 4-5.

Creighton, Thomas H. "The Relationship of Sculpture and Architecture," *Progressive Architecture* XLII (Nov. 1961), 232.

Damerini, Gino. *Scenografi veneziani dell' ottocento: Francesco Bagnara, Giuseppe e Pietro Bertoja* (exhibition catalog). Venezia: Neri Pozza Editore, 1962.

"Dandelion Fountain Sculpture for Perpetual Savings and Loan Association, Beverly Hills, California," *Architectural Record* CXXXIII (Apr. 1963), 310.

Denver Art Museum acquisition. *Art Quarterly* XXIX (Summer 1966), 184.

Flemming, Hans T. "The Challenge of Contemporary Art," *Art in America* XLVIII (Summer 1960), 65 ff.

"Footnotes," *American Artist* XXVII (Apr. 1963), 4.

Frankenstein, Alfred. "Tobey and Bertoia: Fantasy and Geometry," *Art News* XLIV (Oct. 1, 1945), 28.

Friedman, B. H. "Useful Objects by Artists," *Art in America* LII (Dec. 1964), 54 ff.

(Frigerio, S.?) "Exposition de scultures et graphismes chez Knoll International France," *Aujourd'hui* VIII (Apr. 1964), 96 ff.

"Geometric Forms" illustrated. *Art Quarterly* XIX (Autumn 1956), 309.

(Gueft, Olga?) "Bertoia, his Sculpture, his Kind of Wire Chair," *Interiors* CXII (Oct. 1952), 118 ff.

Guirl, Morris E. *How Long the Night; a Modern Morality Play in Four Parts.* Illustrated in woodcut by Harry Bertoia. Grosse Pointe, Mich.: Golden Basket Bookshop, 1943.

Hakanson, Joy. "W. Hawkins Ferry—'Mr. Modern Art,'" *Detroit News,* Pictorial Magazine, Oct. 9, 1966, pp. 13 ff.

—"A Walk in the Shadow of Genius," *Detroit News,* Pictorial Magazine, June 26, 1966, pp. 13 ff.

Huxtable, Ada Louise. "Art in Architecture 1959," *Craft Horizons* XIX (Jan. 1959), 12.

—"Banker's Showcase," *Arts* XXIX (Dec. 1, 1954), 13.

Knoll Associates, Inc. *Harry Bertoia* (biographical statement), n.p., n.d.

(Kroll, Jack?) Review of exhibition at Staempfli Gallery, *Art News* LX (May 1961), 48.

Langsner, Jules. "Harry Bertoia," *Arts and Architecture* LXX (Jan. 1953), 12 ff.

(Lonngren, Lillian?) Review of exhibition at Staempfli Gallery, *Art News* LXII (Apr. 1963), 16.

"Metal Sculpture: Screen for the Manufacturers Trust Company," *Arts and Architecture* LXXII (Jan. 1955), 18-19.

Moritz, Charles (ed.). "Charles Eames," *Current Biography Yearbook.* New York: H. W. Wilson Co., 1965, pp. 139 ff.

Nierendorf Gallery. Review of exhibition. *Art News* XLIII (Feb. 1, 1945), 25.

Nierendorf Gallery. Review of exhibition. *Art News* XLVI (May 1947), 48.

(Porter, Fairfield?) Review of Knoll Associates exhibition. *Art News* LI (Jan. 1953), 44.

Preston, S. Review of exhibition at Steampfli Gallery, *Burlington Magazine* CVIII (Apr. 1963), 183.

"Pure Design Research," *Architectural Forum* XCVII (Sept. 1952), 142 ff.

Quintavalle, Augusta Ghidiglia. *Il Bertoja*. Milano: "Silvana Editoriale d'Arte, 1963.

(Raynor, Vivien?) "Exhibition at Staempfli Gallery," *Arts* XXXVII (Apr. 1963), 56.

"Recent Sculpture USA" (exhibition catalog). *Museum of Modern Art Bulletin* XXVI (Spring 1959), 7.

(Reed, Judith Kaye?) "Monoprints at Nierendorf Gallery," *Art Digest* XXI (Apr. 15, 1947), 22.

Riley, Maude. "Monoprints by Bertoia," *Art Digest* XIX (Feb. 1, 1945), 19.

(Riley, Maude?) "Review of Loan Exhibition on Third Floor of Museum of Non-Objective Painting," *Art Digest* XVIII (Nov. 1, 1943), 12.

Saarinen, Aline B. *The Proud Possessors*. New York: Random House, 1958.

"Song-&-Dance Man," *Time,* Mar. 31, 1961, pp. 56-57.

Sowers, Robert. "Arts in Architecture: The Vista on Fifth Avenue," *Craft Horizons* XXI (Jan. 1961), 38-39.

Speyer, A. James. "Art News from Chicago," *Art News* LV (Dec. 1956), 49.

Staempfli Gallery. Review of exhibition. *Interiors* CXX (Apr. 1961), 26 ff.

Staempfli Gallery. Review of exhibition. *Art News* LXVII (May 1968), 11.

Staempfli Gallery. Review of exhibition. *Arts* XLII (May 1968), 62.

"The Story of Knoll Associates," *American Artist* XV (Sept. 1951), 46 ff.

"Sunlit Straw" reproduced. *American Institute of Architects Journal* XLVI (Nov. 1966), 56.

(Tillim, Sidney?) "Exhibition at Staempfli Gallery," *Arts* XXXV (May 1961), 96.

Bibliography

West, Clifford B. *Harry Bertoia's Sculpture.* Sound and color film, 1965. New York, Radim Films, Inc., distributor.

Whiteside, Forbes. "Sculpture 1950-1958," *Allen Memorial Art Museum Bulletin* XV (Winter 1958), 59 ff.

Whittet, G. S. "Comments on the Current London Triennial Exhibition of Sculpture in the Open Air on View at Battersea Park until the End of September," *Studio* CLXVI (Aug. 1963), 51.

Wolf, Ben. "At Nierendorf Gallery," *Art Digest* XX (Dec. 15, 1945), 10.

Index of Proper Names

Harry Bertoia, Sculptor